T0384032

Lean Transportation Management

Lean Transportation Management

Using Logistics as a Strategic Differentiator

Mohamed Achahchah

Routledge
Taylor & Francis Group

A PRODUCTIVITY PRESS BOOK

First published 2019
by Routledge
2 Park Square, Milton Park, Abingdon, Oxon OX14 4RN

and by Routledge
711 Third Avenue, New York, NY 10017

Routledge is an imprint of the Taylor & Francis Group, an informa business

© 2019 Mohamed Achahchah

British Library Cataloguing in Publication Data
A catalogue record for this book is available from the British Library

Library of Congress Cataloging-in-Publication Data
Names: Achahchah, Mohamed, author.
Title: Lean transportation management : using logistics as a strategic differentiator / Mohamed Achahchah.
Description: Boca Raton : Taylor & Francis, 2019. | Includes bibliographical references and index.
Identifiers: LCCN 2018026354 (print) | LCCN 2018028631 (ebook) | ISBN 9780429490101 (e-Book) | ISBN 9781138592278 (hardback : alk. paper)
Subjects: LCSH: Business logistics--Management. | Shipment of goods--Management.
Classification: LCC HD38.5 (ebook) | LCC HD38.5 .A295 2019 (print) | DDC 658.7/882--dc23
LC record available at https://lccn.loc.gov/2018026354

ISBN: 978-1-138-59227-8 (hbk)
ISBN: 978-0-429-49010-1 (ebk)

Typeset in Minion Pro
by Taylor & Francis Books

To my wife Nasima, my son Ilyas and my daughters Amal and Maysa, who all have been my best supporters in this Lean journey.

Contents

List of Figures

List of Tables

Introduction

In Lean philosophy, transportation is considered to be waste. This triggers the question of how it is possible that there are so many freight movements around the world. With transportation, a company can reach its existing and potential customers around the world fast and without big investments. It is the linking pin between the supply chain processes and partners, who need to work in tandem to deliver the perfect order. From that point of view, transportation is not a waste but an important service differentiator to be used as part of the transportation strategy to create a strong competitive advantage as world-class service experience is becoming the key decision factor, in addition to world-class product capabilities, for awarding business to a world-class supplier. While governments and authorities have been developing many extensive public transportation strategies for a long time, there is still a significant number of private companies that do not have one or, when they have one, it is related to cost reduction. Many studies tried to define world-class and came up with various maturity grids, but there are no international standards to label a company as such. However, these studies taught us the characteristics of world-class performance: a happy customer confirming the high quality of the products, sold against affordable prices, created by engaged employees in a safe environment, delivered fast and in line with the delivery requirements. The characteristics of a world-class company that can deliver this performance include a customer-focused vision, mission, and set of goals that are shared by committed employees who act with integrity and respect laws and regulations. They are responsible for the performance of their processes, benchmarking them and empowered to continuously improve these in a sustainable way by using a structured improvement methodology, as part of the company's operational excellence strategy, to meet their stretched targets in a flat and innovative organization. Examples of world-class companies are Adidas and Amazon, which are using smart transportation networks to increase sales by delivering purchased products faster than their competition. These companies do not treat transportation as a cost center. They are not focusing on transportation spend reduction. They allow customers to buy any product that is available in any close-by store, warehouse, or other storage location, to be delivered at home or any other address such as a store or other pick-up point. Their customers can ask for any omni-channel service they want to pay for and follow the progress of their orders from order entry to delivery on the Internet or choose to receive regular updates on their smartphones. Amazon's Alexa smart speaker system is able to recognize a person's voice requesting the reschedule of a delivery and transfers this command to the shipper's IT systems including the announcement of the new delivery date and time on the trucker's mobile device. Deliveries can be made on the same day the order comes in, in the next hour, in the evening, on Saturday and Sunday. Some logistics service providers offer customers the possibility to change the delivery address and time until only minutes before the original delivery would take place. By being flexible in their extended customer service offer and delivering faster than others, they retain more and attract new customers to increase sales and grow at the expense of the competition. Another way these types of companies try to retain and increase sales is to offer customers a logistics subscription, meaning that they do not have to pay for the transportation costs if they regularly place new orders. At the same time, the companies lower their total supply chain costs as faster deliveries turn out to lead to fewer returns and lower inventories. Lower inventories mean lower investments, financing costs, and inventory carrying costs such as space utilization, handling, obsolescence, scrap, and theft. Reduction of returns means higher sales and lower transportation costs for reverse flows. The result is higher profits while creating more value for the customers, who are happy with the shopping experience. Still, not many companies recognize that transportation is moving from a cost center towards a profit center. Amazon is a good example of an innovative company that is differentiating itself from the rest by working on breakthrough transportation solutions. The traditional logistics service providers are perceived to not innovate fast enough. This is also the reason why the company is setting up its own logistics networks via Fulfillment by Amazon (FBA) to offer third parties that sell products on the Amazon website, and others too, the option to store, pick, and pack their products through the Amazon fulfillment centers and ship the orders via Shipping with Amazon (SWA). This business unit is expected to compete with the established companies like UPS and FedEx. Another Amazon innovation is the business use of drones, but they are also working on a multi-level logistics center from which drones are sent out and received back, while the lowest level is used for the traditional dispatching of trucks. Other Amazon ideas are flying and small mobile truck warehouses. Another solution is the Domino's self-driving robots to deliver pizzas. The idea is not to reduce work force, but to be faster and more on time and to prevent the pizza from shaking. In addition to home deliveries, they can deliver to a park, school, hospital, or office. The expectation is that these types of companies and innovations will inspire the traditional logistics service providers to innovate more and faster to prevent losing market share to the new players. Transportation management professionals understand this philosophy, but top management makes the business decisions. It is therefore important that they understand the transportation management basics and use them in their strategic decision making. Top management should be involved in discussions how to organize the transport management function in the best way and how to use it as a service differentiator. Transportation is more than only the efficient movement of supplies, sub-assemblies, and finished products. It is also more than the key performance indicators on the business-balanced scorecard. Transportation management professionals fail to catch top management's attention due to the use of technical language. Marketing and sales functions are better in doing so as they use key performance indicators that top management understands. They understand profit, loss, and revenue and market share. It is more difficult to understand transportation key performance indicators such as loading degree (also called "load factor"), net and gross pick-up, and delivery reliability. It is easier to get top management's attention when talking about lost sales due to stock-outs, lost tenders due to long delivery times, and high costs due to high inventory levels. Allowing high inventory levels is often used to build up safety stocks to mitigate out-of-stock situations due to long vendors' supply and short customers' delivery lead-times and "plan for uncertainty" to hide problems such as poor raw material and/or finished product quality, suppliers with unreliable supply chains, and inaccurate customer demand forecasting systems. Advocates of high inventory levels say that this approach makes sure that the company always has the products on the shelf to sell and satisfy customers, helps to have enough spare parts for a high customer service level, and benefits from low raw material purchasing prices as these are increasing and buying large volumes leads to quantity discounts. However, all this comes at a high total cost of ownership, as inventories require major investments locking cash flow and working capital, which cannot be used for other business improvement initiatives to increase profit margins, and inventory-related costs lowering the same profit margins that need to go up. The transportation spend is in general twice as high as the warehousing spend, but warehousing gets more attention. This is probably due to warehousing activities being more physically visible. However, transportation processes and the business environment are becoming so complex that working only on the management priorities is not good enough to compete against the best-in-class companies, which have fast, flexible, and transparent supply chains. Due to global sourcing and marketing, both costs and transit-times increase, while inventory levels and customer delivery lead-times decrease creating additional challenges for the transportation function. Also, the booming e-commerce and mass customization require transportation to be agile in complex digital solution designs and tools. Agility refers to a company's ability to adjust to the changing business environments such as customer demand shifts and environmental and market conditions. This puts also a pressure on the transportation branch to hire better-educated employees who can handle the additional complexities. In a Lean culture, all well-educated employees work on improvement activities within their area of responsibility no matter how small or big the contribution to the total company is as many people making many small improvements on a daily basis leads to big achievements. People should not wait until top management tells them what to do. The intention with this book is not to provide an in-depth description of each transportation process. What I think is missing is an overview of the transportation processes and how they interact. This book is written from an experienced shipper's viewpoint to provide managers insight into the added value of transportation as a strategic differentiator, its key drivers, and how to use it in an effective (doing the right things) and efficient (doing the things right) decision-making process. The book can be also a valuable source for students, colleges, and universities.

About the Author

Mohamed Achahchah studied business administration and has 18 years of experience in global distribution management. He started working in a customer service desk handling complaints and claims and learned how important this feedback is for a company. In his further career, he gained experience in transportation management and learned the specifics of this business and the relation between quality, service, and costs. Later on, he worked as project manager leading projects like network redesign studies and simulations, tenders, analyzing customer order behaviors, lead-time and cost reductions, carrier selections and implementations, analyzing self-steering teams and mini-companies, and lead process surveys. Achahchah is PMP® and green belt certified. As advanced Lean certified practitioner, he is currently working as a logistics manager at an international company and involved in implementing Lean in a logistics environment. For feedback, ideas, questions, and so on please send an e-mail to mohamedachahchah@hotmail.com.

1

Lean

Toyota's Lean philosophy is about installing and maintaining a continuous improvement culture and using simple problem-solving tools. It is a process of searching, finding, and eliminating waste throughout a supply chain. The scope includes the company's processes, but also the processes of suppliers and customers. In Lean, it is important to execute only activities, added value, for which the customer is willing to pay. All non-adding-value activities must be eliminated by solving problems and improving processes on a daily basis in a safe work environment. Management visits regularly the "gemba," which is a Japanese word for the workplace where the actual work takes place. Lean is to show respect for people and work smarter, not harder. It is an environment where employees have the responsibility and authority to stop a process if the output is leading to defects. They pull the "andon," which is a Japanese word for "signal," to stop and fix the problem. In Lean, the customer comes first and cost cutting comes second. By making quality and affordable products that customers want to buy, sales will grow. This can be only realized by setting stretched targets that cannot be met by competition. The targets are met by getting rid of complex processes, creating value streams with end-to-end responsibilities and authorities, setting common goals across the company, working in a face-to-face environment, and taking brave decisions when needed. Lean is not a headcount reduction project, but a way to create time for doing more value-added activities with the same amount of people. Freed-up resources are assigned to work on improvement activities. Lean companies work constantly on improving processes, making sure that the improvements stick by standardizing processes, as they will serve as the new baselines for new improvement initiatives. Traditional companies often miss the continuous improvement approach as they "forget" to standardize the new processes and fall back into the old situation. Finally, Lean is not a standalone system. It needs to be seen as part of a broader operational excellence strategy that can consist of process, change, performance, and project management.

1.1 THE VOICES

An organization is like a human being, who needs to use its ears to hear what is happening all around to act accordingly in situations like danger, fire, and other potential safety issues. In the same way, a company needs to listen to the voices of its customers, employees, processes, and businesses. It is good to hear that customers are happy with the service, sales are growing, and the company is profitable. It is also important to find out why customers buy other products, product quality does not meet the requirements, and employees leave the company. The different voices a company can tape from are described in the next section.

1.1.1 Voice of the Customer

Traditional suppliers ask customers to order large quantities to benefit from a discount as the traditional customer is looking for the lowest possible price per product. Nowadays customers look for the best possible value against the lowest possible total cost of ownership. Customers are willing to look for this best combination in their existing global supplier network by requesting and comparing quotations. It is for this reason that companies need to realize that they depend on these customers and not the other way around. Customers give companies the opportunity to show that they care about their customers, understand their needs, and will do their utmost to serve them. The starting point of Lean is to listen to the voice of the internal and external customers and build an emotional bond with them in addition to the perfect delivery of the perfect product. It is a proven concept that companies who are successful in creating both a functional (product) and an emotional (treatment) bond retain their customers for a longer period and manage to increase their sales value. The customer is visited at the workshop, where the actual delivery takes place and the product is used, to capture the customer's expectations and experiences. Listen and understand the feedback of the people doing the day-to-day work. Inform the stakeholders and take immediate action to add more value for the customer. Stop the activities not needed or not appreciated by the customer. With the right partnership and trust, the customer can help with the shipper's challenges such as leveling out the order intake. Customers look for the total value and the total costs of having a product in use; they want to cooperate with suppliers to reduce waste in the supply chain and create meaningful innovations. They look for ways to improve the traceability of the product origins, who produced it, their work conditions, sustainability, and trade compliance. Production technology becomes less and less a competitive advantage due to global outsourcing to suppliers who produce comparable products for competition. Customer service becomes more and more the service differentiator. Customers expect world-class solutions such as 24/7 availability, human approach, and personalized proposals. Customers want to be approached pro-actively, to not spend time waiting, the call taker to be easy to work with, and to be contacted in their preferred way and at their proposed time. It should not cost customers much of an effort and they require fast issue resolution, have high-quality standards, and accept higher prices for good service and green logistics. The customer is looking for a company that is easy to interact with, has nice representatives who handle the requests and questions in a satisfactory manner, leading to more business with each other, and can be recommended to other supply chain partners. Typical issues encountered and reported by customers are the customer service desk is difficult to reach, long waiting times, poor problem-solving capabilities of the call taker, forwarding the customer multiple times to the "right" contact person, not calling back once agreed, and language issues. Table 1.1 shows some examples of transportation-related customer requirements. It is good to hear the voice of the customer in the design phase of a process, as the waste is "planned" here, but also when the process is operational to check if the process delivers what the customer expected. Customer survey tools can support this verification process.

TABLE 1.1

Transportation-Related Customer Requirements

Use a taxi in case of a rush order

Allow the customer to pick up goods

Do not consolidate orders

Use only Euro pallets

Do not use ThrowAway Pallets (TAPs)

Pick up empty pallets upon delivery

Use a carton board layer between pallets when stacking

Do not stack pallets

Maximum height of a pallet is 160 cm

Maximum weight per pallet is 100 kg

Use only black foil

Use trucks with a tail lift

Do not use a standard trailer

Do not use vans

Confirmation of delivery from transporter is required

Send an Advanced Shipping Notification (ASN)

Deliver in room

Bring loading and unloading equipment

Do not use wooden pallets

Do not add invoices to the pouch, package, or pallet

Send the original documents to the receiver by post

1.1.2 Voice of the Employee

Lean is a philosophy and management approach to focus on adding value to customers, but also on respecting people as only employees on the shop floor, and not the managers and/or support functions in the office, are in the best position to identify waste and eliminate it. Studies have shown that supervisors are aware of the majority of the problems faced by the shop floor people, but they do not know all of them. Middle managers know only a small piece of what supervisors know, while top management knows the least about operational issues. Top management can only prioritize the issues they know about. It is therefore crucial that the shop floor workers are heard on a regular basis about the daily issues they encounter dealing with supply chain partners such as customers and suppliers. A top-down and bottom-up daily management (DM) process is required to exchange this information fast. This can be realized by implementing tiered carousel call or meeting sessions. At the start of the day, the front-line workers have a call with the supervisors, somewhat later there is a call between the supervisors and the middle managers and, at the end of the day, there is a call between the middle and the top managers. To prevent an overload of issues for the top management, the shop floor employees need to be equipped with the tools, skills, and authorities to solve problems themselves. Studies have shown that these people have more capabilities than their job strictly requires. This is waste as these people often use their additional skills outside the company by getting roles and responsibilities in sport and social clubs, work on their hobbies, or run their own small business.

1.1.3 Voice of the Process

What is the process telling us? Is the process capable to deliver what we require from it? Can the desired output be achieved in a controlled, stable, and reliable way, meaning that the process operates within the controlled upper and lower limits of the control chart?

1.1.4 Voice of the Business

The voice of the business can be derived from mainly the financial figures such as sales, purchases, labor costs, market value, and taxes. Based on this data, business analysts can take conclusions and make recommendations about the market conditions, profitability per product per business market combination, financial impact of projects, invested capital, research spend, cost levels, creditability, and solvability. This information can help to identify and prioritize potential improvement actions to make the planned goals and targets.

1.2 LEAN THINKING

Lean is a different way of doing things compared to the traditional management approaches. According to Womack and Jones in their book "Lean Thinking: Banish Waste and Create Wealth in Your Corporation," Lean thinking consists of a five-step approach:

- Step 1: Define the customer value from the customer's perspective and express that in terms of quality, service, and costs. Shippers think they know what the customer wants, but they often turn out to be wrong.

- Step 2: Map the value stream: visualize all of the value-added and non-value-added activities to deliver a service to the customer.
- Step 3: Install flow: enable continuous movement of services and information from the beginning until the end of a process. Find the obstacles or hand-over points preventing the service to flow and remove them.
- Step 4: Pull: do not produce anything until there is a customer order.
- Step 5: Strive for perfection: try to eliminate waste completely so that only the value-adding activities remain.

In addition to the elimination of wasted resources used to deliver a product or service to increase the profitability, Lean is about speeding up the supply chain to reduce the working capital. A fast supply chain requires an agile organization to anticipate changes fast, faster than competition, but also to pro-actively drive changes to gain competitive advantages. Figure 1.1 shows the typical division of value- and non-value-added activities of traditional companies. The majority of the total lead-time from order to delivery is consumed by non-value-added activities such as waiting. Non-value-added activities are defined as work that costs money that the customer is not willing to pay. Those activities are not adding value to the service the customer is asking for. Only a very small part of the time, 1%–10%, is used to add value such as transforming information into a service the customer is looking for. Traditional companies try to speed up the value-added activities, but reducing this time by, for example, 50% leads to significantly fewer benefits compared to reducing the non-value-added activities by the same percentage.

The basic idea of Lean is to focus on reducing the non-value-added activities as the potential improvement is much bigger. It is possible that there are activities that do not add value to the customer (e.g., trade compliance), but these cannot be eliminated and have to be executed to be compliant with regulations and laws. In Lean, a company organizes itself

Current process lead-time (10 days)	Non-value added activities (9 days)	Value-added activities (1 day)
Potential improvement (e.g., 50% lead-time reduction)	50% lead-time reduction = 0.5 x 9 days = 4.5 days	50% lead-time reduction = 0.5 x 1 day = 0.5 day

Current process lead-time (10 days)

FIGURE 1.1
Value and non-value-added activities.

in value streams rather than departments. Then it defines the activities that are adding value and those that are not. The latter ones are eliminated. Interrelated indicators to measure the value stream performance are lead-times and inventory levels. The shorter the lead-times, the less inventory is needed to fulfill the customer demand. According to Taiichi Ohno in his book "Toyota Production System—Beyond Large-Scale Production" typical enemies of Lean are activities that do not add value. These are defined as waste ("muda" in Japanese), imbalanced workload ("mura"), and work that creates burden for the team members or processes ("muri"). Examples of "mura" are seasonality, impossible deadlines, and end-of-month rush orders for "making the month." Examples of "muri" are information overload, firefighting, stress, and burnouts. "Muda" causes the biggest wastes, which are grouped in seven categories:

- Transportation: moving (semi-) finished goods to and/or from storage locations and other unnecessary movements.
- Inventories: raw material ("purchased big volumes due to a nice price"), work in progress (being worked upon or waiting for the next process), finished goods ("safety stock" for demand fluctuations or waiting to be sold), spare parts, and other repair material and tools (extra parts for "just to be sure"), but also the storage of too much information not needed ("maybe we can use this in the future").
- Motion: unnecessary walking and/or reaching out to tools that are not adding value to the customer.
- Waiting: people waiting for other people to provide input for the next steps.
- Overproduction: making more products than the customer is asking for. This is the biggest waste as this is creating all the other six wastes.
- Over processing: handling an item more often than the minimum requirement. A multilevel approval process is a typical example of such a waste.
- Defects: producing defective items and other quality issues.

Not using people's skills is also considered as a waste. Another example of waste is a project with shifting deadlines, moving targets, changing priorities, and people leaving the team. A good way to remember the seven wastes is the acronym TIM WOOD. T stands for Transportation, I for Inventories, M for Motion, W for Waiting, O for Overproduction, O for Overprocessing, and D for Defects.

1.3 LEAN PRINCIPLES

Many companies built up extensive Lean experiences in the last century and they are confirming that management needs to follow a few guidelines to come to and sustain a Lean culture. According to Jeffrey K. Liker in his book "The Toyota Way: 14 Management Principles from the World's Greatest Manufacturer," it is required to base the company's decisions on a long-term philosophy, not on short-term financial goals, as the full benefits of Lean will come only after a significant investment in culture change. Start by creating a continuous flow to bring problems to the surface and fix them. This is comparable with the idea of lowering the water level to see the rocks below. By lowering the "water" (inventory levels), the first exposed "rock" (problem) is resolved and the inventory levels are lowered further to resolve other problems. This process is executed repeatedly towards perfection. Use pull systems to avoid overproduction as this one is leading to all the other six wastes. Level out the workload ("Heijunka" in Japanese) to make the ultimate use of the available resources. Build a culture of stopping and fixing problems, compete on quality by getting it right the first time preventing quality inspections and rejects at the end of the process. Use visual controls so that no problems are hidden. Standardize tasks and processes to enable reliable, capable, and stable processes leading to predictable quality levels. Use only reliable, thoroughly tested technology that serves people and processes, not just to have the most modern technology in house. Assign leaders from within the company who understand the work and can teach it to others. Develop people into experienced problem solvers. Respect partners and suppliers and help them improve their processes. Go to the gemba and see for yourself to understand the situation. Plan slowly and act fast. Become a learning organization through reflection ("Hansei" in Japanese) and share lessons learned.

1.4 LEAN CULTURE

The idea of Lean is to add value to the customer in the least wasteful way by focusing on what the customer wants only. It is therefore important to develop a way of thinking in which employees work continuously on improvements by seeing and eliminating waste as they believe there is always a way to do things better. They do not blame people, but they blame processes. In Lean, there is a difference between breakthrough and continuous improvement processes. Continuous improvement, "kaizen," is an incremental way of improving, while the Hoshin Kanri approach, explained further in this book, facilitates breakthroughs. Lean is about eliminating batches or reducing their sizes to preferably one-piece flows, removing or lowering inventory levels and being more efficient to survive in the long term. Lean master Taiichi Ohno, founder of the Toyota Production System (TPS), discovered after the Second World War that Japan required many models in small quantities. At the same time, Toyota faced almost a bankruptcy and could not afford any new equipment, warehouses, or inventories. To anticipate the situation, Toyota reduced changeover times to be able to produce a mix of products on short notice and worked with their employees to increase their flexibility to work in multiple jobs. Taiichi Ohno said, "All we are doing is looking at the time from the moment the customer gives us an order to the point when we collect the cash. We are reducing that time by removing the non-value-added wastes." Lean started within one company, but the scope has been extended to the enterprise level. The Lean approach is rolled out from one company to the whole supply chain in order to create value in all processes from raw material until the delivery to the customer. The supplier is seen as a partner and an extension of the company heading for the same goal. The focus is on building long-term relationships and preventing short-term price reductions leading to lower margins for the supplier. Multi-functional teams across the companies collaborate to eliminate waste with the trust that the companies and their employees will share the benefits. A limited number of suppliers helps to focus the efforts. The best companies have a communication structure in which people are well informed, inform others, are involved in identifying and solving problems, are empowered to take action, know how the business is doing, are recognized and praised at all levels, and see conflicts as an opportunity for improvement, and where everyone's priorities and actions are in line with the company's goals.

1.5 LEAN LEADERSHIP

Lean is not an operational responsibility, which can be delegated to the operations director. Lean is also not about using the Lean tools, as there can be other useful tools for specific situations, not a one-time off event and certainly not a restructuring approach to reduce headcounts in the very short term. According to Toyota, Lean is a long-term lifetime strategic approach to create and maintain a culture of continuous improvement via cross-functional teams in the whole supply chain. Top management needs to create a shared vision and learn and practice this philosophy before they can support and steer any transformation towards a Lean culture. Such a transformation cannot be outsourced to consultants or black belts. The leadership engagement needs to remain after lower-level managerial layers are mature enough for delegating tasks to. To create and sustain a long-lasting Lean culture, potential Lean leaders are carefully developed internally by a lifetime of on-the-job training, learning and one-on-one coaching by mentors ("sensei" in Japanese), who bring problems to the surface and help, encourage, and challenge employees to mature themselves in the problem-solving process by working on actual issues in the company. Lean leaders are humble and take the time to plan and steer all the improvements and employees in the same direction to make sure that their activities are properly linked to the strategic goals. To show the direction and the progress towards the stretched targets, visual management is used there where the actual work takes place to communicate with the team members and the gemba visitors. It is important to become Lean, but it is more important to stay Lean and this can only be learned and sustained by actively using the Lean thinking and approaches in practice. Charles Jennings discovered that a typical employee learns 10% from formal training, 20% from colleagues, and 70% from training on the job. J. Liker and his co-author G. Convis explain in their book "The Toyota Way to Lean Leadership" that Toyota expects for their leaders to work on their self-development by maturing themselves in the Lean philosophy, applying the Lean tools, and leading by example behavior. Lean leaders live and spread the values such as teamwork, standard work, respect for people, go and see for yourself, daily kaizens, and accepting challenging targets. It is important to make the targets (the what), but it is more important to know what the leaders did to realize them (the how). The approach of "make the targets no matter how" is not accepted within Toyota. The Lean philosophy is that the combination of a good approach and clear targets will lead to the right results. The preferred way is to align the targets with the employees by using a top-down and bottom-up counseling process, while keeping the targets challenging, being open-minded, and actively listening to what the people who are doing the real work have to say. As Lean leaders have an extensive knowledge of the company's processes, as they go to the gemba to understand the operations and learn to identify process and performance gaps, the employees are challenged to come up with convincing reasons why something is not feasible. In addition to setting out challenging targets and steadily increasing them, Lean leaders offer at the same time their help and teaching capabilities to their employees to make the targets. The coaches do not give answers; instead, they ask open questions to optimize the on-the-job learning and development. Together they make plans and translate them into actions with clear responsibilities and accountabilities. As Lean leaders are experienced in identifying the strengths and weaknesses of a person, they use the required approaches and tools, depending on the employees' needs, to motivate them towards realizing the stretching company goals. As the coaches are also experienced users of the problem-solving tool, they take the time and energy to guide the people through the process of understanding the problem well for creating the problem definition, goal setting, root cause analysis, and countermeasures. The guideline is to plan slowly and act fast. Only after the potential Lean leaders are recognized as having matured themselves in their self-development process they are rewarded by giving them the possibility, often without direct authority, to coach and develop others. As Lean leaders see possibilities for improvements themselves, they identify and offer the new potential Lean leaders the opportunity to work on real company issues and share the lessons learned with other divisions, business units, and plants with comparable processes. Only mature Lean leaders who have been recognized to have the capabilities to develop themselves and others are involved in creating the company's vision and aligning goals vertically (with their managers and their employees) and horizontally (with their peers).

1.6 LEAN TOOLS

According to TPS, the two technical pillars of Lean are Just in Time (JIT) and Jidoka ("built-in quality" in Japanese). JIT is the delivery of goods in the required quantities and conditions at the right time and place. Goods arrive in smaller quantities on a more frequent and predictable schedule. The main objective is to reduce investments in inventories and inventory holding costs. Jidoka (autonomation, automation with a human touch) is about building in quality at the source, checking the quality continuously and within the process, to prevent inspections and reworks. It is about fixing problems as they show up. The most important Lean tools to help with the Lean transformation are described in the next section.

1.6.1 Breakthrough Improvement

A breakthrough is a major improvement in a key business area. It is a complex, multifunctional problem solved by a dedicated team in a limited period. The goal is often higher than a 50% improvement (also called "Target to Improve" [TTI]) to realize the company's vision. The Toyota-developed Lean tool to use here is Hoshin Kanri ("compass management" or "policy deployment" to manage the company's direction), which is a top-down and bottom-up back-and-forth "catch ball" systematic approach of a strategy planning process to achieve mid-term and long-term goals by aligning the business strategy with the day-to-day activities. Hoshin Kanri has its roots in the 1960s in Japan and the founding father is Dr. Yoji Akao. The tool strives to get all employees pulling in the same direction at the same time by aligning the top management strategy goals with the middle management tactical programs and the operational management projects. Each management level asks the lower level for feedback and adjusts the approaches and targets where needed. This communication leads to realistic and aligned approaches with the buy-in and commitment from the lower managerial levels, who now have a better understanding of the company's direction, the reasoning behind the target setting and their role in it. As the employees see their input is valued and used, they are ready to take the responsibilities to make things happen and accept the related accountabilities. Besides this vertical alignment, there is also a horizontal alignment meaning that the value streams can better cooperate between each other, as they are aware of the higher common company goals and the clearer roles and responsibilities. As this standard strategy planning process is repetitive, the organization gets faster and more efficient through this cycle to generate higher output quality. To keep focus, it is recommended to choose only a limited number of goals. This process requires a strategic vision followed by defining the strategic objectives, which are broken down into smaller ones. Resources are allocated to action plans, which are communicated to all employees. Through a back-and-forth system, the entire organization is involved in delivering breakthroughs. It is about creating a mission, breakthrough targets, and annual goals. The targets are deployed to the organization, where all the employees take their responsibility to add their contribution to realizing the targets. Table 1.2 shows an example of a Hoshin Kanri template.

TABLE 1.2

Hoshin Kanri Template

Strategies × Tactics / Processes / Owners

Strategies ↓ / Tactics	Increase market share	Reduce operational costs	Recruit logistics talent
Take Over Competition	3	1	1
Implement Lean	1	3	2
Hire Recruitment Companies	1	2	3

Processes ↓	Take Over Competition	Implement Lean	Hire Recruitment Companies
Mergers and acquisition	3	1	1
Operational excellence	2	3	1
Human Resources	1	2	3

Owners	Take Over Competition	Implement Lean	Hire Recruitment Companies
John	3	—	—
Eric	—	3	—
Steve	—	—	3

Results	Higher sales	Lower costs	Improved people capabilities
Increase market share	3	2	1
Reduce operational costs	2	3	2
Recruit logistics talent	1	1	3

Legend:
1 weak link
2 moderate link
3 strong link
— no link

A bowling chart is used for reviewing the TTIs by the whole organization on monthly basis. It is a tool to share and track the planned versus actual performance of strategic objectives and highlight their statuses in green if the target is met or in red if the target is not met. The frequency of checking if the projects are on schedule to meet the targets increases further down to the shop floor where DM is practiced. In the interaction between top management and the shop floor, people are asked to share their emotional state, their project status, encountered issues, and what they think can be improved. Table 1.3 shows an example of a Hoshin Kanri bowling chart.

Each TTI is detailed out into an action plan containing the owner, specific tasks, their leads, activity planning, action list, and a resource plan. The progress of these tasks is reviewed regularly and preventive and/or corrective actions are taken to make sure that the original plan is respected. The actual completion date is checked against the planned date and lessons learned are shared in the team to improve future activities. Table 1.4 shows an example of a Hoshin Kanri action plan.

1.6.2 Continuous Improvement

Continuous improvement is about small improvements initiated and implemented by all people throughout the organization to improve the processes they are working in. It helps to identify ways to reduce waste and can be viewed as a formal practice and set of guidelines. Companies are moving to formal approaches such as Lean and W. Edwards Deming's Plan–Do–Check Act (PDCA) cycle. Figure 1.2 illustrates the PDCA cycle. Continuous improvement is a primary focus in these tools, enabling high customer service standards and the reduction of waste. Sustained improvement requires the discipline to create and maintain standards. In the Plan phase, the new standard is set after a kaizen has been executed. In the Do phase, the new way of working is implemented. In the Check phase, the performance is measured and compared with the targets. In the Act phase, countermeasures are defined to go back to the standard if needed. After some time, a new kaizen is started and the PDCA cycle is executed repeatedly. Continuous improvement helps to streamline workflows and constantly improve the way to add value to the customer, saving time and money. The main continuous improvement tools are described in the next section.

TABLE 1.3

Hoshin Kanri Bowling Chart

TTI		Jan	Feb	Mar	Apr	May	Jun	Jul	Aug	Sep	Oct	Nov	Dec
Reduce lead time by 30%	Planned (%)	5	10	15	20	25	30	40	50	60	70	85	100
	Actual (%)	0	20	25	30	40	50	60	70	85	100	100	100
	Status (%)	-5	10	10	10	15	20	20	20	25	30	15	0
Increase delivery reliability to 99%	Planned (%)	10	20	30	40	50	60	70	80	85	90	95	100
	Actual (%)	5	10	15	20	25	30	40	60	70	80	90	100
	Status (%)	-5	-10	-15	-20	-25	-30	-30	-20	-15	-10	-5	0
Reduce costs by 50%	Planned (%)	15	20	25	30	40	50	60	70	80	90	95	100
	Actual (%)	10	20	30	40	50	60	70	80	90	90	90	100
	Status (%)	-5	0	5	10	10	10	10	10	10	0	0	0

TABLE 1.4

Hoshin Kanri Action Plan

Task	Milestone	Lead	Status	Jan	Feb	Mar	Apr	May	Jun	Jul	Aug	Sep	Oct
Train VSM	VSM capabilities	John	Off track	+	=								
Map current state	Current state	Mike	Off track		+	=							
Define future state	Future state	Sara	Off track			+	=						
Identify waste	Waste identification	Emma	Off track				+	=					
Eliminate waste	Countermeasures	Louis	On track					+ =					
Implement countermeasures	Implementation plan	John	On track					+ =					
Set up and measure KPIs	KPIs	Mike	Ahead of plan						=	+			
Sustain new process	Standard work	Sara	Ahead of plan							=	+		
Install monitoring process	PDCA process	Emma	Ahead of plan								=	+	
Review and close actions	Lessons learned	Team	Ahead of plan									=	+

Legend:
+ planned end date
= actual end date

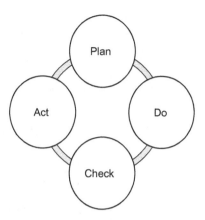

FIGURE 1.2
PDCA cycle.

1.6.3 Kaizen

One of the crucial Lean tools for the continuous improvement process in TPS is the kaizen, a Japanese word for "an improvement" or "change for good." It is in fact not only a tool, but a Toyota-developed way of working to remove waste from processes by following a structured approach to prevent jumping to conclusions and rushing to "solutions." Kaizens are used on a daily basis and they are never ending as they are repeatedly used to improve the same process. What is improved today is considered tomorrow as the starting point for a new improvement activity to meet a higher target. Kaizens are actions to improve processes by eliminating difficult tasks, reducing burdens, and making processes reliable, stable, and capable. The combination of the tool and related improvement process is based on the belief that there are always problems in an organization; the available talent is encouraged to look for problems and not hide them, solve these and work on process improvements, and make mistakes and learn from them without finger pointing. The ultimate goal is to create value for the customer, but this way of working gives also self-confidence to employees and supports teamwork and personal development, leading to a better-motivated work force. Figure 1.3 shows an example of a kaizen template. The improvement process starts with going to the gemba and creating a clear problem statement by answering questions such as: why is it a problem, for whom is it a problem, how big is the problem, when is it a problem? Problems can only be solved if they are deeply understood. Then the current state (as-is flow) is mapped, by using the value stream mapping

Problem:	Date:
Team leader:	Team members:
1. Problem Statement: What is the problem, why is it a problem and why is it important to solve this problem?	5. Countermeasures: What countermeasures can be used to eliminate the root causes? Which part of the problem will be solved by which countermeasure and how much? How sure is this? Is it necessary to experiment before the implementation?
2. Current state: How does the process currently work? What is the actual situation and what is the trend? Is data available to quantify the problem? What is the target? What is the gap between the actual and target situation?	6. Verification: Did the implementation of the countermeasures deliver the expected results? If yes, is there any evidence to support that conclusion? If not, why not?
3. Future state: How should the new process look like? How big is the required improvement?	7. Standardization and sustainment: Has the standard work been created? Have the employees been trained? Is the new way of working embedded in the operations? What measures have been taken to maintain the new process?
4. Root cause analysis: What causes lead to the current performance level? Is it possible to link these with their effects? How much is the individual contribution to the total problem?	8. Follow-up: What additional activities are needed to complete the improvement? Lessons learned: what went well? What could have been done better? What will be done differently next time?

FIGURE 1.3
Kaizen template.

tool, followed by the future state (to-be flow) design. The team members proceed by searching for the root causes that are preventing the process to perform according the future state, which is not necessary the ideal state. After the root causes have been found, the team can think about and try out potential countermeasures, which do not have to be the best and final solutions. Countermeasures are temporary or permanent actions to reduce waste or mitigate problems incrementally, while solutions mean the complete elimination of the issue. After gaining agreement on which countermeasures to go for, it is time to create an implementation plan, which includes who will do what when and how, and anticipate on issues encountered during the implementation. As the Lean philosophy is based on using facts and figures from the gemba and not on assumptions or desk researches, the team members are requested to measure the performance in the new situation to verify that the process has indeed been improved and that the targets have been met. The new process is standardized and described in a standard work template. The process performance is monitored by measuring this and publishing it on a DM board. The new situation serves as the current state for new repetitive kaizens to improve this process repeatedly towards perfection. The value stream mapping, problem solving, standard work, DM tools and processes are explained further in this book. A more extended use of a kaizen approach is the kaizen event. Where a kaizen can be executed on an individual level or in a small team within a few days, a kaizen event is a team activity that can last a few weeks in which a cross-functional team is focused on working only on the chosen topic by using a war-room type of environment. The team members are those who are doing the actual work and are empowered to improve their processes. This way people are brought on board to actively support the change. The team describes the background of the topic, maps the current situation (the Lean term is "current state"), defines a goal statement, works on finding the root causes, brainstorms about temporary and/or permanent countermeasures, gathers evidence that changes have indeed had their impacts and agrees on follow-up actions. Kaizen events support incremental improvements without big financial investments. The team uses an A3 one pager, were the "A3" refers to the paper size, as a guide with instructions how to plan an improvement initiative, lead a team, solve problems, think, discuss and gain agreements, track their activities, and monitor the team's progress and communicate within and outside the team and use it for presentations to report out. It encourages the team members to gain and share insights by writing and rewriting the document to track the development of the problem-solving process. The tool and process combination was originally developed by Toyota and is used by them to facilitate a fast decision-making process. The structured PDCA based approach allows managers to make decisions with confidence, as they know that people have followed the right process to come to the right conclusions and recommendations. Also, team coaches use the A3 for an effective coaching and mentoring process. Within Lean, kaizen is the core activity to remove waste and solve problems, but it is also used as a process to develop people. This is the way to create a learning organization leading to a Lean culture with its specific way of thinking and acting. The preparation of a kaizen event starts four weeks before the actual workshop takes place. Typical activities week-by-week look like:

- Week 1: Define scope, goals, charter, planning and basic information about the current state.
- Week 2: Select team members and team leader.
- Week 3: Organize room, tools, equipment, food, and drinks.
- Week 4: Kick-off and communicate.

Typically, a kaizen workshop takes one to five working days. The day-by-day activities are:

- Day 1: Understand the process. Provide an introduction into Lean, walk and map the current process, and gather data (current state).
- Day 2: Go to the gemba. Observe the process, do time studies, video the process, brainstorm about improvement ideas (future state).
- Day 3: Implement. Walk, simulate, and storm the new process. Implement changes.
- Day 4: Optimize. Work in the new process, identify and fix issues, improve more (sub-) processes, and finalize the details.
- Day 5: Sustain. Document the new way of working and the sustain plan. This is the new current state. Create and roll out a training plan, communicate to stakeholders, and report out to the steering group.

When reporting out to the steering group, it is important for this group to verify if and how much the team contributed to the shipper's strategic goals such as inventory or lead-time reduction, market share increase and/or customer satisfaction improvement. The kaizen team needs to explicitly refer to the goals they worked upon, which Lean tools they used and how they applied them, explain the process of target setting, share what the target was, and show how big the improvement was by providing evidence in the form of validated and confirmed numbers. The kaizen team is also requested to prove that the results are sustainable for a longer period, clarify and share how it is monitoring on a daily basis the actuals and trends against the standards, and immediately see any gap on a DM board. It is also crucial to understand if and how the team applies the PDCA cycle to improve when not meeting the targets or bring the performance to a higher level. The idea is to start working on the high-priority items and show that the approach is successful by fixing real issues for the employees. It is important for the top management to listen to the ideas of all the employees independent from how big or small these ideas are and recognize successful kaizen teams.

1.6.4 Value Stream Mapping

People in the workshop know how a process works in detail. People outside the process think that they know too. This is often based on how the process is described in the quality system documentation. If this is not available, the knowledge is based on interviewing people in the workshop. Then it turns out that people in the same process have different ways of doing the same work. Therefore, it is a good idea to go to the gemba, see the process, and talk with people to know how the work is done in reality. A Lean tool for supporting this process description is the Value Stream Map (VSM). A VSM is a Toyota-developed process map capturing the value-added and non-valued-added activities in a supply chain. Figure 1.4 shows an example VSM. It includes direct and indirect information and material flows to meet the customer demand. Information flows are there to support people in the workshop with planning and work orders.

Examples of material flows are parts supply, inventories, and transportation processes. A VSM is an effective and efficient visual way to understand the goods and information flows from a customer point of view. The added value of a service is created as it moves through a supply chain. A VSM indicates the direct value-added activities, but also the supporting indirect information flows. This method supports the identification and improvement of the whole supply chain and prevents sub-optimizing individual processes. A VSM starts with mapping the current state by using standard symbols and indicating wastes and their root causes. Then a future state, not necessarily the ideal state, is created without the detected waste. It includes key Lean elements such as takt (a German word for "beat") time, one-piece flow, and the pull system. To come to the future state and generate improvement ideas, several tools can be used such as brainstorming, try storming, Pareto, and fishbone diagrams. Then an effort-impact matrix is drawn to prioritize the actions, which will be implemented to come to the future state. Questions to answer for the prioritization session can be:

- Is the action commercial feasible?
- What are the pre-requisites for implementation?

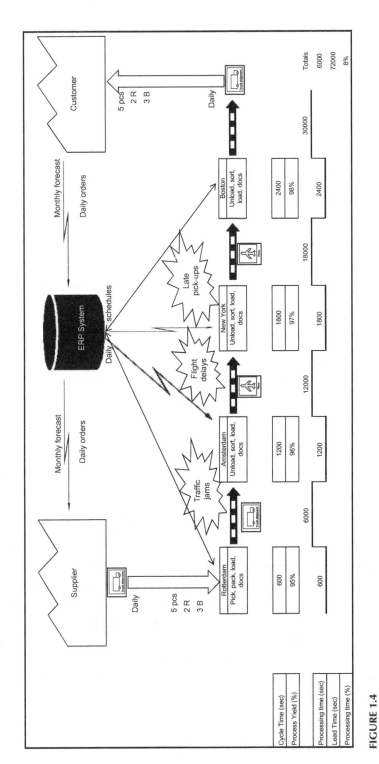

FIGURE 1.4

Value Stream Map.

- What is the best way to implement the action/project as fast as possible?
- Who should be involved in the implementation?
- Are there reference cases?

In addition to the visualization aspect, a VSM creates the starting point for a kaizen. It makes sure that cross-functional team members talk the same language to speed up mutual understanding by looking to the process in a different way than they normally do. It brings data, such as lead-times, inventory, and defect levels, together. People who work in the process and those who are in the supporting functions share their own ways of looking at and measuring process performance. It is not a static map. It is updated when there are changes. The VSM tool is also called "Material and Information Flow Diagram" within Toyota. Rother and Shook describe in their book "Learning to See: Value Stream Mapping to Create Value and Eliminate Muda" an eight-step approach to create a VSM. It is a team activity, wherein each team member has a task to gather actual data by, for example, using stopwatches and videotapes. A VSM captures end-to-end processes from order intake to payment receipt and includes information and material connections. VSMs are used to communicate current and future states regarding improvement initiatives. The objective is to find improvement opportunities to reduce waste and make the process flow. The perfect flow is the ideal situation where a service is produced according to the takt time with leveled workload to meet the customer demand without waiting times, delays, movements, non-value-added activities, and defects.

A VSM exercise consists of two phases. The first phase is a preparation phase, which consists of these activities:

1. Select a value stream to map. VSM pilots are usually started on a multi-process level to create a model line, which can be used as reference for further rollout of Lean. The next level is to draw VSMs on the company level, as this is normally the highest level people can optimize within their span of control. In a mature Lean environment, it becomes feasible to create VSMs on an enterprise level by adding supplier and customer sites to the value stream.
2. Assign a maximum of eight team members and provide them a Lean basics training. As there is no individual who knows all the details

of every process, it is important to include people who work in the process and know the details.

3. Collect process information. Map the process starting from the customer and work backwards to the supplier. Prepare open questions for people working in the workshop for when going to the gemba. Inform them upfront and mention that the team members are coming to measure the process and not the people.

The second phase starts when the team comes together for the VSM workshop and includes these steps:

1. Go to the gemba; draw the process boxes; and gather data such as inventory, lead-time, cycle time, waiting time, and work in process. A process box is a place where material and/or information is transformed into a product or service. Cycle time is the time needed to complete a process step for one unit including the walking, manual, and machinery activities. Waiting time is the time a piece needs to wait before it is worked upon in the next process step. Lead-time is the sum of all cycle and waiting times.

2. Draw the material flow from right to left, starting from the customer back to the supplier. Map the customer demand and the requested delivery times and quality levels. It is possible to draw parallel process flows, but focus on the main process, suppliers, and customers. Sub-processes can be worked upon in separate VSM events. Add the information flows. Material flows from left to right, where information flows the other way around: from right to left. Draw the information flows and their direction and add rework flows.

3. Fill in process box data such as cycle times, yields, lead-times, defect rates, and inventory levels.

4. Sum up the total cycle and waiting times at the bottom of the map.

5. Identify the value-added and non-value-added activities; create kaizen bursts and indicate potential improvements.

A butcher paper is pasted on the wall of the conference room to create a VSM. Markers and sticky notes are used to write down the process steps and paste them on the paper. The sticky notes allow changing the VSM frequently and without losing the overview, which is the case when using pens. This way of working mobilizes team members to walk and think. It improves the communication as people can ask for explaining the input of each individual. It is not recommended to use software, preventing loss of time learning how to use it. Once the mapping is completed, the team can upload the drawings in the software for further communication towards the stakeholders.

1.6.5 Daily Management

DM is a daily routine to make sure that processes are performing well to deliver the customer needs. This tool is developed by Toyota and is a structured and disciplined daily meeting where employees come together to talk about what is going well, what problems there are, and how these can be fixed by using the problem-solving tool, which is discussed in the next paragraph. It is a control system to make sure that the daily objectives are met by using a forward-looking and action-oriented approach. The intention of the meeting or call is not to review only past performance. Taking some time to learn from the past can help, but most of the time should be spent to agree on new actions to make the targets of the day. The meeting should not be longer than 15 minutes. It is important to start and stop on time and to not allow extensions. Running the business this way requires the discipline to join the meetings or calls every day. Processes and business environments are that complex that a less frequent follow-up system is not good enough to survive. Make sure that all the invitees join and that there is an onboarding process for new hires. DM requires the visualization of the performances in such a way that it is easy to see when processes are deviating from the norm. A common way to do this is to place a DM board on the shop floor where the work takes place and stand around it when having the daily meeting. Figure 1.5 illustrates an example of a DM board.

In basis, it is not necessary to make minutes, but to write the agreements and actions on the board. In case of a virtual environment, it is possible to use other presentation and registration tools. This way, employees better understand what is important for the customer and feel more ownership and a greater sense of urgency to detect problems, analyze them, and implement corrective and/or preventive actions. Each team member has the responsibility to use the standard work to prepare and update part of the information on the board before the meeting starts. The board consists of three sections: people, performance, and improvements. In the people section, employees inform each other about their wellbeing and if they can deliver the required output by pasting the

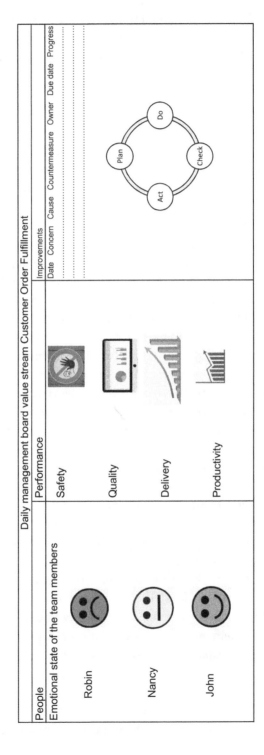

FIGURE 1.5
Daily management board.

applicable smiley colors (green, yellow, red) on the board. The performance section informs the employees about the actual critical process performance, the target, the gap between these, and the trend. Common KPIs measured are safety, quality, delivery, and productivity. Example visualization tools are Pareto diagrams, graphs, charts, checklists, and colors. Make sure that the information is up to date and reliable and do not allow KPIs to stay on red for a long time. Review what the problem is and check whether the target is realistic. The improvements section contains the submission date; concern, describing the problem; cause, indicating the root cause of the problem; countermeasure, showing the action to fix the problem; owner; due date; and progress made. It is important that the agreed actions are followed up on a daily basis to make sure that they are executed in accordance with the plan. Do not allow actions to stay open for a long time. Such a board attracts attention of the employees, who can see in a few seconds if the process is under control or not. If the process produces output outside the control limits, people are allowed to stop it. Then they start working on the root cause analysis by following the pre-defined problem-solving steps. They are encouraged to participate and share their ideas for temporary or permanent countermeasures to make the targets on time. This problem-solving process on a daily basis is easier than analyzing situations that occurred weeks or months ago. It also allows the team to anticipate faster on issues. DM is necessary to manage the right Lean behaviors in the right direction and realize the Lean goals. Visualization of the people's emotional state, KPIs, and improvement status information makes the deployment process easier. Other DM topics are disciplined standard work, leader standard work, and leadership and accountability checks. Basic DM standard work instructions include information about when, how, where, and who to do what. Leader standard work is a daily routine for the value stream leader to verify if the planned work has been done timely and correctly. By using a daily checklist to audit processes, people will start checking themselves before the leader asks. The Lean philosophy is looking for this behavior. This DM routine needs to be executed by all the layers of the organization in tiered meetings or calls. An example tiered meeting approach is to have the first DM in the morning on the shop floor, another one for the middle management around lunch time, and the last one for the top management at the end of the day. In each tier meeting, a representative from the lower tier joins to allow the information to flow bottom-up and top-down on a daily basis to enable an easier management decision-making process. This way of working is also more fact based and less subjective.

1.6.6 Problem Solving

When there is a problem in traditional companies, people try to solve what they think is the problem, immediately. They jump to conclusions without doing a proper root cause analysis and brainstorm about the different ways to solve the problem. This wastes resources without solving the real problem. Toyota developed a structured problem-solving approach to eliminate these disadvantages. A problem can be defined as a customer need that has not been fulfilled or a gap between the as-is and to-be situations. Not constantly meeting the targets can also be seen as a problem. A problem can be time, money, or occurrence based, but they are interrelated and influence each other. A number of line stops, occurrences, leads to loss of time and time can be expressed in money. Countermeasure impact can be expressed in quality levels, lead-times and/or cost improvements. As there are many ways a team can look at a problem, it is important to create a common understanding and problem definition to get all the team members working in the same direction. This enables a faster way to countermeasure the problem and prevents valuable time lost in debating subjective criteria and opinions. A good problem definition is not easy. There are different levels of when and where to see a problem:

- Point of recognition: "symptom" of the problem
- Point of occurrence: "location" of the problem
- Point of cause: "root cause" of the problem

The idea behind this structure is that what people see does not have to be the real problem. It is necessary to dig a bit deeper to find the root cause of the problem. The application of the PDCA cycle is crucial in this process. The first phase is to execute a proper root cause analysis and agree on the countermeasures (P), then implement them (D) and check if the counter-measures did have an impact (C). If the countermeasures did work, then standardize the process (A). If not, then undertake another PDCA, and more if needed, until the issue is solved. It is important to learn to see waste and issues. Once a problem is detected (e.g., after using the "5 times why" tool), it needs to be fixed immediately. Structural problem solving enables people to see the weak points and supports the root causes with facts and figures. After that, countermeasures are agreed upon and implemented to close the gap. Regular reviews are executed to summarize lessons learned and share them within and outside the team.

Figure 1.6 contains the eight steps of the problem-solving cycle. It is important to go through all of them without skipping any step. For clarifying the problem in step 1, the following questions of the "5w + 1h" tool can be asked: What is the problem? Why is it a problem? Where is it a problem? When is it a problem? Who is it a problem for? How much of a problem is it? These questions lead to a problem statement, which is Specific Measurable Achievable Realistic and Time (SMART) bound. A problem statement does not include a root cause and/or countermeasure, as these are unknown at the start of the cycle. If these are known upfront, then the problem seems to be clear and there is no need to go through the problem-solving cycle. These "quick wins" and "low-hanging fruit" can be implemented immediately. This approach needs to be practiced carefully as small, difficult to find, underlying issues can be challenging to identify. Step 2 is to breakdown the problem in workable pieces and choose the sub-problems to work upon. Before doing so, it is necessary to go to the gemba and see the process, learn how the work is done and what issues can pop up. Ask people in the workshop

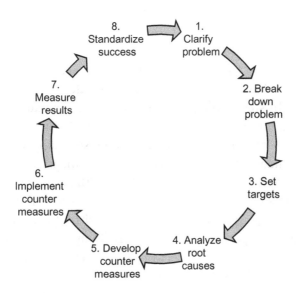

FIGURE 1.6
Problem-solving cycle.

open-ended questions. By visiting the actual workplace, problems become clear and visible. Based on those impressions, improvement ideas can be generated. Before going to the gemba it is important to announce this upfront to the shop floor people and mention that the team is not coming to measure them, but that they would like to know more about the process capabilities. A successful gemba walk requires a solid preparation. It must be clear what the purpose of the walk is: Is the objective to know more about the current state? Or is it for identifying waste? Or measuring process times? Then split the team in small groups and go to the gemba. Once there, try to not judge or think immediately in solutions; be humble, patient, listen actively and make pictures, videos, process maps, and time studies. Take time to stand still and observe the process, the people, and their interactions, and write these down before starting asking questions. Review, comment, and discuss the findings later with the team. Typical questions to ask can include the following: When does this problem occur? How often does it happen? Where is it seen? What is the impact of the problem? What standard work is used? Is this followed? Who are your internal and external customers? What requirements do they have? How often do you talk with them? What do you do first when you start your shift? Why is that necessary? How much time does it take you? Which part of the process is working well? Which part does not? Why not? What aspects of your job do you like the most? Which the least? Why? Instruct all people joining the walk to document their observations to cover as much information as possible. Then summarize the process descriptions and validate them with the people on the shop floor. Step 3 is to set a target for the new situation. This does not have to be the ideal state, but a better situation than before. In step 4, the potential root causes, including the data to support them, are identified. For this step, the "5 times why" tool can be used. The root causes are grouped and presented by a fishbone, also called an Ishikawa diagram, which is a causal diagram that shows the causes of a problem in the form of a fishbone. Then the countermeasures are defined in step 5. This includes a plan with who will do what when. Take the time to plan slowly, but act fast. Prioritize the countermeasures with the biggest impact and the least effort. Temporary countermeasures are implemented to stop the bleeding and mitigate the negative impact on customers, while working on finding the root causes and permanent countermeasures. Step 6 is about communicating and implementing the countermeasures and learning from these experiences. Before going over to the full implementation, it is recommended to do some testing. In case of successful results, standardize the new process, which can serve as the new current state for new kaizens. If not, apply the PDCA cycle again and evaluate the root cause analysis. Find the issues and agree on additional countermeasures followed by a new PDCA cycle. The results are checked against the targets in the gemba and these are made visible by including the actual performance, target, trend, and gap in the performance graph. Verify if the identified root cause analyses and countermeasures were correct and effective by measuring the results in step 7. Good results need to be the outcome of a good problem-solving process and not the outcome of other influences. If bad results are the outcome of a bad problem-solving process, there is room for learning from the mistakes. It is good to learn from what went well and what did not go well. Step 8 is there to standardize and sustain the improvement. In case of successful results, standardize the new way of working and see if the same improvement can be used in other processes and/or locations. In case of unsuccessful results, execute new PDCAs and share the lessons learned. Agree on who will be responsible for auditing which process, when, and where. Focus on those processes with the highest risk by assessing the probability that something can go wrong and how severe the impact can be.

Other analytical tools that can be used in this problem-solving process include the following:

- Flowchart: a diagram representing a process by using boxes to visualize the process steps and connect them with arrows.
- Scatter plot: a way to display the relationship between two variables by displaying coordinates.
- Checklist: a tally sheet in which each data type is grouped.
- Pareto diagram: a chart containing bars and a line graph. The bars are in descending order. The line is ascending and shows the cumulative value.
- Control chart: a chart with upper and lower control limits in between the process values need to stay.
- Ishikawa diagram: a fishbone method to show the relation between cause and effect.
- Histogram: a diagram representing the distribution of data.

1.6.7 Standard Work

Activities that are efficient, designed in the right order, and strictly followed by each team member are called standard work. Taiichi Ohno and Shigeo Shingo at Toyota developed standard work in the 1950s and 1960s. This approach ensures process stability and maintains process knowledge, which can be used as the baseline for kaizens and problem-solving events. It is a good way to sustain implemented improvements. Asking people to write down process steps helps them to think about the most effective and efficient way to do their work. Standard work can be used to train new employees, as it should be written in a simple format that can be understood by any employee. These instructions can also be used for auditing processes as they help to check if the work is taking place in the agreed and documented way. Typical auditing questions can include the following: What is the target condition? What is the actual condition? What obstacles are preventing people from reaching the target condition? What obstacles are addressed now? What is the next topic to improve? What has been learned from the issues? Table 1.5 provides an example of standard work.

Standard work includes information about when, how, where, and who to do what. The objective is to organize the work in a safe and logical way to prevent variances in the process outputs. This limits the number of defects and makes the process outcomes predictable. It allows the company to improve its resource planning and deliver on the committed date and time. All employees need to follow the standard work as it organizes work in the best order and gets the best out of people, machines, and raw material. Standard work prevents performance drops. Recovering from these drops is a waste of energy, which can be used to improve processes instead of returning to the standard. People doing the same work in different ways is leading to different quality outcomes. Each employee tends to train his or her way of working to the new hires. This makes it difficult to retrieve where in a process a problem occurred. Standard work is introduced to agree on one way of working for all operators. This documented and standardized work is then used to train new hires, safeguarding high quality and safety levels. It makes it easier to see when the process differs from the standard. A process in control is reliable and gives the same outcome when executed by an employee repeatedly. It is also repeatable and provides the same outcome when different people execute the same

TABLE 1.5

Standard Work

Process Name: Complete Order Check				Revision Date: 1-1-2017	
Start Process: Order Dropped in SAP				Team Leader: J. Johnson	
End Process: Order Released for Picking				Value Stream: Order Fulfillment	

Process Step	What	Where	How	When	Who
1	Open the order	SAP transaction x	Double-click on the order	Within 30 min	Export control officer
2	Check the customer	Export control tool	Fill in the full name	Within 10 min	Export control officer
3	Find the product	WMS transaction a	Search product code	Within 5 min	Order taker
4	Verify quantity	WMS transaction b	Double-click on product	Within 5 min	Inventory controller
5	Check invoice payment	SAP transaction y	Enter invoice number	Within 10 min	Administrator
6	Reserve products	WMS transaction c	Click "Reserve"	Within 5 min	Order taker
7	Release the order	SAP transaction z	Click "Release"	Within 5 min	Order taker

process. The process is capable when it meets the performance targets. The main steps for setting up standard work are:

- Step 1: Calculate the takt time.
- Step 2: Balance the work.
- Step 3: Sequence the work.
- Step 4: Write down the standard work.
- Step 5: Sustain the new way of working.

Step 1 starts by understanding processes and creating detailed process maps. Do not assume anything, but go to the gemba. Observe the process and execute time studies to measure the cycle time, output per day, yield, number of people per day, etc. Announce the visit to the gemba on time

Takt time = net available time in seconds per day/customer demand per day

FIGURE 1.7
Takt time calculation.

to the people in the process and it should contain the message that the observers are not coming to control them, but to map and measure the process. Based on this information the takt time can be calculated. Takt time is the time in which a service needs to be produced to meet the customer demand. Figure 1.7 shows the takt time calculation.

The net available time is exclusive of breaks, meetings, and sanitary stops. When the customer demand goes up and the working time remains the same, the takt time decreases, meaning the speed of work needs to go up to meet the customer demand. When the customer demand goes down and the working time remains the same, the takt time increases meaning the speed of work can slow down. When the customer demand does not change and the working time increases, the takt time increases, meaning the speed of work can slow down too. When the customer demand does not change and the working time decreases, the takt time decreases, meaning the speed of work needs to go up to meet the customer demand. Cycle time is the time of a worker to complete a task. Cycle time can be measured by a time study and can vary over time due to changes in machine set-up, work force, and ways of working or raw material. The time study gives insight into which processes are fast and which are slow. Step 2 is about bringing the out-of-balance processes under control, meaning bringing back the cycle times to the takt time level. To check if the customer demand can be met with the current process set-up, cycle time is divided by takt time. The ideal situation is total cycle time per day = total takt time per day. However, this approach will lead to delays in case there is any issue with the process, which needs to be stopped temporarily. To allow for these situations, the cycle time needs to be a bit lower than the takt time. The Japanese word for balancing the work is Yamazumi, which is a method to evaluate the work balance by creating a graph with stacked task times and how these can be distributed equally over the available people. It is a useful tool to calculate what the cycle time per person needs to be, to realize the customer demand. It visualizes the identification of bottlenecks and resource issues. The final goal is to create a one-piece flow meeting the customer demand. Variation leads to waste and overburden as it is difficult to plan resources in a good way to meet customer requirements. Figure 1.8 shows a typical process with varying cycle times.

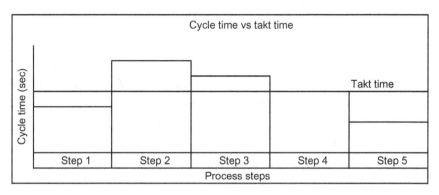

FIGURE 1.8
Cycle time vs takt time.

It is neither cost-efficient nor motivating to plan resources against the maximum possible customer demand, meaning that operators are underutilized in case of a stable process. It is therefore important to level out the daily workload by smoothing out variations based on the takt time. As different products have different takt times, it is recommended to produce daily a mix of products. The idea is to get all the process steps performing on the takt time. This can be realized by re-distributing the work, combining steps, speeding them up, and other mitigation actions. Step 3 defines the optimal work sequence taking into account questions such as which work needs to be done first? Which work can be done in parallel? What needs to be done by an operator? Do they have capacity restrictions? What is the time it takes to move to the next phase? What is the time it takes to pick parts? What are the waiting times? After defining the sequence of work, it is time to create the most efficient, safe, and ergonomic layout. Step 4 is about creating a standard work document and getting this approved by all the stakeholders as confirmation that the new way of working is accepted as the new standard. Step 5 is there to sustain the standard work. This can be realized by using DM boards and audits ("Kamishibai" in Japanese). After having the standard work in place, it becomes less difficult to do audits. Monitor the daily target achievements and related improvement activities by using visual performance dashboards. These boards are set up in the middle of the process to enable immediate process status checks by anyone in the workshop. After stabilizing the standard work, new kaizens can be started to work on realizing a higher target.

1.6.8 5S

A clean, safe, and well-organized workplace helps to see wastes and eliminate them. A nicer and easier way to remember this philosophy is "5S." The five Ss are five Japanese words that start with an "S": Seiri, Seiton, Seiso, Seiketsu, and Shitsuke. The English translations are sort, straighten, sweep, standardize, and sustain. This methodology was invented by Toyota in the 1970s. As it is a cyclical process, it is required to finish the previous step before going to the next one, preventing waste by, for example, cleaning things not needed. The idea is to sort out what is needed and what is not needed. What is not needed can be labeled and processed as follows:

- Trash: Throw away.
- Defectives: Repair, scrap or recycle.
- Not needed: Sell or give away.
- Used daily: Keep at Point of Use (POU). Less frequently used items are stored in a distant area.

With straightening, things are put in a place for easy access. Sweeping means cleaning the floors and equipment. The workplace is standardized in such a way that abnormalities become visible. The use of visual tools such as pictures is recommended as these say more than words. Sustain the process by making it a habit and a daily activity. 5S is a disciplined way of creating and keeping an efficient and effective workplace. Some companies use the term "6S" as they add another "S" for Safety. Incidents can lead to near misses, minor and serious injuries, or even death. Most accidents are caused by people's unsafe actions and/or physical conditions. To increase people's safety in a workshop, it must be clear where to find the nearest emergency exit, escape routes, alarm buttons, fire extinguishers, first-aid kits, and Automated External Defibrillator (AED). In Lean, safety comes first, followed by quality and then efficiency. Typical visual tools used to improve the safety are color codes, signs, lights, sounds, and glass walls. 5S is not only applicable in a production environment, but also in an office setting (e.g., to reduce the time to find an e-mail, a file, or a storage location). According to Taiichi Ohno, 5S is one of the Lean building blocks: "if you cannot do 5S, you cannot do Lean." Lean is about eliminating waste and that is what 5S is doing: it removes hazards, prevents looking for lost items, and reduces motion. The toughest challenge of 5S is the change of attitude. People need to believe that a clean and organized workplace is not only good for the company, but also for their own personal satisfaction. They need to own the process, regularly audit it, and make it a daily habit. Table 1.6 shows an example of a 5S audit checklist.

TABLE 1.6

5S Checklist

Date:		
Scored by:		
Location:		**Score (1–10)**
Sort: Define what is needed and what is not needed	Safety hazards, such as oil and chemicals, exist	10
	Items present in walkways, stairways, fire exit	9
	Unnecessary inventories, supplies, parts present	8
	Items on walls, boards, etc.	7
	Equipment, tools, furniture not needed are present	6
Straighten: A place for everything and everything in its place	No fixed places for items	5
	Tools not in their places	4
	Correct places for items not clear	3
	No indication of walkways and workstations	2
	Items hanging around after use	1
Sweep: Clean and organize	Cleaning material not accessible	10
	Floors, walls, stairs, etc. are not free of dirt	9
	Lines, labels, etc. are not clean	8
	Equipment and tools not kept clean	7
	Other cleaning issues	6
Standardize: Maintain and monitor the progress	Standards not visible	5
	No cleaning checklists available	4
	Cleaning instructions missing	3
	KPIs not easy to read	2
	No standard work	1
Sustain: Sustain the rules	Personal belongings not stored	10
	5S inspection not performed	9
	5S activities not done	8
	5S principles not known	7
	People not trained	6
Total		6.0

TABLE 1.7

Lean Tools and Their Applicability

Lean Tool	Applicability
Hoshin Kanri	Long-term strategy and policy deployment process to realize break-through improvements
Kaizen	Short-term approach to implement continuous and incremental improvements
Value stream mapping	Process of optimizing value streams by identifying and eliminating non-value-added activities
Daily management	Daily event to follow-up the order realization processes and anticipate issues as they occur
Problem solving	Process to analyze and solve a complex problem, which requires a step-by-step deep dive
Standard work	Way of working to standardize processes and make them capable, stable, and reliable
5S	Structured approach to realize a safe, efficient, and effective workplace organization

1.6.9 Overview

Table 1.7 shows a summary of when to apply which Lean tool as described in the previous paragraphs.

1.7 LEAN MATURITY

Although Toyota did not implement Lean assessments, it seems for western companies to be helpful as they are used to the approach of: "you get what you measure." There are assessment tools to measure the Lean maturity of an organization and indicate what needs to be done to reach the next level. The Lean assessment is an audit performance scorecard reported to the top management. Customer feedback provides what is going well and what can be improved. Internal reports provide the data about Lean practices. There are various Lean maturity assessment tools, which can indicate the maturity levels in, for example, 4 phases or a score of "1" to "10." Phase 1, of the 4 phases, means "TTIs are not met;" phase 2 relates to "Some TTIs are met;" phase 3 is "Many TTIs are met;" and phase 4 indicates "All TTIs are met." Likewise, a score of "1" means "No evidence" and "10" means "Clear evidence." Table 1.8

TABLE 1.8

Basic Lean Assessment Tool

Lean Principle	Traditional Approach	Score										Lean Approach
1	Short-term	1	2	3	4	5	6	7	8	9	10	Long-term
2	Batch	1	2	3	4	5	6	7	8	9	10	Flow
3	Push	1	2	3	4	5	6	7	8	9	10	Pull
4	Unbalanced workload	1	2	3	4	5	6	7	8	9	10	Balanced workload
5	Fix problems later	1	2	3	4	5	6	7	8	9	10	Fix problems immediately
6	No standard work	1	2	3	4	5	6	7	8	9	10	Standard work
7	Hide problems	1	2	3	4	5	6	7	8	9	10	Make problems visible
8	Technology in the lead	1	2	3	4	5	6	7	8	9	10	People and services in the lead
9	Tell	1	2	3	4	5	6	7	8	9	10	Teach
10	People are costs	1	2	3	4	5	6	7	8	9	10	Respect people
11	Push partners	1	2	3	4	5	6	7	8	9	10	Respect partners
12	Sit in the office	1	2	3	4	5	6	7	8	9	10	Go to the gemba
13	Plan fast, act slow	1	2	3	4	5	6	7	8	9	10	Plan slow, act fast
14	Repeated mistakes	1	2	3	4	5	6	7	8	9	10	Learn from mistakes

shows an example of a basic Lean assessment tool based on the 14 Toyota principles as described by Jeffrey K. Liker in his book "The Toyota Way: 14 Management Principles from the World's Greatest Manufacturer." It is an indication of how far along a company is in applying Lean principles. A typical Lean implementation starts with training and engaging the leadership team in Lean philosophy. To be ready for the Lean change, the following prerequisites have to be in place: burning platform is clear, potential roadblocks have been removed, project organization is created, and a model line has been chosen. The model line is a limited scope of an organization or process where the first improvements are implemented and which can be used as a success story to market the Lean philosophy in the rest of the company. Then it is time to think about scaling up and standardizing the new way or working by setting up the right organization for further Lean deployment. This organization includes the creation of value streams with a dedicated value stream leader and the adoption of a "train the trainer" approach for rolling out the Lean foundations to the rest of the organization. The continuous improvement culture is sustained by constantly assessing, measuring, and reporting out the Lean level scorecard to the top management. This enables the organization to work towards a world-class level application of Lean. Depending on the organization's size and/or scope, it can take up to five years to implement the Lean concept. The rollout can be done site-by-site, process-by-process, business-by-business, or region-by-region.

2

Transportation

Transportation is part of logistics, which originated in the military to support the troop and equipment movements of military operations. Nowadays it is used for various types of operations in both the public and private areas. Transportation is not a standalone operating system as it is derived from the logistics strategy, which in its turn is created from the company's strategy. Also, for transportation, there is a need for a mission, vision, and deployment approach leading to a transportation policy statement. Logistics deals with the physical movement of goods from one place to another and for just-in-time delivery against acceptable costs and includes inbound transportation, warehousing, inventory management, outbound transportation, customer deliveries, returns, and repair flows. Logistics is part of supply chain management, which covers all market processes such as sourcing, manufacturing, and distribution of products to the market. Complementary processes are supply and demand planning, procurement, subcontracting, product development, and cooperation with external partners. Transportation is the ability to pick-up the right quantity of correct goods within the agreed service and price level and deliver them at the agreed location. The longer the transit times, the higher the inventories, the more space and energy needed. A truck arriving too early needs the driver and the truck to wait. A truck arriving too late requires the warehouse personnel to wait. Transportation can reduce inventory and warehousing costs, while speeding up delivery to the end customer. It is the most central point where a lot of information about production, sales, and marketing comes together. This enables the transportation function to make optimized decisions over the whole supply chain. The ultimate goal of transportation is to be consistent, reliable, and flexible. This needs to be realized in a challenging environment: high customer requirements, cost reduction targets, shorter lead-time requests, personnel shortages, market capacity issues, network complexities, environmental restrictions, increasing congestion, legal requirements, fuel cost increase, and road taxes. Transportation management decisions need to be based on well-understood customer requirements. Customers count on a high level of quality and efficient delivery of their goods by motivated employees using standard processes. Transportation is used to find the optimal balance between costs, inventory, and service levels. Typical costs are transportation and warehousing. Typical inventory-related costs are the costs for purchasing and ordering the raw material, using labor and machines to produce the finished products, and financing the inventory carrying costs for storage, obsolescence, scrap, loss, damage, and other non-quality costs and cost of capital as inventories require investment of money, which cannot be used for other business cases. Figure 2.1 illustrates the mathematical formula of calculating the Weighted Average Cost of Capital (WACC).

The inventory carrying costs can be up to 20%–25% of the product value. Service indicates the product availability on stock once ordered. In traditional understanding, a high service leads to high costs and high inventories. High inventory leads to high costs and high service. High costs lead to high inventories and high service. Another relationship is that the more, especially expensive, inventory is centralized in one central distribution center leading to higher service levels, the lower the working capital and inventory holding costs are, but the higher the transportation costs are as the inbound flows from vendors and outbound good flows to customers need to travel longer distances. In Lean, inventories and costs are reduced while increasing the service. By working on lead-time reduction, all these aspects are addressed at the same time. A balance between the three elements is leading to an acceptable performance of the three

$$WACC = (E/V) * Re + (D/V) * Rd * (1 - Tc)$$

Re = cost of equity
Rd = cost of debt
E = market value of company's equity
D = market value of company's debt
$V = E + D$ = market value of company's financing
E/V = percentage of financing that is equity
D/V = percentage of financing that is debt
Tc = corporate tax rate

FIGURE 2.1
WACC calculation.

variables. However, this strategy does not enable a company to excel in one of them. A customer is comparing the performance of different suppliers; it may turn out that some suppliers who do explicitly choose one of the three is outperforming the rest of the competition. Fast transportation, and thus high costs, can be used as a strategic service differentiator to generate more sales. Transportation in excess of what is required is waste and should be eliminated as much as possible. There are many types of transportation companies. There are asset-based companies who have their own equipment. In road transportation, these are mainly small companies, which can own one or more trucks. The bigger companies mostly do not have their own equipment. These freight forwarders hire the small asset-based companies to handle their customers' cargo. They act as an intermediary between the shipper and actual transportation companies. This process of subcontracting is a way to limit the amount of investments needed to cover a large transportation area. It is also a risk mitigation tool for when volumes go down. The forwarder contracts with the subcontractors are often valid for a year or less, which enables the forwarder to reduce equipment not needed quite fast by not offering the subcontractor a new contract. Besides scaling down, it is possible to scale up quickly. In the air, parcel, and express business there are big freight forwarders, who do not own airplanes. The bigger companies in sea freight do own ships. More and more companies offer a one-stop-shop concept, meaning that they try to sell their customers all modalities to all destinations. However, no company can deliver the best performance in all modalities and regions. DHL is the global market leader offering a wide range of supply chain services. Number two is Kuehne + Nagel, followed by CEVA and UPS. DHL has a global market share of a single digit indicating the high-level fragmentation in the industry. Service providers are constantly adding parts of the value chain to their control to increase profits. The expectation is that there will be further consolidation as there are uneven market shares in the different regions and carriers cooperate more and more in alliances to improve their efficiency. The profit margins are low, which is the result of severe competition and volatile markets with shortening contract durations and local small transportation companies, which are better in adhering to local customer requirements. Forwarders try to differentiate service offers to increase margins. They specialize themselves in complex supply chains, value-added services and specific solutions in specific industries. Other words used for cargo are freight, goods, or products, while the shipper is called "consignor" and the receiver "consignee." A "notify party" is the company to be contacted by the carrier once the goods arrive at the destination. This can be a signal for the receiver's customs broker to start the clearance process. The transportation lead-time is defined as the time between the pickup of a shipment from one place until the delivery at another place. Other words used for lead-time are Turn Around Time (TAT), Transit Time (TT), and transportation time. Many words are randomly used for companies handling transportation, while their exact scope of work can differ significantly. The terms can be grouped as:

- A company managing goods flows on behalf of a customer by picking, packing, and shipping them by using their own, asset- or non-asset-based, network or subcontracted parties: Logistics Service Providers (LSPs), service providers, Lead Logistics Providers (LLPs), xParty Logistics (xPL), where "x" can be a "1," "2," "3," "4," or "5." The xPL structure will be described later in this book.
- An asset- or non-asset-based company moving cargo from one location to another: carriers, freight carriers, freight companies, trucking carriers, suppliers, transporters, transport companies, transportation companies, transport providers, transportation providers.
- A non-asset-based company, which arranges transport of goods on behalf of either the shipper or receiver: freight forwarders, forwarders.

2.1 LOCATION AND FLOW TYPES

Transportation means a movement from one location to another. There are many location and flow types, which are described in the following section, although the exact definitions and characteristics can differ per business and type of goods (spare parts, general cargo, and food):

- Pick-Up and Drop-Off (PUDO) and Hold for Pick-Up (HFPU): a temporary (drive-in) storage location enabling people to pick up and drop off goods at this location.
- Field Stocking Location (FSL): a storage location close to customers to enable deliveries within a few hours if the distance allows this. A FSL is replenished from a Regional Distribution Center (RDC)

or Central Distribution Center (CDC). The non-urgent orders are delivered from a RDC or CDC. Delivery locations can be customer sites, PUDOs, HFPUs, other DCs (also called rebalancing), or scrap locations.

- Local Distribution Center (LDC): a national storage location where products are stored and from where customer orders are delivered on the next or same business day when the distance allows this. A LDC is replenished from a RDC or a CDC. The intention is to deliver only locally required products from this location. The non-urgent deliveries come from a RDC or CDC. Delivery locations can be customer sites, PUDOs, HFPUs, other DCs, or scrap locations.
- RDC: a regional storage location where products are stored, from where customer orders are delivered next or same business day if the distance allows this. LDCs and FSLs are replenished from this location. It receives purchased products from the goods suppliers and rebalancing flows from the other DCs. In addition, unused returns can be sent back to this location. Delivery destinations can be customer sites, PUDOs, HFPUs, (repair) vendor premises, other DCs, FSLs, or scrap locations.
- CDC: a global storage location where all products are stored and delivered within one or more days and from where RDCs are replenished. Both CDCs and RDCs can receive goods that require repacking as the suppliers are normally sending bulk packages. If the shipper is shipping single pieces, the bulky packages need to be repacked into single-piece packages. Even if the supplier delivers single-piece packages, these might require repacking as they might not be strong enough to prevent damage in the transportation network.
- Repair Center (RC): a location where returned goods can be repaired and sent back to a DC or scrapped.
- Scrap Center (SC): a location where waste that has no economic value is scrapped. The raw material can be recovered by recycling.
- Factory warehouse: this is a storage location on the factory site. This is possible when the factory has the space and capabilities to store its Supplier Owned Inventory (SOI), other raw material, and/or finished products. It can be owned by the factory but also outsourced to a third-party service provider.
- Cross-dock location: the incoming shipments are brought directly from the receiving to the shipping lanes for forwarding to the next

destination. The time these goods can stay in this location is limited to a few hours. The goods are not put in stock.

- Merge center: a consolidation center where products from multiple vendors are grouped and sent as one shipment to a customer. This delivery structure is often used in make-to-order concepts.
- Market warehouse: a national storage location where the inventory can be owned and the warehouse managed by the local organization. The local customer orders are delivered on the next or same business day when the distance allows this. A market warehouse can be replenished from a RDC, CDC, or product supplier. The intention is to serve local market needs as they can require specific products.
- Factory: a production site with buildings and machinery where people operate these machines and make products.
- (Repair) vendor site: a location that repairs goods. It can be the location where the goods are produced, but it can be also a warehouse or an office.
- Return warehouse: a location where used and unused returns from the markets and engineers are received, inspected, stored, and sent to a repair vendor, DC, or scrap location.
- Returns consolidation location: a central returns collection point where individual market returns are consolidated into bigger shipments and sent to a RC or a DC.

Flow types can be described as:

- Upstream: an inbound goods flow from a product supplier to a storage location
- Mainstream: a goods flow from an internal to another internal storage location
- Downstream: an outbound goods flow from a storage location to a customer
- Returns: a goods flow from a customer to a return storage location
- Repairs: a goods flow from a return storage location to a repair supplier
- Scrap: a goods flow of no economic or only its raw material value from any location to a scrap location, which can be a disposal company

2.2 OUTBOUND PROCESS

The outbound process starts when a Sales Order (SO) drops from a customer Enterprise Resource Planning (ERP) system, mostly via an Electronic Data Interchange (EDI) interface, into the Warehouse Management System (WMS). When the order drops at the warehouse, a Delivery Note (DN) is created. Based on the order priority, the shipment is picked, packed, and shipped. The shipping process requires the availability of basic information such as the shipper's and receiver's addresses, their opening times, requested pick-up and delivery dates and times, number of shipping units with their weights and dimensions, and priority type such as:

- Urgent: same or next day early morning.
- Standard: next day or later depending on the service level request.
- Economy: lead-time can be up to one week depending on the characteristics (weight, dimensions, hazardous material) of the goods, distance, and transport modality.

Shippers can ask carriers for value-added services, which are not included in the standard carrier service and for which an accessorial might be charged. Accessorials are extra costs for additional services as requested by the shipper. Examples of these services can be in-room collections and/or deliveries, shipment status notifications, milestone exchanges, pro-active exception monitoring, heavyweight and/or oversized cargo handling, SMS and/or e-mail shipment status messages, hardcopy PODs, manual carrier bookings, slot bookings, 24/7 customer service availability, and hand-carry options. Other options are signature, hold for pick-up, Saturday, Sunday, car boot, in-locker, same day, in-night, overnight, and time deliveries. A customer is entitled to drop a SO at any time; however, it depends on the agreed order cut-off time if the order will be processed on the same day. Order cut-off time means the latest time the order can drop in the WMS and can be picked, packed, and shipped on the same day. It depends on the latest truck departure time and the time the warehouse needs to prepare the shipment. A truck needs to start driving at a certain moment to make the following connections in the transportation network. Truck departure times depend on carrier networks and transportation modalities. It is recommended to contract carriers with a late order cut-off time to give customers more time to drop orders for same-day processing. The same is valid for a warehouse provider: the less time needed for processing orders, the better. Carrier selection can be fixed or dynamic. Fixed carriers can be defaulted per trade lane, type of goods, or customer requirements. In case of dynamic carrier choice, the best price-quality carrier is selected taking into account the requested lead-time, destination, weight, measurements, and other shipment characteristics. Carrier selection can be done manually and with simple tools or using a sophisticated Transportation Management System (TMS). Every shipment needs to be packed in such a way that it can survive the travel from the shipper to the customer. Figure 2.2 shares an example of a solid package. Goods need to be properly packed to absorb bumps, drops, and falls during transportation. Each shipping unit needs to have a carrier label with a tracking number so that it can be scanned through the transportation network for status updates on carrier track-and-trace websites and/or the shipper's ERP system. After labeling, the shipment data is transferred from the WMS or TMS to the carrier system

FIGURE 2.2
Solid package. (From www.pixabay.com.)

via an EDI connection. Shippers can use also handwritten waybills, standalone carrier shipping systems or internet-based tools. Each shipping unit needs to be accompanied with the necessary documentation such as a packing list, DN, invoice, or customs document depending on the origin-destination combination. In case of repairable goods, it is possible to include a return label in the outgoing box for returning a product. After the shipment has been picked and packed, the shipper puts it in a shipping lane ready for pick-up. It is common practice that a pre-notification is sent to the carrier to pick up the shipment. The message contains information (number of pallets, parcels, shipping units, destinations, etc.) about the cargo and a copy of the documentation. Such a pre-alert can be done by phone, e-mail, or EDI message from a WMS/TMS into the carrier system. The trucks arrive generally one or half an hour before the truck departure time to check and collect the goods. The actual time needed to check the physical goods and if the same is reflected on the documents, depends mainly on the volume, but it is also impacted by other elements such as type of goods (pallets, parcels), number of destinations, destination types (national, export), and loading process (manual versus automated). Drivers are expected to see the warehouse people load the goods and sign for receipt. After the shipment has left the warehouse, it is up to the carrier to proactively inform the shipper with any status change and/or delay notification including the root cause, improvement action and a new Expected Time of Arrival (ETA) if applicable. Multiple orders on the same day destined for one delivery address should be stacked, consolidated, and shipped as one shipment to safeguard the cargo delivery quality and minimize the payable volumetric weight. Other words used for volumetric weight are chargeable or dimensional weight. This charging concept has been introduced as it turned out that the cost of a shipment is more affected by the amount of space it takes in an airplane rather than the actual weight. A less dense cargo needs more space compared to its actual weight. Shippers are encouraged to use more compact packaging to reduce the volumetric weight. There are also very heavy parts, which would benefit too much from this concept. Therefore, airlines charge the maximum of the volumetric and actual weight. Volumetric weight (kg) is calculated as (length [cm] × width [cm] × height [cm])/6,000. The value "6,000" can differ per carrier and transportation modality and is described as the dim, dimension, or weight conversion factor.

2.3 INBOUND PROCESS

The transportation process at inbound is limited as there are more warehouse activities such as unloading, put-away, sorting, repacking, and putting on stock. Inbound receives shrink-wrapped packages, boxes, crates, full or non-full pallets, and bulky goods. These can be standard, hazardous, fresh, or any other type of goods. The goods type defines the inbound handling and/or storage location. The goods need to be checked on cosmetic and other damages, shortages, surpluses, weights, measurements, and documents such as the waybill, invoice, and Customs Trade Reference Number (CTRN). Incompleteness and/or incorrectness must be mentioned on the transportation document or electronic device. In case of damage, it is required to take pictures. If the goods cannot be checked immediately, this inspection needs to be done within 24 hours after receipt and a notification is sent to the supplier about the findings. Each delivery is normally pre-notified by a Purchase Order (PO) in the WMS or any other means. This is to inform the receiver that the goods are on their way, enabling the receiver to plan resources and processing instructions. A common target for a dock to stock processing time is 24 hours. In case of a backorder or out-of-stock situation, a process can be installed to search and process the specific PO or PO line (one type of product) within a few hours against a surcharge. To safeguard a good master data quality the actual weights and measurements are checked upon receipt and updated in the WMS if necessary. This process prevents wrong carrier selections and potential customs clearance issues. Other issues that can pop up at inbound can be boxes without a label, wrong labels, unknown labels, missing or unknown reference numbers, goods delivered to a wrong address, or wrong goods shipped to a correct address. A company needs to provide the inbound process owners with instructions how to act in such situations. Example instructions can be to send goods back to the vendor, accept the goods under different terms and conditions, or scrap them.

2.4 SHIPMENT PREPARATION

When goods are moved from the pick-up to the delivery address, they are facing quite some forces in different directions, which can lead to damages or losses such as wet cargo, containers falling overboard, theft, and broken goods. These forces can be the result of acceleration, braking, accidents, and vibrations in combination with the gravitational impact. Prerequisites for a perfect delivery are proper packaging and correct labeling. Factories are normally using packaging, which is good enough to protect the products when they are moved on a pallet. The packaging might not be good enough for transporting it as a single shipping unit. A shipping unit is a set of products that are packed together in one physical package, which cannot be divided in more units and has a unique Serial Shipping Container Code (SSCC) identification number on the shipping label. A SSCC barcode on the label is used to identify the shipping unit and is scanned throughout the transportation network. Other words for a shipping unit are package, box, pallet, or parcel. Also, the term "handling unit" is used, which is, for example, a pallet containing multiple parcels for multiple customers. The parcels have their own unique shipping unit labels, which will have their own routing after the first sorting center. A pallet is a logistics tool to move and store goods by a lift, reach or Electric Pallet Truck (EPT). A shipper can buy new or used pallets from pallet providers, but it is also possible to rent them from a rental company. Globally, there are many non-standard pallet sizes; however, there are Euro, UK, North-American, and more standardized sizes with their own specific dimensions and load capacities. The dimensions (l × w × h) of some example pallet types are 80 cm × 120 cm × 15 cm (Euro), 100 cm × 120 cm × 15 cm (UK), 48 inches × 40 inches × 6 inches (North America), and TAPs with various dimensions. The weight of an empty pallet can be up to 25 kg. Each industry has its own standards and requirements, but pallets can be made of various raw materials: hard wood, plastic, pressed wood, metal, and coconut. Each type has its typical characteristics such as quality, lifetime, weight, dimensions, material, and price. It is therefore important to know upfront what type of goods the pallets are supposed to protect and to which destinations the pallets are going to be sent, as various countries can use different standards, before purchasing or renting them. The exact pallet-purchasing price depends on the pallet dimensions and the used raw material, but generally, the raw material accounts for two-thirds of the price and the labor for one-third. The transportation costs per pallet are limited as a standard trailer can load up to 500–600 empty pallets. Figure 2.3 illustrates an example of a pallet. There are no global pallet providers; there are only local or regional players. It is a buyers' market as there are many pallet providers. Only a few of them have a network of production facilities and storage locations. Some players have a European Pallet Association (EPAL) license for Euro

FIGURE 2.3
Pallet. (From www.pixabay.com.)

pallets, which meet the standards and allow the exchange of "pallet for pallet." To enable a pallet exchange process between shippers, carriers, and receivers, an accurate pallet registration system is required. As it is often not possible or economical, because the transportation and management costs are higher than the pallet price, to exchange pallets with other countries, shippers often use the cheaper TAPs. A pallet registration process starts at the unloading of the truck. The unloader counts the number of received pallets, types, their quality, and the presence of the International Plant Protection Convention (IPPC) stamp on the pallet. IPPC is part of the United Nations' (UN) Food and Agriculture Organization (FAO), which issued and maintains this standard. The stamp indicates for international flows that the solid wooden pallet has been heat treated or fumigated to prevent diseases such as wood pests from transferring from one country to another. The standard layout of the stamp includes the IPPC logo; International Organization for Standardization (ISO) 3166 two-letter country code, region, and unique registration number issued by the regional Phytosanitary to the packaging manufacturer; and the Heat Treatment (HT) acronym. The International Standards for Phytosanitary Measures (IPSM) 15 regulations prescribe that the location of the stamp is provided on two opposite sides of a package or pallet so that it is clearly visible for a customs officer. The counted pallets are checked on differences against what is mentioned on the transportation document such as Convention Relative au Contrat de Transport International de Marchandises par Route (CMR) for road transportation. Companies register any difference on the transportation document and communicate these to the sender of the goods and the pallet pool provider. These rental pallet providers require that everyone who rented pallets takes care of their in- and outbound registration. Any missing, lost, or incorrectly registered pallet needs to be paid by the administrative receiver. The number of pallets on the documents, physically received and accepted are registered in the pallet administration tool.

The pallet outbound process starts when loading the truck, where the number of pallets per pallet type and ship-to are registered in the pallet administration tool. This registration can be done in a WMS or any other tool. Registration accuracy is crucial as invoicing is based on the pallets entering the organization minus the ones for which there is evidence that they have been shipped to an approved address. To verify if the registered number and type of pallets are also physically there, a periodic, often monthly, stock counting process is executed. This process starts with creating count lists and assigning employees to them. They check per location the number of pallets and their types and write down any difference. Then the count lists are handed over to the pallet manager to compare the physical numbers with the stock list. Differences are analyzed and explained. The stock list is adjusted to the actual physical situation. Credit or debit notes are created and sent to the shipper, receiver, and pool provider. Part of pallet management is to create a pallet budget, which is reviewed periodically. As pallets are often "lost," it is important to create a culture where this hidden cost is seen as a significant process, which requires discipline and training to understand and control the pallet flows. The pallet registration process is audited and improved regularly. Shippers can receive high charges, because the outbound registration is not accurate enough due to, for example, the long lead-time between the event and the registration. It also happens that pallets are registered on the organization's account, but this did not take place in reality while the registrations are not checked regularly. The ex-factory package is often not good enough to ship individual products via almost any transportation network, but certainly not good enough to be shipped via a parcel & express network. This is the root cause of a high number of damages. The packages are bumping against each other, dropping, and/or falling from conveyors. International shipments suffer more than domestic ones due

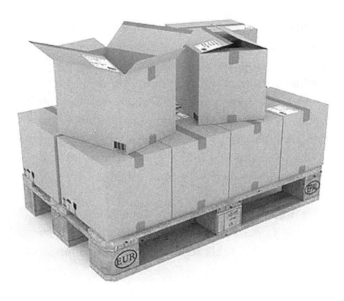

FIGURE 2.4
Goods within the pallet boundaries. (From www.pixabay.com.)

to more loading and unloading activities. It is important to use light and dense, but solid, packaging to keep transportation costs under control. Hazardous material requires more expensive packaging compared to standard cargo. Each shipping unit needs to have a shipping label mentioning the products, country of origin, weight and any other info requested by the destination country. It is crucial to keep the goods within the pallets boundaries to prevent damages due to lift and pallet truck handling. Figure 2.4 shows an example of goods within the pallet boundaries. Another way to prevent damages is to put the most robust packages on a pallet first and then put lighter products on them.

2.5 TRANSPORTATION MODALITIES

In transportation, goods can be shipped by the modalities parcel and express, air, road, sea, train, and intermodal. The key variables are transit times and costs. Faster transportation is more expensive. The actual costs of a shipment depend on the shipper's and receiver's full addresses; dangerous or standard cargo; number of pieces; dimensions; net weight; volumetric weight; net volume; gross volume; stack ability; transportation by air, sea, road, or train; required speed; and carrier. The highest running cost component for a transportation company is labor, followed by fuel, road taxes, IT, repair and maintenance, trains and ferries, insurance, and tires. Shippers generally agree on rates with their transportation companies for a year or longer. The rates are an average over the year and potentially include a market volatility risk mitigation cost part as the actual costs depend on the transportation capacity in the market and the time between the request for quotation and the goods movement. The shorter this time span, the higher the rates as the transportation capacity decreases. The closer to the shipping moment, the lower the transportation capacity, the higher the rates. The potential advantage of fixed longer-term rates can be the security of having enough capacity to move all the goods throughout the whole year including the high season period. The potential disadvantage is higher rates as the shipper does not benefit from the lower rates of the volatile market when the transportation demand is lower than the supply. The other way around, the potential advantage of tendering each shipment directly on the market is that a shipper can benefit from the day-to-day demand versus supply situation potentially leading to lower rates. The disadvantage can be the higher rate in case of high demand. It can also be that there is no transportation capacity at all to move the cargo. Other important information to know is that demand is higher than the average at the end of the month as sales people try to realize the monthly targets and just before and just after holidays to ensure the right stock levels around this period. It also happens that due to holidays such as Christmas and New Year, fewer flights are planned leading to lower capacity. In addition to higher rates, at these times, it is also more difficult to find space for bigger shipments and the lead times can be longer due to backlog situations.

Figure 2.5 shows the typical phases of a transportation flow. A truck picks up the goods from the shipper's location and drives to a port or terminal, where the goods are unloaded. The goods are sorted and forwarded via one or more transshipment points to the next port or terminal. After customs clearance, the goods are delivered to the customer. More or less the same processes and phases are applicable for the inbound, return, repair, and scrap flows. Bookings can be cancelled free of charge until a certain time before the actual pick-up takes place. Not respecting the timelines means that the carrier will charge an amount for the cancelled shipment. The exact timelines and amounts are agreed upon by the shipper and the carrier but depend also on the transportation modality.

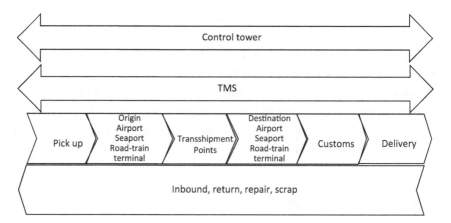

FIGURE 2.5
Typical phases of a transportation flow.

In road transportation it is common practice that no charges are involved when the cancellation takes place at least 24 hours before the originally planned pick-up time. After that, the carriers charge about 75% of the shipment rate. There can be many more flows and location types making the network complicated to manage. An increasing number of shippers uses a TMS and a control tower to manage this complexity. More information, details, and characteristics per modality, TMS, and control tower are shared later in this book.

2.5.1 Parcel and Express

The two words parcel and express are often used to refer to the same service. Parcel means "package" and express means "fast." Together it means a fast package service. A typical parcel is lighter than 70 kg combined with a door-to-door service. There are global, regional, domestic, and local service providers. The industry has enabled and benefited from trends such as globalization, e-commerce, and Lean inventory management and just-in-time philosophy. Carriers offer several services and rates and they use their own commercial names for day- and time-definite services. A day-definite, but not guaranteed, service is also named "economy" and has a TT of one or more working days, while a time-definite and guaranteed service is called "express" and means a Next Business Day (NBD) delivery before 09:00, 10:30, 12:00, or End of Day (EOD). For every service, there are specific weight, dimensional, and girth (2 × width + 2 × height) limits that apply for conveyable and non-conveyable pieces. Conveyable pieces are relatively small packages, which can be sorted by the standard sorting belt and fit in the standard parcel transportation network. Non-conveyable pieces are often long and heavy, cannot be sorted by the standard sorting belts, and need to be handled manually, but might still fit in the transportation network. Some carriers allow also pallets in their parcel network; however, these pallets are not sorted in the standard sorting belt and are handled manually. Table 2.1 shows the common service names and delivery commitments. These services are available for both national and international shipments. The exact lead-times and delivery commitments depend on the ship-from, ship-to, and products characteristics. Express shipments are not always flown as nearby destinations can be serviced by cheaper road transportation. However, express shipments are loaded first (priority boarding), as these are prioritized above economy shipments. Once the shipment is in transit in the carrier's network it is often not possible to up- or downgrade its service level. Most of the shipments are delivered to the customer's door; however, more and more companies offer the option to pick-up the shipment from a PUDO, HFPU, or any other pick-up location. This service option is introduced to make the delivery process more efficient for the carriers as customers are often not at home or not available to sign upon delivery. The other advantage is that the carrier can ship big volumes to one location instead of many. The added value for the customer is that he or she does not need to stay at the delivery location till the driver comes. The customer can now pick up the shipment at a date, time window, and location that suits him or her best. The success of the parcel industry is based on the combination of speed and relatively acceptable costs. By transporting the product more quickly to the customer,

TABLE 2.1

Parcel and Express Services

Service Name	Delivery Commitment
Same day express	Emergency delivery on the same business day
Express critical	Fastest possible shipping option on the same or next day
Express 9:00	Urgent delivery on the next business day by 9:00 a.m.
Express 10:30	Urgent delivery on the next business day by 10:30 a.m.
Express 12:00	Urgent delivery on the next business day by 12:00 noon
Express end of day	Time-sensitive delivery by end of next business day
Economy	Less urgent: delivery within certain number of business days
HFPU	Delivery to a HFPU location using available service options

the shipper benefits from having cash faster, lower inventory levels, and short lead-times. Another important element is the high delivery reliability. Tracking and tracing technology, combined with guaranteed service levels, allow customers to plan shipments with confidence. The market is advanced in IT-enabled technology such as Global Positioning System (GPS), tracking and tracing, and automated pre-notifications. This eliminates error-sensitive manual work and speeds up the information exchange processes in this high-margin market. The GPS market is growing due to new trucks equipped with this functionality and the declining purchasing price of the tracking device. It improves the asset's safety and security and provides truck performance data to track and trace vehicles, which are loaded with high-value goods. Unfortunately, the adoption of the GPS tools is limited as a result of their still relatively high purchasing prices.

Parcel and express providers offer a global coverage and deliveries within a few days. They are mainly known for their flown express service, but the ground transportation is becoming more important due to the increasing e-commerce shipments. In times of economic downturn, customers tend to migrate from express to economy service levels to reduce costs. However, even in hard times, premium services are used to recover from production backlogs at suppliers, who need to speed up deliveries, stock-outs due to wrong forecasting and/or higher sales, freight capacity issues with economy service modalities such as sea and road freight, damaged or lost shipments, and limited knowledge of the transportation function. Parcel and express providers tend to have capacity issues during peak demand periods such as Christmas and the end of the year. The market is highly competitive. The parcel process starts with the driver who picks up the package from the customer location and scans it. This scan serves as a pick-up confirmation. It is possible to ship multiple packages as one shipment. All packages have their unique tracking numbers; however, they are identified as part of a shipment by using one of the numbers as the master reference. An indication such as "1 of 3," "2 of 3," and "3 of 3" reflects on each package. When tracking one of them, all other packages will show up. This way of working is also called "mother-and-child" structure. Then the driver goes to the nearest carrier's sorting location. Here the shipments are sorted based on destination, service level, and mode of transportation. It is the first point to check if all the picked-up packages can be re-confirmed by this location as received. Figure 2.6 provides an example of a parcel-sorting belt. Some parcel providers operate two sorting belts in parallel. The two belts are powered

FIGURE 2.6
Parcel sorting belt. (From www.pixabay.com.)

from two different power stations to make sure that in case of a disaster, such as power outage, the sorting capacity can continue on 50% of its capacity until the issue is resolved. After the sorting process, the package is shipped with other packages by air or road to the next sorting center. From here, a truck drives to the delivery center, which is a local hub, from where the parcels are delivered to the customer. Upon delivery, the driver hands over the package and receives a signature on the handheld Delivery Information Acquisition Device (DIAD). A DIAD enables the printing of a digitalized POD, including the delivery date, time, and consignee name, from the carrier's track-and-trace website. The DIAD allows the immediate transfer of shipment status change to the carrier's website, the use of the pick-up scan as the pick-up confirmation, and the delivery scan as the delivery confirmation. The pick-up and delivery truck can be the same but can vary daily depending on the optimal route planning. An Air Way Bill (AWB), which contains information such as weights, dimensions, consignor, consignee, and service level, is pasted on each package for track-and-trace purposes.

Heavy or oversized parcels, pallets, hazmat, and in-room deliveries do not fit in some parcel networks and some carriers do not accept them in their network as they disturb their standard flows. Those who do accept them require the customer to go through a carrier approval process, which can delay the pick-up by 24 hours. In this approval process, carrier locations that will handle the shipment check if they have space and equipment to handle the specific shipment. If so, then the customer is instructed to forward the shipment in the carrier's network. The carrier invoices a surcharge for the additional space and handling. The carrier terms and conditions can indicate that these kinds of shipments can have a longer TT due to their physical characteristics. Table 2.2 shows the parcel weight and measurement restrictions of a few carriers. The international rates are generally offered in volumetric shipment weight brackets from one country to another or from one zone to another, where a zone can consist of multiple countries. These country-to-country and zone-to-zone pricing has been introduced to simplify the rate cards, as there can be millions of zip-code-to-zip-code combinations, which are difficult to maintain in the carriers' invoicing systems. The domestic rates are often offered as a price per package or package weight brackets. Carriers use a discount system to offer rates to customers. Based on the volume and other contract terms and conditions, carriers offer customers a discount (e.g., 10%) as a reduction

TABLE 2.2

Parcel Weight and Measurement Restrictions of a Few Carriers

Criteria	Carrier x	Carrier y	Carrier z
Maximum weight for conveyable goods (kg)	30	70	68
Maximum weight for non-conveyable and non-palletized goods (kg)	70	70	68
Maximum weight per pallet (kg)	1,000	Pallets are not accepted	1,000
Maximum measurements for conveyable goods (l × w × h) (cm)	120 × 80 × 80	$(2 \times w + 2 \times h) = 419$	$L + (2 \times w + 2 \times h) = 330$
Maximum length for non-conveyable and non-palletized goods (cm)	300	270	274
Maximum measurements for a pallet (l × w × h) (cm)	120 × 100 × 160	Pallets are not accepted	302 × 203 × 178
Volumetric weight calculation ratio	1/6,000	1/6,000	1/6,000

on their basic rates. This way of working simplifies the rate management in the carriers' invoicing systems. Frequently used volumetric calculation ratios are 1/4,000; 1/5,000; or 1/6,000. It is important to consider this when comparing rates to prevent wrong conclusions. Include also the Fuel Surcharge Costs (FSC). The FSC is applied as a percentage, which can vary from 1% to 10%, of the invoice value and is different per carrier-service level combination. The next paragraph contains more information about FSC mechanisms. Do not forget to add surcharges and accessorials, applied by some carriers for deliveries to extended areas, on Saturday, cargo exceeding the standard weight and measurement restrictions, in room deliveries, DGs, cash on delivery, and residential addresses. The top 10 parcel and express carriers are DTDC, Japan Post Group, YRC Worldwide, PostNL, Schenker, Royal Mail, Blue Dart, UPS, FedEx, and DHL. Parcel and express modality is used for:

- Long and short distance coverage
- Low and high goods value density
- Low shipping volume
- Time- and not time-sensitive shipments

2.5.2 Airfreight

Airfreight is the expensive, but reliable, transportation of high-value goods in cargo or passenger planes. Cargo planes shipments are also called "freighter" deliveries and shipments with passenger planes are also called "belly" deliveries. The shipping capacity of this transportation modality is expressed in tons per year and is often used to support the JIT strategy, as this modality is fast and flexible, to keep inventories and inventory holding costs low. There can be only a positive financial business case if the lower inventory costs outweigh the additional transportation costs. The goods go out via cargo and passenger aviation gateways to other airports. Passenger planes form the bigger part of the airfreight capacity. Freight forwarders buy transportation capacity from airlines and sell it to shippers. Some of the airlines have longer-term contracts with the forwarders and fly only for them. Other airlines are used when needed and when they have capacity for incidental shipments. Some integrators, companies offering domestic and international door-to-door airfreight services owning aircraft and road delivery trucks, like UPS and FedEx, own part of the cargo planes and operate as airlines. This industry applies other labor terms and conditions than those of truck drivers and warehouse personnel. Fuel and labor form the majority of the transportation costs. Airfreight is a good option for the delivery of time sensitive shipments to anywhere in the world. It is also a safe way of transportation due to the strict airport controls. Typical airfreight shipments contain pallets or packages >70 kg and sent from one to another continent. The "70 kg" is an average as the exact value depends on, for example, the trade lane, alternative rates of parcel carriers versus airfreight forwarders, service levels, and distances. "Airfreight" shipments within a range of around 500 km of an airport are often not flown. It is faster and cheaper to drive them from one location to another under AWB terms and conditions, even if the shipper ordered an airfreight service. It is cheaper as driving costs are lower than flying. It is faster as the goods do not need to be trucked to the airport, sorted there, and offered to the airline a few hours before the uplift. Airport-to-airport flows within the same range of distance are also driven for the same reasons. Airfreight business offers both an economy service of around 1 week and a premium service of around two days lead-time. However, the airfreight industry offers rates and lead-times for more specific services such as:

- Economy: the standard slow service of around one-week lead-time.
- Express: the premium faster service of two or three days.
- Next Flight Out (NFO): the fastest possible service of one day, depending on the first available flight there is.
- Hand carry: an employee takes the package at hand and flies to the customer for a personal delivery. This option can be used in any mode of transportation and to any country; however, as this very expensive option is considered only for extremely urgent situations it is not feasible to countries that require the potential visitors to apply for a visa first. The messenger needs to follow the right processes such as going through the destination customs clearance offices upon arrival. It is possible that the goods are checked and immediately released for further transportation, but sometimes customs authorities ask the carrier to come back at a later time to pick up the goods and pay any duties and taxes. It is also important to have all the applicable export documentation in place when crossing a border to prevent the confiscation of the goods and/or other problems for the person or company. More information about export documentation and potential issues of non-compliance are explained further in this book.

TABLE 2.3

Maximum Cargo Plane Capacities

Airplane Type	Front Part: Cargo Hold		Lower Deck		Back Part: Cargo Hold		Bulk Hold:
	Length (m)	Volume (m³)	ULDs (LD-3) (#)	Air Pallets (#)	Length (m)	Volume (m³)	Volume (m³)
A380-800	17.40	89.55	44	14	17.90	107.46	18.40
747-800	14.79	88.25	36	11	13.88	88.25	14.70
777-300ER	19.82	107.46	44	14	15.73	89.55	17.00

Source: www.airliners.net

The exact lead times and costs depend on criteria such as the shipment characteristics (weight, dimensions, hazardous material), distance, number of daily or weekly available flights, and under- or overcapacity in the market. It is not allowed to ship some hazardous material by passenger aviation. Cargo planes can carry those although there are airlines whose policy is not to accept these. Table 2.3 shows the maximum cargo plane capacities when it is fully used for freight only, meaning without any passengers.

An airplane can load air pallets, Unit Load Devices (ULDs), and loose cargo. An air pallet is a rectangular metal plate, which can be pushed manually over the plane rails. Figure 2.7 illustrates an example of an air pallet.

FIGURE 2.7
Air pallets. (From www.pixabay.com.)

FIGURE 2.8
ULD. (From www.pixabay.com.)

There are different air pallets, but the typical measurements (l × w × h) are 318 cm × 224 cm × 163 cm. There are also different ULD types. Figure 2.8 shows an example of an ULD. The external measurements of the most frequently used LD-3 are 154 cm × 152 cm × 162 cm. The maximum gross weight it can handle is 1,588 kg and the maximum gross volume is 4 m³. There is an upper and a lower deck in an airplane. The maximum accepted height in the lower deck is 1.60 m. Airfreight cargo flying in the lower deck is less expensive compared to those items flying in the upper deck as the latter one can carry heavier and bigger goods, but the available space in the market is limited.

The available number of cargo airplanes is low, while there are many more passenger airplanes, which offer lower deck space leading to a lower market price. Relatively small air shipments below 500 kg, which have been booked in the morning, are picked up in the afternoon on the same day. The carrier accepts the booking requests by default. Bigger shipments or bookings not made in the morning are picked up the day after as they require a formal booking acceptance from the carrier. A booking confirmation is the communication of flight details, AWB numbers, and departure and arrival data. Depending on the shipper-carrier connectivity, this information can be shared by EDI, e-mail, or other means of communication. Smaller shipments are easier to book with both passenger and cargo airlines, while big shipments can often be moved only via cargo airlines, which are designed to handle bigger shipments, which cannot be moved in passenger airplanes due to their limited weight and size capabilities. Some goods such as lithium batteries and some dangerous goods (DGs) are allowed to be transported only in cargo airplanes. As there are more passenger than cargo airplanes, it is easier for the carrier to uplift shipments fast with passenger airlines. The majority of airfreight cargo is moved in passenger flights. Table 2.4 shows the maximum cargo an airplane type can load in case all the passenger seats are fully occupied.

Once the goods have been picked up from the shipper's location, or delivered by the shipper to the carrier's location, they go to a local carrier consolidation point or directly to the airport if it is an urgent shipment. Then they go to the carrier consolidation point or the airline location at the airport. From here, the goods are moved to the airplane, where they are loaded. The exact routing depends on the carrier's network and ordered service level. Urgent shipments such as NFOs are often taxied directly to the airport to be loaded on the airplane. After taking care of the export customs clearance process, which can also be done by the shipper, the carrier tries to uplift the goods with the first available flight to the requested destination. On-board carriage means that a person takes the package in hand, flies to the destination, and hands over the package to the receiver. Economy service shipments are normally routed through a local carrier consolidation point, grouped with other customers' shipments, sent to the carrier consolidation point at the airport, consolidated with other customers' shipments, and brought to the airline location at the airport to be loaded in the airplane, which flies to the destination airport. There, the goods are customs cleared

TABLE 2.4

Maximum Cargo-Passenger Combination Capacities

	Passengers and Cargo Load				
Airplane Type	First Class Passengers (#)	Business Class Passengers (#)	Economy Class Passengers (#)	ULDs (LD-3) Cargo (#)	Air Pallets Cargo (#)
A380-800	22	96	437	2	8
747-800	24	65	450	0	7
777-300ER	22	70	368	2	10

Source: www.airliners.net

by the carrier, receiver, or receiver's customs broker. Then the goods are delivered to the receiver or they are picked up, depending on the delivery agreement. The shipper and the carrier can decide differently, but in general, the lead-time calculation starts on the pick-up day and stops on the delivery day. Based on the pick-up date and the agreed lead-times the latest possible delivery day can be calculated. The lead-time agreements can be made in calendar or business days. The complexity with calendar days is that the majority of the receivers are closed on the weekend. Airlines do fly also on the weekend, which means that once a plane arrives on the weekend and the carrier is willing to deliver the shipment to meet the target lead-time, it is not possible to do so. This is leading to disputes on whether the shipment is delivered on time or not. A carrier can deliver the goods earlier, unless other agreements have been made between the shipper, the receiver, and the carrier. It is possible to ask the carrier to call the receiver for a slot time. Such requirements need to be communicated from the receiver to the shipper and from the shipper to the carrier. All the supply chain partners then monitor the shipment's progress pro-actively. In case it becomes impossible to make the delivery date or time, the carrier is expected to send exception messages within the pre-agreed timeframes. These messages include the issue description, resolution, and a new delivery date and time. Not all carriers can deliver this status information fast enough, which is often caused by slow information processing or incapable information systems, but also by the limited carriers' customer service opening times of, for example, 8 a.m. to 6 p.m. Before they process the received shipment status information and exchange this with the shipper, it is already 10 a.m. or later. This is too late for express shipments with an expected delivery time of before, for example, 9 a.m. The impact of a delayed shipment is severe in a "system down" situation, where machines, systems, and people are waiting for a spare part to fix the problem and continue production. Carriers can provide shipment status information to customers by using the following date and time terms:

- EDD: Expected Date of Departure
- ETD: Expected Time of Departure
- ADD: Actual Date of Departure
- ATD: Actual Time of Departure
- EDA: Expected Date of Arrival
- ETA: Expected Time of Arrival
- ADA: Actual Date of Arrival
- ATA: Actual Time of Arrival

Although these milestones are sufficient for most of the customers, there are shippers who require a more detailed visibility with more milestones and shorter time spans between these. A good example of such an improvement is Delta Air Lines, which is implementing a real-time tracking system to locate the exact position of ULDs by equipping these with Bluetooth-enabled tracking devices. This increased digital visibility provides the control tower of the airline the possibility to monitor and reroute shipments if needed. The most important information is probably the ETA as the recipient of the goods uses this arrival date and time as the starting point for planning production, assembly, or re-distribution activities. This is also the reason why customers ask for regular ETA updates to adjust this planning if needed, because forecasting a reliable ETA when processing the order in the warehouse and/or booking transportation can be difficult. It can happen that originally communicated ETAs are not met due to transportation issues such as adverse weather conditions, mechanical failures, traffic jams, and more of these "uncontrollable" root-causes. It is not possible to prevent these situations in all cases; therefore, the best way to mitigate their impacts is to share the shipment status information immediately with the supply chain partners. The ideal situation would be that customers log in on the Internet to see at any moment where their shipments in transit exactly are real-time or receive these updates pro-actively on their smartphones; however, the logistics industry has not progressed that far yet.

Airfreight flows can be divided into three legs, offering a customer the possibility to choose from the service options described in the next section, which indicate who is responsible for which part of transportation, bears the risk, does the customs clearance, and absorbs the costs:

- Door-to-Door (DD): the goods are picked up by the carrier from the shipper's and delivered to the receiver's address. Shipper's export declaration can be created by the carrier, the shipper, or the shipper-assigned third-party broker. The carrier, the receiver, or the receiver's assigned third-party customs broker can execute the import customs clearance at destination. The carrier is not responsible for the customs clearance, through-put time, or costs if a third-party broker is used.
- Door-to-Port (DP): the goods are picked up by the carrier from the shipper's address and delivered to the agreed destination airport. Shipper's export declaration can be created by the carrier, the shipper, or the shipper-assigned third-party broker. The receiver can

take care of the customs clearance and the last mile from the airport to the receiver's address or outsource one of those or both to a third party. The carrier is not responsible for the customs clearance, its throughput time, last mile, or related costs to the receiver's address. The receiver can do these activities or assigns these to a third-party broker.

- Port-to-Door (PD): the shipper or by the shipper-assigned third party is responsible to pick up the goods at the shipper's address and deliver them to the agreed origin airport from where the carrier is taking care of the shipment till delivery to the customer. Shipper's export declaration can be created by the shipper or by the shipper-assigned third-party broker. The carrier, the receiver, or the receiver's assigned third-party customs broker can do destination import customs clearance. The carrier is not responsible for the customs clearance, its throughput time, or costs in the last situation when the receiver assigns this work to a third-party broker.
- Port-to-Port (PP): the shipper or the assigned third party is responsible for picking up the goods at the shipper's address and delivering them to the agreed origin airport from where the carrier is taking care of the shipment till delivery to the destination airport. Shipper's export declaration can be created by the shipper or by the shipper's assigned third-party broker. The receiver can take care of the customs clearance and the last mile from the airport to the receiver's address or outsource one of the two or both to a third party. The carrier is not responsible for the customs clearance, its throughput time, last mile, or costs to the receiver's address.

An airfreight carrier can organize all the three legs, door-to-door, but it is also possible to use three different carriers, as by sourcing in this way can lead to lower rates and higher service and quality levels. The limited number of big airlines dominate the port-to-port market, while for door-to-port and port-to-door transportation there are many players in the market, which leads to more competition. It is also possible to use alternative modes of transportation for the first and the third leg (e.g., use the cheaper train, instead of the more expensive road freight, to move freight to and from airports).

When the shipper creates a delivery in the carrier transportation-ordering tool, a House Air Way Bill (HAWB) is generated. A copy is attached to the goods, while the original one is handed over to the driver together with other documents, which will be described later in this book. The driver-signed HAWB serves as confirmation of receipt of the shipper's goods by the carrier and acts as a contract between them and contains information such as carrier's liabilities, claims procedures, goods description, and transportation charges. There is a standard HAWB format, which is used throughout the world for both domestic and international airfreight. This document is not negotiable, does not specify on which flight the shipment will be sent or when it will reach its destination. The airline consolidates customers' HAWBs into a Master Air Way Bill (MAWB). To enable customers to order until late in the afternoon or early evening, and still ship out the goods on the same day, it is important that shipping locations are located near big airports from where the maximum number of destinations can be reached. There are few airlines who can fly from small airports to many destinations. Forwarders are expected to deliver the goods to an airline a few hours before the uplift unless the carrier and the shipping location are located at the airport. In such cases, it is possible to agree upon shorter times due the cargo coming from a safe origin. Any airfreight cargo needs to be screened through x-ray machines, sniffed by dogs, routed through explosive trace detectors, or physically opened by the security personnel to make sure that the cargo is safe to fly. Shippers need to have the Authorized Economic Operators (AEO) or "Known Consignor" status. The purpose of this status is to make sure that a business complies with safety and customs requirements. The status of "reliable exporter" offers benefits such as simplified export procedures and faster throughput times due to less strict customs inspections. The consignor invests in increasing the security of its supply chain by using and maintaining compliance procedures for employee training, products classification, licenses, and sanctioned party screening tools. This way the shipper is relieved from having its goods controlled and avoids delays and screening costs. The certificates are issued and audited by local authorities. Example audit questions can be:

- What type of goods (chemicals, weapons, consumer goods, etc.) are stored? Are these stored in the same area?
- Who has access to these goods? Is access to cargo restricted to authorized people only? Are the truck loaders and unloaders being screened? When was the last time?
- How is the inbound flow made secure before storage (unbroken seal, consignor is AEO certified, carrier is Customs and Trade Partnership Against Terrorism [C-TPAT] certified, physical conditions, number of

units, weights and dimensions are in line with the documents)?
Is this process also available for the outbound flows? What is the
follow-up process in case of differences?

- Which tools (cameras, badges, seals) are used to manage these
restrictions?
- What is the policy (procedures, instructions, trainings) to sustain
this process?
- How are the carriers assessed to check if they meet the security
standards (certification, measures, policy)?
- How often is stock counting executed to compare the outcomes with
the inventory management system numbers? What processes are
there to analyze discrepancies?

If not certified as "Known Consignor," the shipper can submit its goods
for a security scan to a third party before they are loaded. This causes
throughput time delays and generates screening costs. If a company uses
only parcel and express, it is not necessary to be registered as "Known
Consignor." Express carriers, certified as "Regulated Agent" as they do
not own the goods, guarantee that all shipments are screened within their
own locations before flying. This standard process is executed within the
agreed TTs and without additional costs. The shipper is relieved from
administrative expenses, procedures, and investments.

Airfreight rates are generally defined as $/kg (volumetric weight). These
are often broken into a few components to align them with the service
options (D-t-D, D-t-P, P-t-D and P-t-P) a shipper can choose. The rate
components can look like:

- Pick-up from the shipper to the airport
- Terminal handling charges at the origin airport
- Export customs clearance activities
- Air transportation from the origin to the destination airport
- Destination airport terminal handling charges
- Import customs clearance activities
- Delivery from the airport to the receiver

The actual costs depend on:

- Cargo type: light volumetric cargo can lead to higher costs compared
to small heavy cargo.

- Trade lane: the rates are lower from west to east due to imbalance in volumes.
- Fuel prices: higher oil prices lead to higher kerosene prices.
- Currency exchange rates can be positive or negative.
- Packaging: increase of volumetric weight due to repacking.
- Service levels: shorter lead-times mean higher rates.
- Carrier rates: each carrier has strong- and weak-priced lanes.

Carriers often charge minimum weights of, for example, 30 kg, even if the shipment weight is only 10 kg. The standard rate per kg does not cover all the costs involved in handling such a small shipment. Carriers charge the maximum of the volumetric and actual weight. Figure 2.9 provides insight in the calculation of the volumetric weight (kg): (length [cm] × width [cm] × height [cm])/6,000. The maximum height of the pallet needs to be used to calculate the volumetric weight, even if the top of the pallet is not flat or optimally utilized. This means that the customer needs to pay also for this empty space, as the carrier cannot utilize it. As the biggest cost component is fuel and as this is fluctuating on a daily basis, fuel mechanisms are agreed between the shipper and the carrier to charge these costs on a variable basis. Fuel surcharge can be agreed as a fixed amount per chargeable or actual weight, but also as a percentage of the invoice value. There is no regulation indicating how to calculate the surcharge. Each carrier can apply its own mechanism. Many carriers

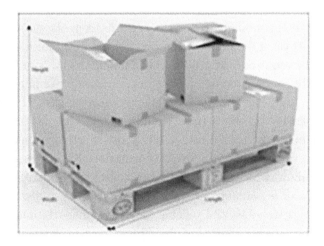

FIGURE 2.9
Volumetric weight. (From www.pixabay.com.)

apply the following way of working: start by fixing the fuel price baseline (e.g., $1.50 per liter) and calculate the average number of kilometers an airplane can fly per liter (e.g., 10 km per liter). Check the fuel price when the shipment takes place (e.g., $1.60 per liter). The fuel surcharge is then $1.60 − $1.50 = $0.10 per 10 km or liter. This amount can be recalculated to a surcharge per kg, percentage of the invoice amount, or any other metric. An example road FSC mechanism can look like:

- Baseline price per liter (pump price exclusive Value Added Tax (VAT): $0.80
- Rate increase/decrease per € 0.05 fuel price change per liter (exclusive VAT): 1.5%

The fuel price change is calculated by taking the average price of the previous month on the pre-agreed source, such as www.shell.com or www.bp.com, and comparing it with the baseline price.

Top 10 air freight forwarders are DHL, K+N, Schenker, Expeditors, Panalpina, UPS, Nippon, DSV, Kintetsu, and CEVA. They account for one third of the market. DHL is the largest with a single-digit market share. The market shares differ significantly from one market to another. In regions like India, southeast China, and the UAE, local or regional carriers dominate the markets.

2.5.3 Road Transportation

Road freight is the modality to transport goods from one place to another by road. To cover the route between two destinations motorized vehicles are used. The required investment in equipment is low, compared to the other modalities, which makes it easy for competition to enter the market. The result is that there are many small carriers, who compete on mainly price. The cost of constructing, operating, and maintaining roads is cheaper than, for example, railways. It is a cost-effective means of carriage and it enables door-to-door delivery of materials. Road transportation is often the only way for carrying goods to and from rural areas where no rail, water or air is available, and between cities, towns, and small villages. It is also a relatively fast and reliable mode of transportation, which can be ordered at any preferred day and time. However, a truck can load a limited volume, has weight and measurement restrictions, is frequently impacted by adverse weather conditions and traffic jams. A Full Truck

Load (FTL) is used to move big volumes, while Less than Truck Load (LTL) is used for relatively smaller shipments. LTL shipments typically consist of 1–10 pallet places; however, this depends on criteria such as the distance between the ship-from and the ship-to, carrier rate and loading equipment type. Above the average of 10 pallet places, shippers use a FTL, as that is cheaper. The lead-time is also shorter as a FTL drives from the pick-up directly to the delivery address. Single pallets are often routed through a hub-and-spoke network. Another way of working is that shipments are picked up, combined with other shippers' loads, and driven directly to the customer address without going through any consolidation or deconsolidation point. The last type of transportation is also called direct deliveries or groupage. A hub-and-spoke system consists of carrier terminals and spokes, which are line hauls between the terminals. A line haul is a truck driving constantly between two terminals. When a truck arrives at a terminal, the shipments are unloaded and loaded in other line hauls going to other terminals. The terminals can be reached relatively fast and cheap, as they are located near to the center of gravity of the transportation flows. The nearest terminal to the receiver's address takes care of the last mile by using optimized routings for standard deliveries. Dedicated trucks or any other transportation means are initiated in case of special last miles, which require, for example, special unloading tools for an in-room delivery, need to be faster than the standard routing can offer or support a swap service (deliver the new product and bring back the old one). A taxi delivers urgent and small shipments. When it becomes too big for a taxi, a courier van is used to transport the oversized packages or pallets. Other time-critical transportation means are sprinter trucks or 7.5-ton box trucks with or without a curtain side or tail lift. Sprinter trucks can load a maximum of 10 pallet places, while a box truck can load 18 pallet places. Trucks transporting DGs, also called "Accord Dangereux Routier" (ADR) goods, need to be equipped with at least fire extinguishers, wheel chocks, pocket lamp, warning signs, warning vest, and the right cargo documentation. Drivers need to be certified for the Good Distribution Practice (GDP) training. Road carriers use the most extensive rate structures there can be in the industry: per package, package weight, actual or volumetric weight categories, volume brackets, FTL, pallet, pallet place, or loading meter. A loading meter is one linear meter of the length of a truck. This metric is often used for goods that cannot be stacked. It is important to know upfront if the goods are stackable or not. In general, it is the packaging and/or fragility of the goods that define if a pallet is stackable or not; however, it is also possible that carriers use other criteria such as a maximum pallet height of 120 cm or a maximum weight of 1,000 kg. It is therefore important that these criteria are aligned upfront and during the sourcing process. In case the goods are not stackable, the carrier cannot use the empty space above each pallet and needs to be compensated for that. This is also necessary to prevent damages, as the carrier will stack the goods if the rates are based on stackable goods. A Euro pallet (80 cm × 120 cm) is generally counted as 0.4 loading meter. A block pallet (100 cm × 120 cm) is counted as 0.5 loading meter. Another translation is that one loading meter is counted as 1,750 kg chargeable weight and 1 m³ = 330 kg. The most common equipment is a trailer with a length of 13.6 m, a width of 2.4 m, and a height of 2.6 m. Figure 2.10 provides an example of a truck, also called tractor, with a standard trailer.

Another frequently used transportation equipment is the mega trailer, which has the same length and width as the trailer, but it can be up to 40 cm higher. For big volumes, the swap body system is used. This is a combination of two boxes, which can be linked and moved as one unit. To make transportation more efficient, carriers use trailers with double floors, also called "double-deckers," and can carry twice the original number of pallets. This way of working also prevents damages as pallets and other shipping units are not stacked on each other. In general, it can be said that big and inflexible trucks are used to move big volumes over long distances

FIGURE 2.10
A truck with a standard trailer. (From www.pixabay.com.)

TABLE 2.5

Road Transportation Equipment Characteristics

Truck Type	Internal Dimensions (m)			Weight (kg)			Volume (m³)
	Length	Width	Height	Gross	Empty	Net	
Single swap body	7.82	2.40	2.40	20,000–60,000 Depends highly on the truck specifications (e.g., number of axles and the distance between them)			45
Standard trailer	13.60	2.40	2.40				78
Mega trailer	13.60	2.40	3.00				98
2 Swap bodies	15.64	2.40	3.00				113
Road train	21.42	2.42	2.40				124

between two locations, while small, flexible, low-noise and safe trucks are used for city deliveries to and pick-ups from multiple customers. Table 2.5 shows the common road transportation equipment with its characteristics.

To prevent waiting time for the drivers and the warehouse personnel, drop (mega) trailers, swap bodies and containers are parked at the shipper's location. This is empty equipment made available by the carrier on the shipper's premises to be loaded and unloaded when required. A local driver is moving the dropped equipment to and from the docks. This enables the arriving driver to put away an empty equipment and pick up immediately a full one or the other way around. This prevents waiting for the warehouse personnel to load or unload the equipment. Road cargo in Europe is accompanied by a CMR transportation document, which indicates the responsibilities and liabilities of the parties. The CMR is not negotiable and it is addressed to the receiver and the carrier. The shipper fills in the CMR form, or any other local transportation document, with accurate shipment information and signs it when the carrier collects the goods. The driver compares the physical number of shipping units with the documentation and signs for receipt in case of no discrepancy. The consignee will also sign the form as the goods are received upon delivery. This signature serves as the proof that the carrier did deliver the complete shipment in good order and that the carrier can be paid for the service. Road transportation has its restrictions. Accidents and breakdowns lead to delays and unsafe situations. It is less organized compared to other transportation modalities. The speed is relatively low; transporting goods over long distances is difficult, costly, and not good for the environment as vehicles emit pollution leading to respiratory health effects and global warming. The road transportation market is very fragmented with many regional and local players. The international integrators have a very limited market share. The top 10 European road companies are Schenker, DHL, Dachser, DSV, GEODIS, K&N, Rhenus, ND, LKW Walter, and Gefco. Their cost structure depends highly on the network design, such as direct deliveries and hub-and-spoke networks, and other country-specific situations regarding, for example, labor costs and tax levels. The cost structure depends on the carrier's organization and network, but in general, the majority of the total costs are variable (fuel, maintenance, labor, subcontracted vehicles), while only a small part is fixed (terminals, management, owned vehicles). In case of direct deliveries, a driver with a tractor and a trailer goes to, for example, six addresses to pick up relatively large loads and drives directly, without going through a cross-dock location, to the six delivery addresses. The largest part of the driver's time is used to drive from one address to another and not to load and unload cargo. In case of a hub-and-spoke network, there can be, for example, 30 pick-up addresses, as the shipments consist of one to a few pallets only. After the pick-ups, the truck goes to a cross-dock location, where the pallets are unloaded, de-consolidated, consolidated, and loaded in the respective line hauls to another cross-dock location close to the customers, where the goods are unloaded, sorted, and put on box trucks to go to the customers. A hub-and-spoke network requires more manual handling, less transportation, more waiting times, cross-dock locations, and different equipment types, meaning that the cost components vary in type and value compared to, for example, direct deliveries. See the following section for an example cost structure of a hub-and-spoke network:

- Labor: 37%
- Fuel: 26%
- Repair and maintenance: 11%
- Insurance: 3%
- Taxes: 2%
- Tires: 1%
- Toll: 1%
- Train and ferry: 1%
- Gross margin: 18%

Road freight is used in cases like:

- Short distance coverage
- High and low goods value density
- High and low shipping volume
- Time and not time sensitive

2.5.4 Sea Freight

Sea freight, also called ocean freight, is used for intercontinental low value product flows and moves the majority of the world's volumes. The biggest seaports in terms of the number of handled containers are Shanghai and Shenzhen, in China, and Singapore. Together they handle almost one hundred million containers per year. Sea freight has a global coverage, is less expensive compared to the other modalities and can carry extreme sizes and weights, but it has also longer TTs. The gas pollution of sea freight is limited and is one of the greenest transportation modalities as it can carry high volumes against relatively limited fuel consumption. The equipment is the container, which can be stacked upon each other on a ship, but trucks, airplanes and trains can also move them. One container costs a few thousand Euro depending on size and quality and lasts up to a few decades. Purchasing and repairing containers forms around 20% of the total operating costs of a typical shipping line. Containerization means the transportation of goods in containers, where the content is loaded at the shipper's location and unloaded at the receiver's location only. The content can be pallets and loose packages, which remain untouched in-between. The container is loaded on a truck, moved to a container terminal, unloaded, and loaded on a ship. Sea freight can be divided in three legs called pre-carriage (door-to-port), carriage (port-to-port) and on-carriage (port-to-door). An ocean carrier can organize all the three legs, door-to-door, but it is also possible to use three different carriers, as sourcing in this way can lead to lower rates and higher service and quality levels. The limited big carriers, also called shipping lines, dominate the carriage market. If the container is transported from the shipper's location to the origin seaport or from the destination seaport to the receiver's location under control of the shipping line, it is called "carrier haulage." This means that the shipping lines use and pay their sub-contracted trucking companies to move the container under their responsibility. For the pre- and on-carriage legs, there are many players in the market, which leads to more competition. It is also possible to use alternative modes of transportation for the first and the third leg (e.g., use the cheaper train, instead of the more expensive road freight, to move containers to and from seaports). If the container is transported from the shipper's location to the origin seaport or from the destination seaport to the receiver's location under control of the shipper and/or receiver, it is called "merchant haulage." This means that the shipper and/or receiver use and pay their sub-contracted trucking companies to move the container under their responsibility. Figure 2.11 shows containers on a ship. In addition to the standard container or loose cargo lo-lo (lift on-lift off) ships that use cranes for loading and unloading, there are ro-ro (roll on-roll off) vessels, which are designed to move cars, trucks, and trailers on and off the ship on their own wheels.

Shipping lines do not always sail from the origin port (port of charge) directly to the destination port (port of discharge). They often use transshipment points, which are locations where containers are transferred from one ship to another to bring them to another transshipment point or the final destination. The container transfer can take place on the water, where ships are side by side and cargo is transferred from one vessel to another. The other way is to unload the containers from the incoming ship at a container terminal and load them from there on the outgoing ship. The objective is to reduce costs by limiting the number of ports a ship needs to visit to maximize sailing time and make sure that a ship is fully loaded

FIGURE 2.11
Containers on a ship. (From www.pixabay.com.)

from one port or transshipment point to another. Full and empty containers can be stacked on a ship or at a container terminal. An upcoming innovation is the collapsible container. The walls of the empty container can be collapsed to save space on the ship. Loose packages are often used to optimize the container space usage but loading and unloading take longer. To speed up these processes, pallets are used as a lift truck can be used to move these. There are many container types, but these are the frequently used ones:

- 20': standard, flat rack, open top, reefer and tank
- 40': standard, high cube, flat rack, open top, reefer and tank
- 45': standard and high cube

One 40' container can be stacked on two 20' containers and vice versa. A standard container truck can load one 40' or two 20' containers. Road trains can load more containers and a combination of container types, depending on the local laws and regulations. Also, high cubes and 45' containers are used, where high cubes are used to benefit from the extra height and the 45' container to load more volume. The shipper is responsible for the loading degree, stacking, and content. The container is sealed at origin and can be opened only at the customer premises. The lead time can vary from a few days to a few weeks depending on the distance; carrier network; and DD, DP, PD, or PP service option. To protect the products against insects, pests, and other diseases and to be compliant with destination country requirements, the containers are gassed after loading. For the shipper in the country of departure it is mandatory to provide the right papers and labels with a gassed container. The (dangerous to human health) gas is active when the container is in transit, but it is often still there when the container arrives at the unloading address. Opening such a container can be dangerous for people. Because it is not always clear if a container is gassed and contains gas, it is recommended to do a gas measurement followed by degassing before opening the container. The degassing process consists of ventilation by routing fresh air into the container.

To describe the cargo capacity of a containership and terminal, the terminology Twenty-foot Equivalent Unit (TEU) or Forty-foot Equivalent Unit (FEU) is used. Table 2.6 shows the common container types with their characteristics.

A container fully loaded by only one shipper is called a Full Container Load (FCL). A trucking company picks up the container and brings it to

TABLE 2.6

Container Type Characteristics

Container Type	Internal Dimensions (m)			Weight (kg)			Volume (m³)	Door Openings (m)	
	Length	Width	Height	Gross	Empty	Net		Width	Height
20′ standard	5.89	2.35	2.39	30,480	2,280	28,200	33	2.33	2.27
40′ standard	12.03	2.35	2.39	32,500	3,700	28,800	67	2.34	2.27
40′ high	12.03	2.35	2.69	32,500	3,880	28,620	76	2.34	2.57
45′ high	13.55	2.35	2.69	32,500	4,900	27,600	85	2.34	2.58

the container terminal at the origin port, from where it is loaded on a vessel. The reverse process takes place once arrived at the destination port. It is possible to send single pallets by sea freight. Here the terminology Less than a Container Load (LCL) is used. The forwarder picks up the pallets from the shipper's site; brings them to its own consolidation facility, which is also called a Container Freight Station (CFS), where the goods are loaded in a container at carrier's risk and expense; combines these with other customers' goods; and creates a FCL. When this FCL arrives at the destination port, it goes to a deconsolidation facility from where a road network delivers the individual customer shipments. LCL lead time can be up to a few weeks longer than for a FCL. The FCL rates are per container, while the LCL rates are per m^3 or weight brackets, where $1 \ m^3 = 1,000$ kg, with a minimum charge of $1 \ m^3$. However, these rates can consist of various components to align them with the service options (D-t-D, D-t-P, P-t-D and P-t-P) a shipper can choose. The rate components can look like:

- Pick-up from the shipper to the seaport
- Terminal handling charges at the origin seaport
- Export customs clearance activities
- Sea transportation from the origin to the destination seaport
- Destination seaport terminal handling charges
- Import customs clearance activities
- Delivery from the seaport to the receiver

In addition to these rather standard rate components, the sea freight industry uses many surcharges. A key cost driver is the fluctuating fuel price, which cannot always be passed to customers. When fuel prices increase, shipping companies can introduce a Bunker Adjustment Factor (BAF) as compensation. Other surcharges used in the sea freight industry are additional fees for war risk, piracy, overweight, currency exchange rate fluctuations (Currency Adjustment Factor [CAF]), port security (International Security Port Surcharge [ISPS]), hazardous material, peak season, using Suez Canal, and fuel with lower emission. This way the carriers try to justify rate increases and/or offer shippers the possibility to choose and pay for additional services. Although the intentions are good, the reality is generally that if one carrier starts applying surcharges the rest soon follow. The number of surcharges confuses shippers, who also do not consider these when calculating costs and are often confronted with a higher invoice value than originally planned. It is therefore important to reduce the number of surcharges to the minimum and include the "standard" surcharges for, for example, port security and peak season as much as possible in the basic rate. The previously mentioned surcharges lead to higher actual shipment costs than the basic rates, but also other variables influence the invoice value. Examples of other cost drivers are cargo type (light volumetric cargo can lead to higher costs compared to small heavy cargo), trade lane (the rates are lower from west to east due to imbalance in volumes), packaging (increase of volumetric weight due to repacking), and service levels (shorter lead times mean higher rates). Carriers can offer different rates for the same shipment characteristics as they have strongly and weakly priced lanes.

The transportation document for a container is the Bill of Lading (BOL), which is issued by the carrier to the shipper as a contract for carrying the goods. It includes shipper's and receiver's names, departure and destination port names, name of the ship, departure and arrival dates, list of goods mentioning the number and kind of packages, marks and package numbers, weight, volume, and transportation costs. The BOL must be shown to receive the goods at the destination port. The ocean carrier is consolidating the BOL with other customers' BOLs into a Master BOL. The big ocean carrier companies own both the ships and containers. LCL freight forwarders do not own ships but often own the containers. Other terminologies used in sea freight are Non-Vessel Operating Common Carrier (NVOCC) and Vessel Operating Common Carrier (VOCC). A NVOCC is defined as a carrier providing ocean freight services by buying slots or space from a VOCC and reselling them to its customers. The top 10 sea freight forwarders are DHL, K+N, Sinotrans, Schenker, Expeditors, Panalpina, Hellmann, Nippon, DSV, and Bollore. To improve the operational efficiency on some trade lanes, ocean carriers cooperate in an alliance, which is a group of companies that share ships, but every carrier has its own individual contracts, with probably different rates, with the same customer. The three alliances currently moving the majority of the global sea freight volumes, limiting the number of freight movement options for the shipper as they use the same vessel, are:

- The Alliance: K-Line, Yang Ming, Hapag Lloyd, MOL, and NYK
- 2M: Maersk, HMM, and MSC
- Ocean Alliance: OOCL, CMA-CGM, Evergreen, and Cosco Group

These alliances have their pluses and minuses. The pluses are related to operational efficiency improvements for the carriers. The minuses are related to operational performances as the individual carriers can differentiate themselves on rates and customer service but the containers are moved on the same vessel. If this vessel is delayed, then all the individual carriers are impacted. To mitigate this risk and increase the choice, it might be a good idea to cooperate with two different carriers in two different alliances on the same lane. The market is growing at the cost of airfreight as more customers ask for low-cost shipping options as result of the increased production in low-cost countries far away. Sea freight is used in cases such as:

- Long distance coverage
- Low goods value density
- High shipping volume
- Not time sensitive

2.5.5 Train

Railway transportation is a reliable modality for low-value bulky goods as it is the least affected by weather conditions, which is an important factor of delays in transportation. It brings also less pollution than road and air. The routes and schedules are fixed. There are already trains from China directly to European countries with a TT of 18–20 days. Only airfreight is faster over long distances. It is relatively cheap, as it can move tens of trucks at once, and fast. It is safe and the accidents and mechanical breakdowns are minimal. The carriers operate with a minimum number of employees, but they have high fixed equipment costs, while only a small part is variable. A large investment of capital is needed and the cost of construction, maintenance, and overhead are high. It is therefore not easy to enter the market, where only a few big players compete against each other on price and service combination. The processing times of terminal operations are long and come with high costs. Another disadvantage is its inflexibility as its capacity, routes, and timings cannot adhere to individual customer requirements. There are also no door-to-door services and a road delivery is always needed. Trains cannot be used for short distances, small traffics, or rural areas. Booking and taking goods need quite some time. Figure 2.12 shares an example of train

FIGURE 2.12
Transportation by train. (From www.pixabay.com.)

transport of cars. Cargo by train is accompanied by an internationally standardized freight document "Convention Internationale concernant le transport des Marchandises par chemin de fer" (CIM), which serves as the legal basis for freight contracts in international rail transportation. The global top 10 train operators are Union Pacific, Canadian National Railway, Central Japan Railway, East Japan Railway, MTR, Norfolk Southern, CSX, Canadian Pacific Railway, Daqin Railway, and West Japan Railway.

2.5.6 Intermodal

This option involves multiple modes of transportation like air, sea, road, and train. The loose cargo is packed in a container, which is transported to its destination via multiple modes like ships, airplanes, rails, and trucks without removing the cargo from the container. Since there is not much cargo handling, it is both economical and safe. The main objective of this modality is to reduce costs by preventing flying and/or driving and benefit from trade imbalance between, for example, Europe and China. As there can be less volume from one region to another, airfreight rates can be lower in one direction compared to the other way around. As the imbalance depends on the airport-to-airport lanes, it is sometimes beneficial to use road, train, or sea to come to the relevant airport and fly from there. An example of a service name is "sea-air," which is cheaper, has longer TT, and is used for flows ex Asia Pacific (APAC). Airfreight forwarders are the major service providers in this transportation sector. The tariff structure is similar to that of the airfreight industry. The shipments are accompanied by a multimodal BOL, which serves as the carriage contract between the shipper and carrier. A multimodal BOL is not negotiable and only authorized forwarders can issue this document, which is addressed to the shipper, carrier, and receiver. Intermodal companies often do not own the equipment. They have contracts with third-party carriers, which buy cargo space and sell it to their customers. The global top 10 intermodal companies are Hub Group, C.H. Robinson, Pacer, J.B. Hunt Transport Services, UTi, Expeditors, Burlington Northern Santa Fe, Union Pacific, Norfolk Southern, and CSX. A new upcoming mode of transportation is the synchro modality. Where the intermodal service has a predefined and fixed routing, the synchro modality does not have that meaning that the routing and modes depend on the real-time situation of the demand versus supply in the market, congestions, and carriers network capabilities on that specific moment. The customer provides the carrier shipment requirements such as pick-up and delivery dates and times, ship-from and ship-to addresses, volumes, weights, and dimensions. It is then up to the carrier to decide how to pick up and deliver the shipment in line with the customer requirements. The idea behind this approach is to better utilize the real-time transportation network capabilities by being flexible to change the routes and modes real-time leading to a higher operational efficiency for the carrier and lower rates for the customer.

2.5.7 Overview

Table 2.7 shows a summary of the plusses and minuses per transportation modality.

TABLE 2.7

Plusses and Minuses Per Transportation Modality

Transportation Modality	Plusses	Minuses
Parcel and express	Very fast, very reliable, very high trackability and traceability, very high availability, very safe, door to door, relatively flexible, useful for long distances	Very high costs per m³, high pollution, sensitive for adverse weather conditions, not useful for: heavyweights, oversized dimensions, DGs, and pallets
Airfreight	Relatively fast, relatively reliable, relatively high trackability and traceability, relatively high availability, very safe, relatively flexible, useful for long distances	Relatively high costs per m³, high pollution, not useful for bulky goods, relatively limited DGs capabilities, sensitive for adverse weather conditions
Road transportation	Fast on short distances, reliable, high availability, high flexibility, low costs per m³, relatively safe, door to door	Relatively low trackability and traceability, relatively high pollution, sensitive for adverse weather conditions and traffic, limited load capacity, not useful for long distances
Sea freight	Can handle all type of goods and bulky volumes, low pollution, very low costs per m³, safe, door to door, useful for long distances	Slow, less reliable, low flexibility, sensitive for adverse weather conditions, low trackability and traceability
Train	Can handle all type of goods and bulky volumes, relatively low pollution, relatively reliable, relatively low costs per m³, safe, useful for long distances	Relatively slow, relatively low availability, relatively low flexibility, no door to door service, low trackability and traceability
Intermodal	Relatively fast, relatively reliable, relatively low costs per m³, relatively safe	Relatively low trackability and traceability, relatively high pollution, relatively low flexibility

2.6 COSTS AND TRANSIT-TIMES

The two key variables in transportation are costs and transit-times (service). Quality is not a discussion point anymore, but a prerequisite to play a role in the market. The word "transit-time" is used when it refers

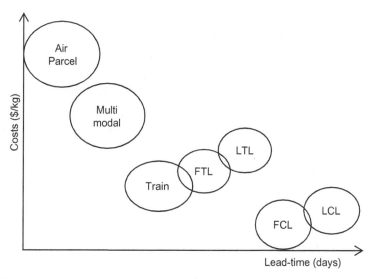

FIGURE 2.13
Costs and transit-times per modality.

only to the transportation time, while "lead-time" contains all activities such as transportation, processing, and waiting times. Figure 2.13 provides insight into the relationship between costs and transit-times per modality. In this figure, it is possible to compare the modalities against each other. Generally, shorter transit-times mean higher costs, but this is not valid in all cases. The transportation costs of a shipment with specific type of goods, weight, dimensions, lane, and carrier rate can be lower when shipping by air compared to sea. This is the result of market conditions where carriers apply different pricing strategies. Some carriers go for the lowest possible price to survive. By offering low prices, carriers try to increase the volumes to improve the equipment and network utilization. This is supposed to lead to lower costs per unit and increase the margins. Other carriers offer only profitable prices. This way they try to attract customers with high-end products, where quality and service are more important than the price, to maintain a relatively high margin. Some carriers attempt to go for a larger market share by offering a low price in combination with one or more unique selling points. After having a considerable market share, the carriers can try to increase prices and their margins. In fact, all the previously mentioned pricing strategies lead to shifts in market shares, as transportation is an indirect demand meaning that lower prices will not lead to a larger transportation market. This is different than lowering the price for, for example, televisions, which probably will lead to more people willing to buy a new one and generate a higher demand for transportation. All these considerations depend on the market situation where the supply is equal, lower, or higher than the demand. The best way forward is to create a tool in which all the carrier rates are uploaded independent from the modality type and let the tool propose the best cost and transit-time combinations. An example of such a tool is the TMS, which will be discussed further in this book.

2.7 INCOTERMS® RULES

When doing business, it is important to specify who is responsible for paying the transportation costs from which ship-from to which ship-to address, who bears the risk of losing the goods, who needs to insure them, what mode of transportation to use, who needs to create the applicable documents, and who will do customs clearance. Eleven Incoterms®, an abbreviation for international commercial terms, rules are used to clarify these responsibilities and support the business; however, they do not include information about the ownership of the goods and other contractual agreements between the seller and the buyer. The use of Incoterms® rules is not obligatory, but it is recommended when the seller and the buyer agree this in the sales contract. The available Incoterms® rules to use are based on the transportation modality. Incoterms® rules for any modality are EXW, FCA, CPT, CIP, DAT, DAP, and DDP. Incoterms® rules for sea freight and inland waterway are FAS, FOB, CFR, and CIF. Incoterms® rules is a trademark of the International Chamber of Commerce (ICC). Table 2.8 shows the exact description of the Incoterms® rules (Source: ICC website. The full text of the 2010 edition of the Incoterms® rules is available at http://store.iccwbo.org/). ICC provides documentation explaining the terms of delivery used in international business.

TABLE 2.8

Incoterms® Rules Description

Modality	Incoterms® Rules	Description
All modalities	EXW	"Ex Works" means that the seller delivers when it places the goods at the disposal of the buyer at the seller's premises or at another named place (i.e., works, factory, warehouse, etc.). The seller does not need to load the goods on any collecting vehicle, nor does it need to clear the goods for export, where such clearance is applicable.
	FCA	"Free Carrier" means that the seller delivers the goods to the carrier or another person nominated by the buyer at the seller's premises or another named place. The parties are well advised to specify as clearly as possible the point within the named place of delivery, as the risk passes to the buyer at that point.
	CPT	"Carriage Paid To" means that the seller delivers the goods to the carrier or another person nominated by the seller at an agreed place (if any such place is agreed between parties) and that the seller must contract for and pay the costs of carriage necessary to bring the goods to the named place of destination.
	CIP	"Carriage and Insurance Paid to" means that the seller delivers the goods to the carrier or another person nominated by the seller at an agreed place (if any such place is agreed between parties) and that the seller must contract for and pay the costs of carriage necessary to bring the goods to the named place of destination.
	DAP	"Delivered at Place" means that the seller delivers when the goods are placed at the disposal of the buyer on the arriving means of transport ready for unloading at the named place of destination. The seller bears all risks involved in bringing the goods to the named place.
	DAT	"Delivered at Terminal" means that the seller delivers when the goods, once unloaded from the arriving means of transport, are placed at the disposal of the buyer at a named terminal at the named port or place of destination. "Terminal" includes a place, whether covered or not, such as a quay; warehouse; container yard; or road, rail, or air cargo terminal. The seller bears all risks involved in bringing the goods to and unloading them at the terminal at the named port or place of destination.

(Continued)

TABLE 2.8 (*Continued*)

Incoterms® Rules Description

Modality	Incoterms® Rules	Description
	DDP	"Delivered Duty Paid" means that the seller delivers the goods when the goods are placed at the disposal of the buyer, cleared for import on the arriving means of transport ready for unloading at the named place of destination. The seller bears all the costs and risks involved in bringing the goods to the place of destination and has an obligation to clear the goods not only for export but also for import, to pay any duty for both export and import, and to carry out all customs formalities.
Sea freight and inland waterway	FAS	"Free Alongside Ship" means that the seller delivers when the goods are placed alongside the vessel (e.g., on a quay or a barge) nominated by the buyer at the named port of shipment. The risk of loss of or damage to the goods passes when the goods are alongside the ship, and the buyer bears all costs from that moment onwards.
	FOB	"Free on Board" means that the seller delivers the goods on board the vessel nominated by the buyer at the named port of shipment or procures the goods already so delivered. The risk of loss of or damage to the goods passes when the goods are on board the vessel, and the buyer bears all costs from that moment onwards.
	CFR	"Cost and Freight" means that the seller delivers the goods on board the vessel or procures the goods already so delivered. The risk of loss of or damage to the goods passes when the goods are on board the vessel. The seller must contract for and pay the costs and freight necessary to bring the goods to the named port of destination.
	CIF	"Cost, Insurance and Freight" means that the seller delivers the goods on board the vessel or procures the goods already so delivered. The risk of loss of or damage to the goods passes when the goods are on board the vessel. The seller must contract for and pay the costs and freight necessary to bring the goods to the named port of destination. "The seller also contracts for insurance cover against the buyer's risk of loss of or damage to the goods during the carriage. The buyer should note that under CIF the seller is required to obtain insurance only on minimum cover. Should the buyer wish to have more insurance protection, it will need either to agree as much expressly with the seller or to make its own extra insurance arrangements."

Source: http://store.iccwbo.org/

2.8 TRADE COMPLIANCE

This is the process of complying with the laws and regulations of the ship-from and ship-to countries. Goods are classified correctly, country of origin is mentioned, right goods value is declared, and duties and taxes are paid. It is also required to screen new customers, suppliers, visitors, and goods for security and have the right licenses to operate. The end-use check is necessary to make sure that the bona fide trading partners can be trusted, that they will not forward the goods to disapproved parties, and that the products are not used for military purposes. Such a check can be executed before providing the export license or after the shipment has taken place. The check requires the handover of, for example, the company profiles of the exporter and the importer, contracts with sales terms and conditions, and shipping documentation. Suspicious situations can be a missing end-user address or a last-minute address change, when high delivery costs are not an issue, third party paying the invoice, false IP address, non-physical company address, or rerouting via another country. The main objectives are to protect critical products, technology, and information from falling into the wrong hands. Another requirement is to create and assess clear anti-corruption and anti-bribery guidelines as any non-compliance can have severe consequences for the involved companies and employees. Such behavior deregulates the process of a fair supply versus demand mechanism in the market. Not being compliant can lead to repayments, reputation damage, business suspensions and exclusions, increased audits, additional authority requirements, fines, seized goods, employee disciplinary actions and contract termination, and jail. It is required to have an Export Control Officer (ECO) in house for understanding, training, implementing, maintaining, addressing, and adhering to the local and international export control and trade sanction laws and regulations and their potential impact on the business. The main objective is to create and maintain lists of unauthorized individuals, customers, parties, groups, companies, and countries that cannot have some technology, software, goods, and services as they can use them for mass destruction weapons or any other harm of people. A common way to show that a company is compliant is to hand over the right documents to the driver. For domestic flows, it is often sufficient when a packing list and a waybill accompany the goods. When a business decides to export, it has to deal with numerous documents. A set of paperwork needs to be put on the physical goods and another set is handed over to the driver to be used by the carrier's clerical departments for the customs clearance process.

2.8.1 Documentation

Which exact documents are needed depends on the country of origin, final destination, and the nature of the items shipped. There are two types of origin: non-preferential and preferential. The customs authorities use the non-preferential origin to define in which country the product has been manufactured for statistical purposes, but also to check if the product is subject to import restrictions and anti-dumping duty application. Preferential origin is the shipping country and is used to apply and benefit from potential free trade agreements to pay no or less duties. Information on documents, such as invoices and packing lists, needs to be in line with the information on the physical product and ERP systems. The frequently by the exporter produced documents are:

- Export license: a governmental document that authorizes the export of a certain number of specific products to a certain destination. Key in determining whether a license is needed is finding out if the products have an Export Control Classification Number (ECCN) and if U.S. jurisdiction is applicable and a Strategic Goods Indicator (SGI). An ECCN categorizes products based on their nature: type of commodity, software, technology, and technical info. The five characters of an ECCN are there to check the potential dual-use of the product for civilian or military purposes like mass destruction weapons. The SGI classifies goods of which export, import, and transit to certain countries is prohibited or only allowed under certain conditions due to their potential dual-use.
- Export Accompanying Document (EAD): a shipper needs to request approval at the customs office of export before moving a shipment. When the request has been approved, the customs authorities release the shipment and give permission to start the shipping process. An EAD, to identify the export and to inform the customs office of exit that the shipment complies with all the safety and security requirements, is then created and added to the shipment documentation.
- Commercial goods invoice: an original and wet-stamped bill signed in blue ink by the shipper and/or chamber of commerce for the goods from the seller to the buyer. The invoice is also used to determine the

amount of customs duties and taxes to pay. The amount of duties to pay is based on the "Harmonized Commodity Description and Coding System" six-digit code (HS code in short), which is a worldwide standard created and managed by the World Customs Organization to describe and classify physical goods, also called "modalities." Other words used for HS code are harmonized, tariff, and customs code. In addition to reporting any import to customs authorities for applying the right duty rates and taxes, it is also used to manage trade agreements and gather trade statistics. Despite the standard, customs authorities of some countries can interpret the codes in different ways leading to other duty and tax rates. Incorrect usage of codes can be seen by those authorities as misleading, which can result in penalties. Some destination countries require the invoices to be legalized by their consulate or embassy in the shipper's country (consular invoice). A standard invoice contains information such as the full invoice-from, invoice-to, ship-from and ship-to addresses including the country names, detailed description of the goods, quantities, weights, dimensions, commercial value of the goods, country of origin (manufacturing), and transportation costs. There can be also a triangular invoice. In such a situation, the ship-from and/or ship-to addresses are not located in the country of the exporter. The buyer can request to leave out a copy of the invoice in the pouch attached to the package, preventing the receiver of the goods from seeing the purchasing prices of the reseller (also called "neutral delivery").

- Pro-forma invoice: a preliminary invoice sent by the seller to the buyer in advance of a shipment to prepare the customs clearance process at the importing country.
- Packing list: an as-original stamped list that provides information about the package type, gross weight, and dimensions of each item in the shipment.
- BL/BOL/AWB/CMR: a freight contract between the owner of the products and the carrier and contains information such as weights, dimensions, consignor, consignee, and service level. In case of a BOL, the buyer needs the original as proof of ownership to receive the goods at the port of discharge. There are two BOL types:
  - Straight: the ownership of the goods can be transferred to a third party.
  - Order: it is not possible to transfer the ownership of the goods to a third party.

- Certificate of Origin (COO): a document legalized and/or signed by the chamber of commerce and/or shipper, which indicates the origin of the exported item. Some countries require also an EUR statement on the invoice as evidence that the goods originate from the European Union (EU).
- Certificate of Conformity (COC): an inspection certificate as evidence that the quality of the goods is declared to be good as they have been checked with positive results. Pre-requisites for issuing a COC are often the handover of laboratory-created test reports and, occasionally, a physical inspection of the shipment. The inspection institutes ask for the complete shipment documentation as preparation before visiting the inspection location. In addition, some local authorities can require that a letter stamped and legalized by the chamber of commerce accompanies the certificate to clear the goods through customs. Other words for this document are certificate of conformance, certificate of compliance, technical inspection report, and certificate of inspection.
- Certificate of insurance: a document issued by the insurance company to serve as evidence that the goods have been insured to take away the concern of liability and potential loss. It contains, for example, the validity date, type of coverage, and liability amounts.
- EUR1 certificate: a document issued by the chamber of commerce that enables importers in certain countries to import goods at a reduced or zero rate duty under trade agreements between the EU and beneficiary countries.
- T-document: a transit document used to transport goods from one country to another without paying customs duties and taxes. This is only applicable between the countries included in the transit agreement.
- Dangerous Goods Declaration (DGD): this is to certify that the DGs have been packaged, labeled, and declared in accordance with the standard international shipping regulations.
- ATR (Association Turkey): a customs document for doing business between the EU countries and Turkey. This document can be used to prevent paying duties if a company can approve that the goods originate in the EU or Turkey.
- Export Declaration: a document required by the U.S. authorities for exporting controlled products to pre-defined countries. This document can also be required for a shipment that exceeds a certain value.

- Non-Wood Declaration: to pass the China entry and exit inspection and quarantine processes, the goods have to be accompanied by a declaration that the shipment does not include any wooden packaging material.
- Letter of Credit (LC): a document from a bank to the buyer of the goods that guarantees the payment of the seller's invoice. The bank will pay the seller if all the conditions are met and the buyer fails to pay.
- Delivery instructions: a shipper's document providing the carrier information about where, when, how, etc. to deliver the goods.

Some destinations require also the handover of some documents to import and pick-up the shipments. These are often local documents, but examples of generally known and accepted ones are:

- Arrival notice: a document with the shipment details such as the number of packages, goods description, and weight, to inform the consignee and the notify party (e.g., customs broker) about the arrival date and time
- Delivery order: an approval document from the consignee to the carrier to handover the cargo to another last-mile carrier
- Freight release: a document created by the consignee to serve as evidence that the freight charges have been paid to allow the pick-up of the goods from, for example, a seaport
- Customs entry: a document issued by a customs broker to declare the imported goods details such as the HS code, country of origin, value, and estimated duty amount to customs authorities
- Carrier's certificate and release order: a document with shipment details created by the consignee and handed over to customs authorities to certify that the importing company is the owner or receiver of the goods.

2.8.2 Customs Clearance

The customs clearance process varies per exporting and importing country combination, product type, mode of transportation, and more. However, it always starts with the seller providing the buyer the shipment documents. The buyer forwards these and other documents, such an import license, to the port authorities before the arrival as preparation to speed up the clearance process. Upon arrival of the goods, authorities are notified to inspect and release the goods. There is a variety of documents that can be requested, but a very important one is the goods invoice. Typical customs requirements for a correct invoice to allow a fast clearance process and prevent penalties or any additional fees are:

- Header: invoice number, date, incoterm, and currency.
- Item: description, HS code, country of origin (manufacture), value, number of pieces, weight, and dimensions.
- If the items have been repacked and the invoice does not contain the correct package details, a packing list can be required.
- Item value cannot be zero, even if the seller delivers to the buyer free of charge. Mentioning "value for customs purpose" is often not accepted.
- Invoice header names such as "Pro-forma invoice," "Import invoice," "Export invoice," or "Customs invoice" are often not allowed. The use of "Invoice" is sufficient.
- Some authorities can request the invoice to be stamped and signed as original in a certain color by the shipper and/or legalized by the chamber of commerce.

When importing, payment of duties, taxes, and customs clearance fees apply to the Importer of Record (IOR) or Exporter of Record (EOR), depending on the agreement between the seller and the buyer. The duty and tax rates depend on the importing country, trade agreements between countries, and HS code, while the customs clearance fees depend on the rate agreements between the shipper and the carrier. There are duty calculators available on the Internet to estimate the expected duties to pay. The basis for these calculations is the import value including freight costs, unless specifically excluded. The customs clearance costs for importing, for example, a shipment into U.S. depend on the number of invoices, due to the rate per invoice, Food and Drug Administration (FDA) clearance fee, and Merchandise Processing Fee (MPF). Incorrect product descriptions, wrong prices, incomplete addresses, or proofs of origin are pitfalls that can lead to high costs and loss of time. Repeated mistakes raise the suspicion of customs authorities leading to stricter requirements and time-consuming audits. For a correct determination of the HS code, a complete description of the goods such as the purpose and material quality are needed. Incorrect classification may result in additional assessments or high tariffs. Only a few percent of the imported goods are checked. Errors can therefore go unnoticed for years. Customs authorities reject declarations where the number of pieces and weight on the invoice differ from the physical numbers. Without a valid declaration of origin, customs cannot define the origin of a product. This leads to delays and surcharges. In case of false proofs of preferential origin and involvement in tax evasion, penalties or fines may apply. Customs clearance can be done internally or outsourced to specialized companies. The outsourced party can be the actual transportation company or another third party, which is also called a customs broker. Some countries require that third party brokers hold a valid (digital) Proof of Attorney (POA), which is a legal instrument with a validity period authorizing an entity to act as the customs agent and represent the importer towards the authorities. Proper customs knowledge helps to smooth flows by preventing extended customs checks or delayed shipments due to missing and/incorrect documentation. This process allows the shipper to be also compliant with the local customs laws and regulations and reduce costs by using the right HS codes.

2.8.3 Supply Chain Security

Supply chain security programs require that there have to be documented processes, procedures, and work instruction in place to make sure that the truck loading, actual transportation, and unloading processes eliminate any security risk. Warehouses are often well secured, while the transportation network is seen as the responsibility of the carrier. When leaving the warehouse, the goods are routed through several locations. They are handed over to various subcontractors and can be transported by multiple drivers. It is probably here that the goods and their environment run the highest security risks. It is therefore expected that the transportation network will get much more attention in the near future. Security starts with hiring the right people by screening them and doing background checks. This screening process should not be limited to new employees. Also, existing personnel should be screened regularly as people's lives change overtime. All employees need to go through a security awareness training to know how to act in unsafe situations, such as unknown people walking unguided in the warehouse. The security measures should also apply for visitors such as product suppliers, catering, cleaning, and audit companies. This screening process is applicable for everyone, independent from the visitor's professional position. Unauthorized people cannot have access to goods, hazardous material, intellectual property, offices, warehouses, and other buildings. It is necessary to screen all the goods flows, use only trucks with hard-sided walls and ceiling and without a brand name on the outside, to prevent theft, a GPS to track and trace the cargo, and an emergency alarm system. People security can include employees' identity badges, access control systems, and lockers. Typical building security items are alarms, fences, cameras, high value cages, security guards, and sprinkler systems. Any incident needs documentation and investigation. A way to check the physical safety is to inspect the cargo before unloading the truck, airplane, container, or any other transportation equipment. If the seal is found broken, the cargo needs to be considered as unsafe. It is also possible to equip transportation tools with door opening sensors. Another example is to prevent IT systems going down by cyber-attacks as companies rely heavily on these. Any disaster here can shut down the company completely. Limit access to computers and other information; do not allow people to have access to multiple ERP transactions such as both generating and approving invoices, use personal and no generic or departmental IDs and passwords, lock computers when leaving the workplace, and use protection technology against viruses. As security is about the whole supply chain, it is the shipper's responsibility to work only with carriers and other partners who are also actively working on a security program. Although the primary responsibility is with them, it is recommended to regularly review who exactly has access to the shipper's systems and execute risk assessments both internally as well as externally to expose any risk and work on mitigating and/or eliminating these to protect all the supply chain partners. Such cyber security requirements and review processes can be included in partner contracts. Potential disasters such as power outages, fires, accidents, hurricanes, strikes, earthquakes, and bomb threats, but also bankruptcies and cyber-attacks, are described in a Disaster Recovery Plan (DRP). The objective of a DRP is to get the operations up and running again within the shortest possible time by using predefined contingency plans and crisis management processes. It includes communication plans and matrices of the internal organization, public safety agencies, customers, carriers, and other supply chain partners. It also includes review, update, audit and training plans and processes. There are many supply chain security certification institutes, but the most known one is C-TPAT, which is a program to improve supply chain and border security. Both importing and exporting carriers are supposed to be C-TPAT certified, but this certification is not only required for the actual transportation company carrying the goods. The certification is required from all supply chain partners such as forwarders and customs brokers. A certification allows for a faster throughput time, as fewer strict cross border checks will be executed. Each certified company can be viewed on the website https://ctpat.cbp. dhs.gov/. To become certified, a company is requested to conduct and document a security risk assessment, then submit an application via the C-TPAT website and complete a supply chain security profile how to meet the security requirements. If the supplied material is satisfactory, the company is certified for three years.

2.8.4 Dangerous Goods

DGs, also called Hazmat as the abbreviation for Hazardous Material, are goods that form a risk for people, animals, and environment if not properly packed and handled in transportation. Hazmat packaging includes risk and safety instructions with one or more symbols. They describe the hazard and the actions to take in case of accidents. The shippers or their product suppliers provide this information in the form of a Material Safety Data Sheet (MSDS), which contains information on the health, fire, reactivity, and environmental hazards and how to use, label, store, pick, pack, and ship goods and how to recognize emergency situations and act safely. DGs such as explosives can be easy to identify, but other goods can be difficult to recognize. Only trained and certified people can do the Hazmat packing and labeling activities. The transportation of DGs is regulated to prevent accidents. Each modality has its own regulations, but there is a classification system, where the potential danger is the key decision criteria. The transportation, packing, labeling and documentation requirements for shipping a Hazmat depend on regulations per modality: ADR for road, International Maritime Organization (IMO) for sea and

International Air Transport Association (IATA) for air. Hazmat goods are classified by three elements:

1. UN code: this marking system categorizes goods based on their packaging and hazard level characteristics and test outcomes of the substance.
2. Hazard class: this classification defines the hazardous material type of risk. The nine classes are:
   - Class 1: explosives
   - Class 2: gases
   - Class 3: flammable liquids
   - Class 4: other flammables:
     - 4.1: flammable solids
     - 4.2: substances liable to spontaneous combustion
     - 4.3: substances which, in contact with water, emit flammable gases
   - Class 5:
     - 5.1: oxidizing agents
     - 5.2: organic peroxides
   - Class 6:
     - 6.1: toxic substances
     - 6.2: infectious substances
   - Class 7: radioactive materials
   - Class 8: corrosives
   - Class 9: miscellaneous; asbestos, airbags, batteries, and others that do not fit in other classes
3. Packing group: this classification defines the hazardous material degree of danger in transportation. It indicates the required packaging type and product quantity limits. Packing group I indicates a high danger, packing group II refers to a moderate danger, and packing group III means low danger.

In addition to the previously mentioned classification and related packing, labeling, documentation, and transportation requirements, there are "packing instructions" (PIs) to follow. In case of shipping, for example, lithium ion and/or lithium metal batteries, packing instructions PI 965, PI 966, PI 967, PI 968, PI 969, and PI 970 need to be respected. For lithium ion batteries, the exact packing instructions depend on the watt-hour capacity of the cells and the battery, the weight of the battery and the number of batteries in one box. For lithium metal batteries, the exact packing instructions depend on the lithium metal content of the cells and the battery, the weight of the battery and the number of batteries in one box. PI 965 for loose lithium ion batteries is divided in three sections: 1A, 1B, and II. Section 1A applies for batteries of more than 100 watt-hour with cells of more than 20 watt-hour or a higher number than allowed in section 1B of batteries packed in one box. Section 1B applies for batteries of less than 100 watt-hour with cells of less than 20 watt-hour or a higher number than allowed in section II (Table 965-I) of batteries packed in one box. Section II applies for batteries of less than 100 watt-hour with cells of less than 20 watt-hour or a higher number than allowed in section II (Table 965-II) of batteries packed in one box. Managing the complex hazmat requirements in a proper way requires specialization. Shippers often outsource this activity to specialized service providers, especially in case of a high diversity of hazardous goods. There are many laws, regulations, exceptions, and restrictions that require specific knowledge and problem-solving skills. For example, only cargo planes can carry lithium batteries, as it is not allowed shipping these by passenger flights for safety reasons. The challenge is that there are no cargo planes flying to some countries or airlines do not accept lithium batteries on their planes. The remaining options are to use road or sea freight; however, their lead-times are longer. These carriers need to work with loading plans, as it is not allowed to co-load some classes for safety reasons.

2.8.5 Embargoed and Sanctioned Countries

Embargoes and sanctions, such as export bans, freeze of bank accounts and travel restrictions, are political trade restrictions to change behavior for the good. These are often imposed on countries' regimes violating human rights, democratic principles, and/or other laws and regulations, but they can also be applied to specific companies and individuals. In addition to the limited logistics infrastructures, transportation to embargoed countries like Cuba, Iran, Sudan, Syria, and North Korea can be even more challenging, as American companies and citizens are not allowed to discuss, handle, and/or ship goods to these destinations. Sometimes it is allowed only by going through an approval process. American warehouse companies need to receive an approval from their headquarters before they can pick and pack any shipment towards any embargoed country. American transportation companies are not allowed to transport goods to these countries, while the limited non-American transportation companies that do ship goods to these countries often have to ask for an approval at their headquarters. Some limitations are valid for specially designated nationals, and/or blocked persons, either directly or indirectly, including subcontractors, even when these transactions are fully in accordance with the applicable regulations. In addition to embargoed countries, there are sanctioned countries like Libya. American companies are allowed to ship to the last-mentioned group, but restrictions and additional requirements apply.

2.8.6 Local Authorities

Companies that do business with other countries have to be compliant with the regulations of local authorities. For example, in the U.S., FDA is responsible for protecting the public health by assuring that foods are safe, sanitary, and properly labeled. They ensure that human and veterinary drugs, vaccines, and other biological products and medical devices are safe and effective. FDA is also protecting the public from electronic product radiation, assuring cosmetics and dietary supplements are safe and properly labeled, regulating tobacco products and advancing the public health by accelerating product innovations.

2.9 TOTAL COST OF OWNERSHIP

The Total Cost of Ownership (TCO) approach is a concept to visualize all the service related costs by identifying and quantifying the people-, process-, and product-related expenses. This helps to make better decisions on service purchases taking into account financial and non-financial factors. It provides a better understanding of all of the costs involved in purchasing and using a service. TCO is an assessment of all costs of an item over its lifetime and calculated at the beginning of a tender process to make the most cost-effective choice. It helps to make a better choice of suppliers or services as the purchasing price is not the only cost that will occur when using a service. All other cost factors need to be mapped to complete the total overview. Other people in the organization know many cost components and they need to be involved in the decision-making. Typical overlooked costs are the costs of non-delivery, payment terms, non-quality, packing, transportation, set-up, training, and maintenance. Thinking in TCO terms should help to provide a clearer understanding of all of the costs associated with acquiring, operating, and maintaining a service. To quantify the different carrier management cost components, it is recommended to use a TCO tool. The key cost drivers, in addition to the basic transportation rates, are the number of man hours involved in these activities:

- Carrier sites to manage:
  - New carrier implementations
  - KPI measurements and follow-ups
  - IT costs for supporting an EDI set-up
- Carrier account managers to approach:
  - Monthly Business Reviews (MBRs), Quarterly Business Reviews (QBRs), and Annual Business Reviews (ABRs)
  - Continuous improvement meetings and calls
  - SOP set-ups
- Carrier sites to audit:
  - Travelling: flights, hotels, taxis
  - Preparation, execution and after care
  - Number of invoices to check
- Customers order desks to contact:
  - Customer meetings and calls
  - Trainings
  - Issue resolutions
- Transportation modalities to use:
  - Daily planning
  - IT support for TMS and WMS set-ups
  - Daily calls and e-mail handling
- Benchmarks to execute every year:
  - Collecting market information
  - Purchasing costs for market research books
  - Costs of outsourcing to a specialized company
- Shipping sites and regions to implement new carriers:
  - Travelling: flights, hotels, taxis
  - Trainings
  - IT support for EDI set-ups
- Tenders to execute:
  - IT support for e-auctions
  - Carrier communication
  - Project management costs

After quantifying the cost per activity, it becomes possible to measure these drivers in the as-is and to-be situation to calculate the TCO impact of any potential change.

2.9.1 Cost and Budgetary Control

In the competitive transportation business, companies are challenged to find creative ways to lower their costs while keeping high quality, service, and compliancy levels. They are also expected to optimize their activities and balance the impacts of the competing elements such as regulations, customers and suppliers input by investing in their core activities and optimizing the management of their non-core activities. In the Annual Operating Plan (AOP) process, a budget is prepared at the beginning of each year. Budgeting means setting aside financial resources for carrying out activities in a given period. The budget is agreed upon by and communicated with all the stakeholders. After that, it is important to monitor the actuals by creating and adjusting quarterly forecasts. The quality of this process depends highly on the monthly cost bridging and accrual processes. In the bridging process, people look back one month and try to explain the plusses and minuses. That information, together with information about new events is used to adjust the figures for the coming months. An event can be defined as a process change resulting in higher or lower costs. In the accrual process, people try to indicate the costs to expect regarding activities in the previous month, based on logistics indicators such as volume, weight and number of shipments. To control the budget, a cost reporting system is needed to capture the actual costs. Budgetary control is a technique where actual costs are compared with budgets. Differences are analyzed and explained. Comparing the actuals with forecasts is called value tracking. This information can act as input for cost reduction initiatives and stop cost increases. One way to brainstorm and gather ideas is to organize a cost reduction kaizen. Common reasons why the actual costs deviate from the budget are:

- Price mix: higher or lower carrier rates per m^3
- Modality mix: more or less volume per modality
- Volume mix: more or less volume; net versus gross volume, full or non-full trucks or containers, and average volume per shipment
- Service level mix: premium versus economy services

- Destination mix: more or less volume to destinations far away versus close by
- Frequency mix: shipped more or less frequently
- Customs mix: paid more or less duties and customs clearance costs
- Complaints and claims mix: paid more or less for complaints and claims due to damaged or lost goods (cost of non-quality)

Table 2.9 shows an example of a more detailed cost and root cause analysis. By filling in values and the PIs in a certain period in the cells, comparing those with each other and with another period, it is possible to detect how much, when, and where the costs changed and what countermeasures to take. Cost control performance indicators can be:

- Labor productivity: number of shipments per employee
- Transportation costs per kg, m³ or shipment
- Outbound costs as % of sales
- Inbound costs as % of purchase
- Claims value as % of transportation costs
- Invoice accuracy as % of transportation costs
- Loading degree of a truck as % of maximum possible volume a truck can load

In case the shipper manages its own fleet, there are more detailed performance indicators to take into account for analyzing asset utilization, finding root causes of inefficiencies, and implementing countermeasures. The main cost drivers to focus on can be:

- Number of delivery stops: depending on the shipment size, a truck is planned for a number of stops to be made in a certain time. It is important to measure the actual versus planned stops to verify the planning accuracy, but also the execution efficiency by the driver. If the planned stops have not been made, it is necessary to analyze why not and improve the next planning and/or execution cycles. Making more stops due to, for example, traffic jams or additional last-minute stop requests can lead to delayed deliveries. Making less stops might indicate a truck driver efficiency issue.
- Time per delivery stop: for each customer delivery, time needs to be planned for allowing the driver to enter the premises, unload the cargo, and take care of the administrative process before leaving.

TABLE 2.9

Cost and Root Cause Analysis

			Inbound	Outbound	Return	Repair
Cost Analysis						
Cost drivers	Price mix	Carrier x (k$)	Δk$			
		Carrier y (k$)	Δk$			
	Modality mix	Parcel & express (k$)	Δk$			
		Air (k$)	Δk$			
		Road (k$)	FTL (Δk$)			
			LTL (Δk$)			
		Train (k$)	Δk$			
		Sea (k$)	FCL (Δk$)			
			LCL (Δk$)			
		Intermodal (k$)	Δk$			
	Volume mix	Net shipped volume (m³)	Δm³			
		Gross shipped volume (m³)	Δm³			
		Shipments (#)	Δ#			
		Trucks (#)	Δ#			
	Service level mix	Economy (k$)	Δk$			
		Express (k$)	Δk$			
	Destination mix	Domestic (k$)	Δk$			
		Intraregional (k$)	Δk$			
		Interregional (k$)	Δk$			

(Continued)

TABLE 2.9 (Continued)

Cost and Root Cause Analysis

			Inbound	Outbound	Return	Repair
	Frequency mix	Daily (k$)	Δk$			
		Weekly (k$)	Δk$			
	Customs mix	Duties (k$)	Δk$			
		Customs clearance (k$)	Δk$			
	Complaints and claims mix	Damages (k$)	Δk$			
		Losses (k$)	Δk$			
Root Cause Analysis						
Cost PIs	Price mix	Carrier x ($/m³)	Δm³			
		Carrier y ($/m³)	Δm³			
	Modality mix	Parcel & express ($/m³)	Δm³			
		Air ($/m³)	Δm³			
		Road ($/m³)	FTL (Δm³)			
			LTL (Δm³)			
		Train ($/m³)	Δm³			
		Sea ($/m³)	FCL (Δm³)			
			LCL (Δm³)			
		Intermodal ($/m³)	Δm³			
	Volume mix	Net/gross volume ratio (–)	Δ–			
		Average shipment (m³)	Δm³			
		Loading degree (m³/truck)	Δm³			

(Continued)

TABLE 2.9 (Continued)

Cost and Root Cause Analysis

			Inbound	Outbound	Return	Repair
Service level mix	Economy ($/m³)	Δm^3				
	Express ($/m³)	Δm^3				
Destination mix	Domestic ($/m³)	Δm^3				
	Intraregional ($/m³)	Δm^3				
	Interregional ($/m³)	Δm^3				
Frequency mix	Daily (#)	$\Delta \#$				
	Weekly (#)	$\Delta \#$				
Customs mix	Duties (% of goods value)	$\Delta \%$				
	Customs clearance ($/#)	$\Delta \$/\#$				
Complaints and claims mix	Damages (#)	$\Delta \#$				
	Losses (#)	$\Delta \#$				

Big locations require more time than smaller ones. A delay at one customer can have a negative impact on the on-time delivery performance of all the other shipments in the truck.

- Loading degree: transportation rates are generally set up on weight, volume, or piece level taking into account how much of these can be loaded in a truck. It is therefore necessary to measure and review if a truck has moved enough cargo to be profitable to improve the planning parameters and/or the execution. An example question can be: why did we use a big truck to move a small volume?
- Empty kilometers: driving an empty truck does not generate any value and is only costing money in the form of, for example, fuel and driver's time. The ideal situation is a full truck driving the whole day. However, although this is not possible for different reasons, it must be clear that after offloading goods at a customer the truck needs to drive as little as possible before picking up the next cargo. A typical review question can be: why did we plan truck A for this trip instead of truck B, which was much closer to the pick-up address? The objective should be to maximize the revenue and minimize the costs per km. One option to do so is to use route optimization tools to calculate the best route taking into account restrictions such as requested delivery times, traffic jams, and regulated working hours of the driver, but also the opportunities of picking up cargo from vendors and/or return flows from customers.

2.9.2 Freight Payment and Auditing

About two-thirds of the total logistics costs are generally spent on transportation. There is much to gain by ensuring that the invoices are accurate and paid on time, preventing late payment fees. Freight payment and auditing (FPA) is often outsourced to specialized companies. In addition to checking and paying invoices, they can deliver data that can be used for improvement purposes. Shippers negotiate contracts with carriers to ship products around the world and hire FPA companies to audit the incoming invoices. The audit ensures the bills' validity, and checks mileages and the correct application of rates and accessorials. It verifies if it is correct to pay the invoice and confirms the bill is not a duplicate. The FPA company submits payments on the shipper's behalf and provides reports that help the general ledger account coding. Following is an explanation of the most frequently used words in transportation accounting:

- Quote or quotation: a document with the price of in detail described service proposed by a carrier to a shipper. If requested, it can contain a breakdown of components such as labor, material, and VAT. It includes also terms and conditions such as delivery time, payment terms, and validity period. Once the quotation is accepted by the shipper it becomes a binding agreement.
- Rate or price: the amount of money in a certain currency in- or exclusive VAT to be paid by a shipper to a carrier for a delivered service.
- Cost or costs: the carriers spend to deliver the agreed service to the shipper. The cost of a specific shipment can be higher or lower than the agreed rate. In the first case, it is a loss-making shipment, while in the latter one it is profitable. Such a situation is possible as the rates are often based on the average shipment characteristics of, for example, one full year, while the actual deliveries can deviate from these.
- Invoice or bill: a document sent by a carrier to a shipper with the amount of money for the described and delivered service to be paid within the agreed period. The minimum required information, such as service description, VAT number, bank account number, and invoice-to and invoice-from names and addresses on an invoice can differ per type of service, country, and origin-destination combination.
- Payment terms: a specification of the period, generally 30 days or more, allowed by the carrier to a shipper to transfer the amount of money mentioned on the invoice.
- Invoice audit: the process of checking if the invoiced amount is according the agreed rates between the carrier and the shipper.
- Payment: transfer of money from the shipper to the carrier in the form of cash in advance, cash on delivery, check, or from one bank account to another.
- Late payment fee: a charge from a carrier to a shipper who paid the invoice after the due date. This instrument, a flat rate or a percentage of the outstanding invoice amount, is often used to encourage the shipper to pay on time.

- Spend: an amount of money paid and given by a shipper to a carrier for a delivered service.
- Expense: money spent in the form of cash (e.g., to pay the drivers) or depreciation costs of an asset (e.g., due to owning a truck) made to generate revenue.

2.9.3 Spend Analysis

A tool to analyze spend data is "spend analysis," which is the process of collecting, categorizing, and evaluating expense data to identify wasteful spending. First identify all the sources from which the spend data can be derived. Example sources can be departments, locations, functions, systems, and persons. Then gather the data as much as possible in one data file to make data crunching easier. Clean up the data, get rid of errors, and standardize the data elements such as modality, region, lanes, products, and markets and cost categories like surcharges, waiting, and fuel costs as the devil is in the details. Then group and categorize the data as much as possible. Analyze the data by creating a graph, Pareto diagram, pie chart, or the rest of the seven quality tool as mentioned elsewhere in this book.

3

Transportation Management

The transportation function is not a standalone activity, as it should be derived from the logistics strategy, which itself is based on the business strategy. It is broken down into a strategy per commodity, which is a set of services with similar characteristics and can be purchased as one package. Transportation commodities are parcel and express, airfreight, road and sea freight, train, and intermodal. Each commodity strategy is translated into business, customer, process, and people requirements. These are used as input for the carrier selection and review processes. The outcomes of the carrier selection process, such as carrier allocations and rates, are uploaded in a TMS. In the carrier review process, the agreed carrier KPIs are measured, analyzed, and improved. This information is useful as input for the carrier selection process. Figure 3.1 illustrates the carrier management cycle, which will be discussed in the following paragraphs.

3.1 COMMODITY STRATEGY

Commodity strategy is used to determine what issues and risks currently there are and how these can be solved in the next purchasing cycle. The commodity strategy needs to be in line with the transportation, logistics, and company strategies. The commodity strategy development helps to understand service requirements, search the market for potential carriers who can provide the required services, set up a strategy how and when to approach the market to maximize the sourcing results, and build a continuous improvement process to maintain the quality, cost, and service levels once the strategy is implemented.

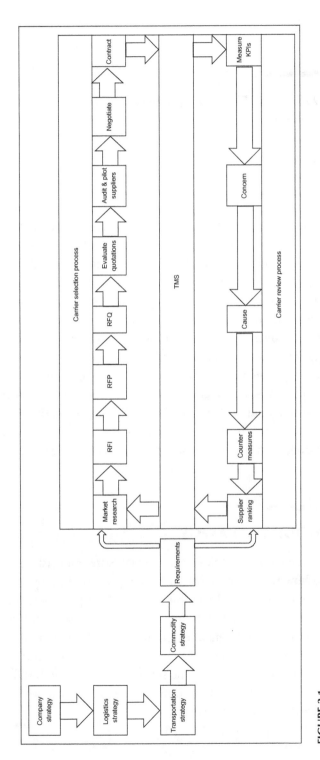

FIGURE 3.1

Carrier management cycle.

Different ways and tools are used to develop a commodity strategy. The following strategy development process, as applied to the transportation management specific processes, is based on the five-step approach of Dr. Robert Monczka Ph.D. and his co-authors as described in their book "Purchasing and Supply Chain Management" (6th edition, page 208 and further) and is elaborated as follows:

1. Build the team and the project charter.
2. Conduct market intelligence research on suppliers.
3. Strategy development.
4. Contract negotiation.
5. Supplier relationship management.

3.1.1 Build the Team and the Project Charter

In this process the typical project management activities, such as creating a project charter, team, stakeholder analysis, communication plan, scoping document, and project plan, are worked out. These activities are not discussed in this book, as they are widely known and educated skills.

3.1.2 Conduct Market Intelligence Research on Suppliers

The objective of this phase is to understand the transportation market in terms of pricing, capacity, number of players, and trends and review the current strategy. This review is done by comparing the actual with the planned performance of the sourcing objectives such as delivery reliability, quality, cost, IT capability, customer service, contract terms and conditions, validity period, and contract coverage. Contract coverage means at what level the shipper managed to adhere to the agreed carrier and volume allocation. A high coverage encourages carriers to invest in sharp rates and account management team set-ups. It gives a signal of commitment to invest in the partnership and it stimulates ownership to solve problems. Both parties respect the agreed allocation unless the carrier is structurally underperforming or lacking capacity. The most important elements of delivery performance are transit times and their reliability. Carriers provide KPI reports on regular basis and share the performance details. Non-performance is analyzed and exception codes are used to group the root causes. Carrier uncontrollable factors and customer-related issues are excluded from the "net" carrier performance measurement.

Typical quality issues are under- or over-deliveries, losses, damages, and billing errors. However, customers feel the gross performance, which includes all carrier- and non-carrier-related misses. Shippers and carriers need to work together to improve this gross performance and meet the targets. A Cost Price Indicator (CPI) measures the price performance by dividing the new rates by the old ones. The comparison is based on all-in rates and includes all surcharges, such as FSC, Security Surcharge (SSC) and Peak Season Surcharge (PSS), for an easy understanding. FSC fluctuates with the oil price and SSC depends on the international security environment. FSC varies by airline, origin, and destination and can be based on volumetric or actual weight. PSS is paid by the shipper to the carrier to guarantee transportation capacity during peak season. As the demand is higher that the supply in this period, airlines and the ground infrastructure experience high pressure due to space limitations in cross-dock locations, shortage of warehouse personnel, lack of trucks and parking space and limited number of slots leading to congestions at ports. Each relatively small operational issue results in service disruptions as the supply chain is planned without any buffer. Airlines try to sell the available capacity as an Express service against higher rates and prioritize big loyal customers. SSC is paid to finance the activities to secure the cargo. Shippers and carriers agree on surcharge mechanisms as the surcharge amounts change overtime. IT capabilities to provide better supply chain visibility are key. There is a growing need for EDI communication and it is becoming a standard requirement. Carriers are requested to provide messages such as the confirmation of pick-up, ASN, on board confirmation, arrival at destination, Confirmation of Delivery (COD), and POD. A dedicated account management team is necessary to support a long-term relationship and provide support to the business. There are global, regional, and country account managers to drive improvements and schedule ABRs, QBRs, and MBRs. The responsiveness of the account management team and the customer service desk are key for timely problem solving and ongoing relationship building. A SLA is created to write down terms and conditions regarding payment terms, liabilities, sustainability, and security agreements. It is important to standardize these pre-defined terms and conditions for all carriers to prevent discussions during contract negotiations and implementations. Accepting these, together with other requirements, can be used as a pre-requisite for tender participation and can be communicated in the RFI phase. They can be managed as non-negotiable items in the tendering process. It is good to have an idea about the optimal number of carriers and leveraged volume is key to achieve competitive pricing. To support the conclusions regarding the current strategy it is important gather data. Relevant data of the current situation can be:

- Customer feedback
- Performance and reliability level per trade lane
- Proactive problem solving by carriers
- Track and trace availability per carrier
- Contract coverage of endorsed carriers. Carrier status: strategic, niche, commercial, or preferred
- Current carriers and their performance per trade lane
- Scope of services per carrier
- Effectiveness of carrier account management structure and relationship management
- Carrier strategy: laid-back or aggressive rating
- Number of shipments, weight, spend, and rate level per carrier
- Market information such as imbalance in trade lanes and its impact on rates

3.1.3 Strategy Development

In this phase, the new business requirements and related goals are defined. Table 3.1 shows an overview of the current, competition, and best-in-class performance and the targets for the coming years.

Tools to define the future strategy are the Strengths Weaknesses Opportunities Threats (SWOT), the service portfolio, and the suppliers

TABLE 3.1

Goal Setting

Sourcing Objectives	Current Performance	Competition Performance	Best-in-Class Performance	Target 2018	Target 2019	Target 2020
Delivery reliability (%)	95	98	99	96	97	98
Costs ($/m³)	250	260	200	230	200	190
Number of carriers (#)	15	15	5	10	7	5

	Strengths	Weaknesses
Internal	Increasing volumes Strong brand image Financial stability Purchasing expertise Market knowledge	No volume commitments Complex organization Multiple decision makers Challenging requirements Price focused
	Opportunities	Threats
External	EDI Buyers' market Logistics market places TMS	Increasing fuel prices Road taxes Limited number of suppliers Shortage of drivers
	Strategy: capitalize	Strategy: risk management

FIGURE 3.2
SWOT analysis.

view analyses. A SWOT analysis evaluates the organizational strengths and weaknesses and the market threats and opportunities. Figure 3.2 shows an example of a SWOT analysis.

In the service portfolio analysis, the service types based on the supply risk and related costs are defined: strategic, leverage, or routine service. Each type of service requires a different purchasing strategy. Figure 3.3 provides an example of a service portfolio analysis.

The supplier view analysis gives an idea about how a supplier sees the shipper based on the shipper attractiveness and spend. The four categories are "core," "exploitable," "development," or "nuisance" customer. Each of these qualifications requires a different purchasing and negotiation strategy. Figure 3.4 provides an example of a supplier's view analysis.

High	Leverage Parcel & express	Strategic
		Air
Relative cost		
	Road 　　　　Intermodal Train 　　　　　　Sea	
Low	Routine	
	Low　　　　　Supply/Risk　　　　High	

FIGURE 3.3
Service portfolio analysis.

High	Exploitable customer	Core customer
Relative	Carrier y	Carrier z
value	Carrier x	
	Nuisance	Development customer
Low		
	Low Company attractiveness High	

FIGURE 3.4
Supplier's view analysis.

Creating the future strategy is defining the way to realize the newly agreed sourcing objectives. Typical elements of a strategy are:

- Services: which modalities, rate structures, and performance targets to use.
- Carrier base: who will be the allocated suppliers and back-up suppliers and what is the supplier reduction target?
- Purchasing: agree on single, dual, or multiple sourcing and tender road maps.
- Contracting: define the contract duration, terms and conditions, and spot quote strategy.
- Carrier development: set out quality improvement plans, audits, and efficiency improvement plans.

Example commodity strategies are:

Parcel and express:

- Minimize the usage.
- Cherry pick (choose the cheapest option with any carrier to any destination).
- Include regional players.
- Better manage the breakeven point: the weight or volume at when airfreight becomes cheaper than parcel and express.
- Simplify rate structures.
- Contract period is one year.
- No volume commitment.

Airfreight:

- Use only forwarders, which can deliver any shipment to any destination (global coverage).
- Spot quote rates for shipments >3,000 kg.
- Allocate volume per trade lane.
- Do not accept any surcharge.
- Limit the use of niche players.
- Improve contract coverage.
- Agree on a variable fuel surcharge mechanism.

Sea freight:

- Use only shipping lines (no forwarders).
- Reduce carrier base.
- Allocate two carriers per trade lane.
- Safeguard sufficient capacity for the high season.
- Minimize volume commitments.
- Purchase as a group of sites.
- Improve pick-up and delivery performance.

3.1.4 Contract Negotiation

The objective of this phase is to sign a contract. Before doing so, it is possible to negotiate the terms and conditions with the carriers, based on a negotiation plan. A good knowledge of the transportation industry and specific carriers' capabilities, and weaknesses, are pre-requisites for successful negotiations. Also benchmarking rates is a good habit, but acting tough is not always a good approach; instead, the parties need to be prepared to move towards a mutually beneficial relationship.

3.1.5 Supplier Relationship Management

The final phase is to measure the carrier performance, create a carrier development plan, and continuously improve processes to realize the targets. Suppliers should be treated as equal partners and as part of the supply chain. Without their contribution, it is impossible to satisfy customers. Especially in tough times, it is not recommended to squeeze suppliers and lower their margins. Show that the shipper trusts the supplier by not telling them what to do and how much to contribute. Instead, both parties need to collaborate to remove waste from the whole supply chain leading to a win-win situation. It is important to explain the potentially bad situation of the shipper to suppliers and ask them for help by brainstorming on improvement opportunities. The best way to do this is on one-on-one basis as the suppliers are more open to share ideas, even it is tempting to call and bring in all the suppliers in one room and ask them the same questions as this perceived to be "faster" and "more efficient." Although the plan phase is faster, the act phase will take longer as suppliers will not easily share their thoughts and ideas with competition being in the same room. In Lean philosophy, it is preferred to plan slowly and act fast.

3.2 CARRIER SELECTION PROCESS

The starting point for any source or tender activity is to install an effective and efficient team with sufficient negotiation skills and transportation market and carrier knowledge. Examples of such market intelligence and benchmark information are the number and key players, their sizes, specialties, quality levels, selling strategies, rate components, and contacts. The team also needs to have information and data about the cargo characteristics like fragility, packing, and stackability allowing them to provide the carriers a clear picture of what is expected from them. The team gathers business, customer, people, and process requirements. Meeting only the customer requirements is not sufficient, as the proposed carrier solutions need to be workable for an organization. There is also no value to select a cheap solution with a lengthy implementation period. Typical process requirements can be EDI connectivity, daily performance reporting, self-billing, single point of contact, availability of drop trailers, exchange of pallets, returns and tracking, and tracing capabilities. Tenders are widely communicated to encourage competition and receive a sufficient number of quotations. Figure 3.5 shares an example content list of a tender document.

The ultimate goal is to choose the right carriers that can meet the requirements against competitive rates. Carriers reply on the invitation to tender by sending responses that explain the quotation, pricing, terms, and conditions. They emphasize their competitive advantages, value for money, certifications, competencies, experience, and why they think the

1. Introduction
2. Scope
3. Goods flows
4. Objectives
5. Customer and operational requirements
6. Business and people requirements
7. Submitting the proposal
8. Proposal format
9. Timing
10. Confidentiality
11. Communication matrix
12. Dataset
13. Cargo pictures

FIGURE 3.5
Tender document content list.

business needs to be given to them. A point of attention is that tendered lanes are awarded to the best carrier. It is a not an appreciated habit to "abuse" invitations to tender for gathering market information only. They do support these requests, but this needs to be mentioned upfront as benchmarking process requires a different approach than a tender. Carriers invest time in a tender process and they want to make sure that there is something to win. Finding out that there was no real tender is frustrating and leads to carriers not accepting invitations to tender, mistrusting the shipper, and providing only standard solutions. The tender responses need to be evaluated fairly and honestly. In addition to providing good rates, the carriers are required to fill in a quality assessment questionnaire. After that, their physical sites are visited for audits, using the same questionnaire, as carriers tend to score themselves higher than shippers do. A market research is executed to get an indication of which carrier long list could meet the requirements and can be invited for the Request for Information (RFI) phase. A RFI is the process to collect written information about carrier capabilities. Table 3.2 shows an example of such an assessment questionnaire based on the sourcing objectives. A typical questionnaire contains questions about technological capabilities and support, pipeline visibility, real-time tracking and tracking, customer service, service areas, transit times their and reliability, urgent delivery services, damages, and claims. Other topics are account structure and management, EDI and web connectivity, carrier management, carrier selection, customs processes, continuous improvement, sourcing and contracting, control tower (CT), cost, proactive exception notification and management,

TABLE 3.2

Carrier Assessment Questionnaire

Evaluation Criteria	Description	Weight Factor	Score	Target
	QUALITY			
Damage prevention	How is the service provider preventing damages?	20	6	9
Quality certification	What quality certifications does the service provider have?		7	9
Quality measurement	What KPIs are reported?		8	9
Measurement of subcontractors	How does the service provider measure and develop subcontractors?		9	9
Complaint and claim handling	What processes are there and how are these measured and improved?		5	9
Sustainability	What are the service provider's sustainability efforts?		6	9
Supply chain security	What measures are taken to be compliant with supply chain security requirements?		7	9
	DELIVERY			
Delivery reliability	Percentage of shipments arrived on (SLA) time.	20	5	8
Shipment accuracy	Percentage of shipments arrived complete.		6	8
Pick-up accuracy	Percentage of shipments picked up on (SLA) time.		7	8
Invoice accuracy	Percentage of correct invoices.		8	8
	SERVICE			
Transportation capacity	Capacity per day/month/quarter/ year (m^3, # trucks).	20	9	7
Global coverage	Can the service provider deliver to all countries?		8	7
Equipment	Is the equipment owned or subcontracted?		7	7
Flexibility and responsiveness	What is the response time between booking and loading?		6	7
Single point of contact	Is there a dedicated single point of contact for the customer?		5	7

(Continued)

TABLE 3.2 (Continued)

Carrier Assessment Questionnaire

Evaluation Criteria	Description	Weight Factor	Score	Target
Issue resolution	What is the time, efficiency, and effectiveness of the issue resolution process?	4	7	
Proactive exception management	Is it possible to receive pre-alerts on time?	3	7	
	COST			
Price level	How competitive is the financial offer?	20	5	6
Price transparency	Is it possible to receive the price components?	6	6	
Rate structure	Is it a simple or complicated (e.g., many surcharges) rate structure?	7	6	
Cost reduction targets	Is the service provider willing to agree cost reduction targets?	8	6	
	IT			
EDI and web communication	How much is the service provider using EDI and web communication tool?	20	9	5
EDI/web industry standards	What type of EDI/web communication standards are used?	8	5	
Labeling and barcoding	Does the service provider use RF scanning and (SSCC) label barcodes?	7	5	

shipment creation, milestone tracking, and transport mode selection. Additional ones are shipment consolidation and transport network optimization, shipping instructions and documents, sub-contractor management, shipment visibility and proactive monitoring, business analytics, billing accuracy and financial solidness, digitalization, organization, globalization, performance indicators, and reporting.

Based on the RFI feedback it is possible that some of the carriers are taken off the long list as they cannot meet some mandatory requirements, also called "knockout criteria," or the sourcing team does not think they can meet them. The short list carriers proceed to the Request for Proposal (RFP) phase. A RFP is a request towards the carriers to come up with proposals how they will meet the requirements. It is not required to include their financial offer yet. It is possible that some carriers are taken off the short list, as their proposals do not meet the requirements. Carriers who did not made it through the RFI and/or RFP phase are explained why they have not been selected for the next phases. Sometimes, it turns out that carriers did not provide the requested information, as they did not understand the questions or the shipper did not interpret the information in the right way. The next step is to ask the suppliers for a financial offer, which is also called a Request for Quotation (RFQ).

The next step, after rating the potential carriers based on the sourcing objectives, is to audit their processes. This is to prevent carriers from giving a too-positive picture of their company. It remains the shipper's responsibility to verify the presented capabilities. Another idea is to execute a pilot to check in practice if the carrier indeed can deliver what is promised in the tender process. After the audit and pilot have been executed, the tender outcome should be validated against other strategic considerations such as: does the solution fit in the shipper's long-term logistics strategy? Does the carrier support continuous improvement? What are the implementation risks, timings, and costs? Table 3.3 shows an

TABLE 3.3

Overall Decision Matrix

Decision Criteria	Weight Factor	Carrier x	Carrier y	Carrier z
Quality assessment	10	0.1	0.2	0.3
Audit	15	0.2	0.3	0.4
Pilot	20	0.3	0.4	0.7
TCO	25	0.4	0.5	0.6
Cost-reduction target	5	0.1	0.7	0.8
References and track record	5	0.2	0.8	0.9
Lead-times	20	0.3	0.9	−0.1
Neutrality	10	0.9	−0.1	−0.2
Fits logistics strategy	15	−0.1	−0.2	−0.3
Improvement idea generation	10	−0.2	−0.3	0.1
Implementation time and resources	5	−0.3	0.1	0.2
Total weighted score	—	31.5	46	40
Ranking	—	3	1	2

example of an overall decision matrix. The decision criteria, weight factors, and scoring system can be freely chosen. The data will provide information about what the carriers can deliver and if the sourcing objectives can be met. Potential gaps are identified and checked if and when they can be closed. It is better to have gaps that can be closed on short term. As some gaps are more important than others, it is good to give them a weight factor and score the carriers. The weighted scoring for the audit, pilot, and strategic considerations will provide the information to take conclusions and come up with recommendations. After approval, it is time to work on a communication plan and inform all the stakeholders. Then describe the lessons learned in the form of what went well and what could be done better. Sit together with the carriers who did not win and review with them the process and the results.

A more detailed systematic RFQ process can consist of these activities:

1. Collect historical shipment data of the previous year. If necessary, adjust this data with forecast information to provide the carriers reliable data that they can use to quote. Do not take the actual spend and compare this with the calculated costs, as the actual spend can contain costs for waiting time, taxi, late payments, and special services. Instead, calculate the as-is and the to-be costs by using the rates.

2. Invite carriers to quote for the first round and request them to use the communicated standard formats to prevent spending too much time comparing quotes with each other as carriers tend to submit quotes in their own ways. This approach should also help preventing delayed and/or incorrect responses jeopardizing the tender successfulness. It is recommended to use transportation-specific tender tools. The standard purchasing tools cannot cover the complexity in transportation. There is a wide range of rate structures per mode of transport, geographies, accessorials, surcharges, currency conversions, rounding rules, equipment types, pallets, weights, dimensions, and break-even point calculations. These business rules need to be well understood and processed for a correct comparison of carrier offers.

3. Analyze the carrier quotes and compare them. Table 3.4 shows an example of a detailed carrier quotes comparison. Share this benchmark information per lane with the carriers as input for step 4.

4. Invite the carriers to quote for the second round. Carriers tend to not immediately offer their best possible rates and

TABLE 3.4

Detailed Carrier Quotes Comparison

Process	Category	Sub-Category	Required Capabilities	Capabilities Carrier A	Capabilities Carrier B	Costs Carrier A (k€/year)	Costs Carrier B (k€/year)
PUDO	General	Owned locations	>75	80	100		
Deliveries		Agent locations	<10	20	10		
		Drop boxes	<5	5	0		
		Opening hours	09:00–18:00	09:00–17:00	08:00–18:00		
		Maximum weight	<25 kg/parcel	<20 kg/parcel	<30 kg/parcel		
		Track & Trace	100%	80%	100%		
		Transactional rate	0	1,95 €/parcel	0	120	0
		Management fee	0	2,26 €/shipment	0	10	0
	Outbound	Order cut-off time	19:00	22:30	18:00		
		SLA	09:00	09:00–18:00	08:00		
		Performance	99%	97%	98%		
		Rate	10 €/parcel	12 €/parcel	13 €/parcel	300	400
	Returns	SLA	NBD	NBD 10:30	2BD 12:00		
		Frequency	Daily	Daily	Weekly		
		Performance	95%	90%	92%		
		Rate	5 €/parcel	6 €/parcel	7 €/parcel	100	90

service levels. Some of them hope the shipper to accept the initial proposal, while others would like to get an idea how they quoted against competition. Another reason is that carriers try to build in some room for negotiation. Make clear towards the carriers how many rounds there will be.

5. Organize face-to-face negotiation meetings. Prepare the carrier profiles with the turnover, service portfolio, unique selling points, TCO, and SWOT analysis. Gather market price and benchmark information, negotiation targets, and alternative sources, such as switching to another carrier, in case of threat or no agreement. Define strategies on supplier arguments and the least favorable point at which the deal will not be accepted, think of potential new business to offer, build in room for negotiation, and do not come immediately with a take-it-or-leave-it proposal. Stay on speaking terms with the carriers and go for a win-win situation to maintain their high cooperation level.

6. Agree on volume and carrier allocation. Use dual sourcing, where one carrier is in the lead, while the other is the back up. On another lane it can be the other way around. This concept keeps competitors sharp and is a good risk mitigation tool, where the back-up can take over from the lead carrier in case of disaster. Carriers try to force single sourcing by offering lower rates, but it is important to map the potential benefits and risks and decide if single sourcing is worth the risks. It is possible to ask carriers to quote rates for full allocation or only part of the volume.

7. Communicate the volume and carrier allocation to all stakeholders such as carriers who did and who did not win the tender, the shipping and receiving locations, project team, and steering group. Share also the starting and end dates of the volume allocation and rate validity.

8. Implement the new volume and carrier allocations. Start with generating a scoping document so that is clear for all stakeholders what is going to be implemented, what is not, when, how, and who. Such a document contains the project lead, team, steering group, and time planning.

To allow for accurate and reliable quotations, it is import to share the correct weights and dimensions of the parcels and/or pallets. A gemba walk with the carrier is recommended to explain and show the products so that they can assess stackability, above and/or below other customers' products, hazardousness, fragility and packing material, risk of losing small products or damage due to goods hanging over the pallet boundaries, and pallet configuration. It is important to share the exact ship-from and ship-to addresses, including the street name, number, zip code, and the city and its nature, commercial or residential, to define whether additional equipment, and thus additional costs, such as tail lift and in-room delivery are needed. The more specific the information is the more accurate the quotation will be. In case of incomplete information, the carrier will build in safety margins to cover this risk, which means higher rates.

An important element of tendering and sourcing is negotiating. Before starting a negotiation, the carriers need to be informed upfront about the why, objectives, planning, and way of working. The reasons for a negotiation can be diverse. An example is that the carriers did offer a promising proposal, but the target is not met yet or the market circumstances changed. The change can be an opportunity or a threat. An opportunity can be the increasing, while a threat can be the decreasing of the transportation market capacity. Other reasons can be supply constraints due to bankruptcy, volume developments, changing raw material and energy prices, lower profitability, changing inflation and labor costs, higher unemployment, or lower interest. Objectives can be rate reductions, better financial terms and conditions, supply base rationalization, and risk mitigation. These objectives can be realized by agreeing on some tactics: prepare fact and figures such as the market conditions and benchmark information and focus on the carriers with the biggest spend. Analyze how carriers see the shipper, set ambitious targets, and use the right momentum as tendering in a low season will bring more savings compared to tendering in a high season. Install a cross-functional and capable negotiation team to work on a negotiation book, agree on roles and responsibilities and decide on allocation strategy such as take it or leave it or the lowest cost. Do not take the as-is situation for granted and propose new ways of working. Execute carrier SWOT analyses and find out what their strengths and weaknesses are and what external elements offer opportunities and which threats there are. Example opportunities or threats are order intake and market development (stable, declining, increasing), marketing budgets, insourcing to avoid lay-offs or outsourcing for extra capacity to meet the higher production targets, unemployment figures, and lay-offs due to restructuring. Other examples are the volume trend changes towards emerging markets, raw material and energy price developments, travel bans, changing laws and regulations, cargo capacity, which carriers have unique capabilities, product supplier locations, and supply distances. The best offer meeting all the requirements and providing the best value for money wins the tender. This process is completed by creating and signing a Letter of Intention (LOI) and a Service Level Agreement (SLA). It is recommended to include the company's legal department when agreeing and signing these documents. A LOI captures the binding and non-binding terms and conditions of an upcoming deal between two parties. It contains elements such as who will write the contract, when to sign it and a Non-Disclosure Agreement (NDA). Both parties write down in a NDA which information needs to stay confidential and which can be shared with others. A LOI is a preliminary agreement and describes how to come to a contract. After signing a LOI, it is still possible to talk about and negotiate certain topics, but the exact elements need to be written down before signing the document. Figure 3.6 illustrates an example of LOI content list.

It is possible to create a LOI or take an existing one and adjust it to a specific situation. One party can propose a concept and the other one can come up with change requests. The final goal is to protect both parties in the discussions after signing the LOI. A SLA is a contract between a shipper and a carrier that documents what both parties will provide against what performance levels and terms and conditions. It includes the shipper's expectations of the carrier performance by using KPI targets. A SLA can include also a plan how the carrier will compensate the shipper in case of contract breach. There are situations where the SLA guarantees do not apply. These situations can be natural disasters, cyber-attacks, or terrorist acts. Figure 3.7 shows a typical SLA content list.

Purpose
Terms and conditions
Services
Implementation costs
Liability and insurance
Rates and invoicing
Binding and non-binding factors
Assignment
Non-disclosure
Governing law and jurisdiction

FIGURE 3.6
LOI content list.

General
Article 1: Definitions
Article 2: Scope of agreement
Article 3: Service requirements
Article 4: Prices, invoicing, and payment terms
Article 5: Contract duration and termination
Article 6: Volumes
Article 7: Service requirements
Article 8: Trade compliance
Article 9: Supply chain security
Article 10: Sustainability
Article 11: Quality and regulatory requirements
Article 12: Miscellaneous
Article 13: Contract coordination
Exhibits
Exhibit 1: Service definition
Exhibit 2: Lead-times
Exhibit 3: Volumetric weight
Exhibit 4: Fuel surcharge clause
Exhibit 5: Duties and taxes
Exhibit 6: Rates
Exhibit 7: Key performance indicators
Exhibit 8: Complaints, claims, insurance, and liability
Exhibit 9: Packaging
Exhibit 10: Terms and conditions
Exhibit 11: Reporting
Exhibit 12: Standard exception codes
Exhibit 13: Non-disclosure agreement and data protection
Exhibit 14: Shipping tools
Exhibit 14: Contract change requests

FIGURE 3.7
Example SLA content list.

Many shippers use a manual approach to manage tenders by using Word and Excel templates. This might be sufficient for simple and small tenders, but the complexity and time spend increase when the tenders become bigger in terms of number of lanes, shipping and receiving points, flow types and invited carriers, types of transportation equipment, customs, and packaging requirements. The risk of an incorrect tender outcome is higher due to this complexity and the amount of work leading to an uncontrolled processes and outcomes. The same as within many other industries there is tender software available for the transportation market. The shipper saves time and money by sharing tender information via such a system, reducing the number of questions and other communication from and to stakeholders. Using standard reports out of the tender tool simplifies analyses. Carriers understand and process the information better and faster leading to better offers, as carriers treat the tender more seriously and do their utmost to offer a competitive proposal. Both e-procurement tools and specialized companies, such as the tendering software of TenderEasy and the e-auction software of Easibuy, are available in the market to support these processes. E-procurement is the electronic procurement of services via Internet, EDI, or ERP systems. E-Auction is a virtual environment where suppliers bid against each other for a contract. It encourages competition to offer their best rates. After the business has been awarded to a carrier, it is time to create an implementation plan. This process starts with generating a scoping document to agree on what is in and what is out of the project scope, the responsibilities and accountabilities of each team member, and how the deliverables will be assessed and approved. It specifies the goals, deliverables, tasks, costs, deadlines, change request procedures, and planning. Table 3.5 shows an example of a carrier implementation plan.

A standard part of project management is to create, update, distribute, store, and maintain an action list so that all team members know what is expected from them when and to hold them accountable for the progress. It is recommended to use an implementation checklist to verify if all elements are in place for a successful go-live. Important to remember is that each change is tested before it is implemented. An important input for the implementation plan is a Standard Operating Procedure (SOP). SOPs contain detailed written instructions to achieve the required performance per individual process and distilled agreements from contracts into easy-to-understand work instructions. A SOP can serve also as a training program for new and existing employees and needs to be regularly updated to be taken serious by the employees and respect the predefined ways of working. Changes can be processed through change requests. An example SOP content list is shown in Figure 3.8.

TABLE 3.5

Carrier Implementation Plan

	Activity/Deliverables by Week	1	2	3	4	5	6	7	8	9	10
1	Design project plan	▓									
2	Deliver draft to senior management		▓								
3	Kick of project		▓								
1	Mapping of planning and booking process			▓							
2	Mapping of pick up and collection process			▓							
3	Collect customer requirements			▓							
4	Map organization and communication customer requirements			▓							
5	Mapping of complaint handling and troubleshooting			▓							
6	Mapping of system settings			▓							
7	Mapping of return process			▓							
8	Mapping of invoicing procedure			▓							
9	Mapping active reporting requirements			▓							
10	Map reporting transport costs			▓							
11	Map incorrect/missing master data			▓							
1	Describe planning and booking process				▓						
2	Describe pick-up and collection process				▓						
3	Describe organization and communication customer requirements				▓						
4	Describe complaint handling and troubleshooting process				▓						
5	Describe system settings				▓						
6	Describe return process				▓						
7	Describe invoicing procedure				▓						
8	Describe track and trace				▓						
9	Describe pallet exchange procedure				▓						

(Continued)

TABLE 3.5 (Continued)

Carrier Implementation Plan

	Activity/Deliverables by Week	1	2	3	4	5	6	7	8	9	10
10	Describe emergency procedures										
11	Describe active reporting										
12	Organize reporting transport costs										
13	Refresh incorrect/missing master data										
14	Describe SOP										
15	Describe fall back scenario										
16	Risk assessment										
17	Go/no-go										
1	Close gap of planning and booking process										
2	Close gap of pick-up and collection process										
3	Close gap organization and communication customer requirements										
4	Close gap of complaint handling and troubleshooting										
5	Close gap of system settings										
6	Close gap of return process										
7	Close gap of invoicing procedure										
8	Close gap of active reporting requirements										
9	Close gap reporting transport costs										
10	Close gap incorrect/missing master data										
1	Communication stakeholders										
2	Training operations										
3	Implementation of system settings										
4	Implementation KPIs, daily and active reporting										
5	Go Live										
1	Monitoring KPIs										

1. Introduction
   1.1   Standard Operating Procedure
   1.1.1 Purpose
   1.1.2 Audience
2. Change requests
3. Scope
4. Terms and conditions
5. Operations
   5.1   Locations
   5.1.1 Shipper
   5.1.2 Service provider
   5.2   Shipment preparation
   5.2.1 Pick-up process
   5.2.2 Delivery process
   5.3   Customs, duties, and taxes
   5.3.1 Importer of record
   5.3.2 Incoterms® rules
   5.3.3 Customs clearance
   5.4   Hazardous material
   5.5   Volumes, weights, and measurements
   5.5.1 Volumes
   5.5.2 Weights
   5.5.3 Measurements
6. EDI
   6.1   Shipping tool
   6.1.1 Data exchange
   6.1.2 Labels
   6.1.3 Track and trace
7. Visibility
   7.1   Delivery information
   7.1.1 Non-deliveries
   7.1.2 Partial deliveries
   7.1.3 Confirmation of delivery
   7.1.4 Proof of delivery
   7.2   Claims
   7.2.1 Damages
   7.2.2 Shortages
   7.2.3 Terms and conditions
   7.3   Billing
   7.3.1 Account numbers
   7.3.2 Payment terms
   7.3.3 Rates
   7.3.4 Invoicing
   7.3.5 FPA
   7.4   Reports and reviews
   7.4.1 Reports
   7.4.2 Reviews
8. Communication matrix
   8.1   Shipper
   8.2   Service provider

FIGURE 3.8
Example SOP content list.

3.3 CARRIER REVIEW PROCESS

After the business has been awarded to the carriers, it can be that they need help to deliver world-class performance. In this process of supplier development, the shipper works with the carriers to improve their performance and increase their capabilities. A pre-requisite for a successful supplier development process is to act as partners and maintain a good relationship management in order to create value in all processes from raw material to delivery to the customer. Carriers need to be considered as the extension of the shipper and both are working towards the same goals. Build long-term relationships and prevent short-term price reductions leading to lower margins for the carrier. Limit the number of carriers, focus on cost reduction, and share the benefits: two thirds for the shipper and one-third for the carrier. Create multi-functional teams across the companies and collaborate to eliminate waste with the trust that benefits will be shared. After implementing the carriers, start measuring the agreed KPIs in line with their definitions and compare the actual performances against the targets. Analyze the KPIs by asking questions like: what is the actual performance? What is the trend: stable, improving, or declining? Is the standard met? If the standard is not met in combination with a stable or declining performance it is needed to sit together with the carrier and talk about performance improvement actions they have to implement to meet the standard. This improvement process starts with describing and quantifying the issues. It is then important to find the root causes behind these issues to take temporary and/or permanent countermeasures. Carriers are ranked and labelled as a preferred carrier to keep, a potential carrier that could be used in the future or a carrier who needs to be eliminated from the carrier list. Installing, measuring, and reviewing KPIs on a daily basis is crucial, as transportation networks cannot be managed only through incidental network redesigns and tenders. Disciplined daily management is necessary to identify and eliminate waste. Set targets, check actual condition to the plan, find root causes, and solve the problems by using the Lean problem-solving tool. Each carrier is supposed to provide performance and exception reports in the agreed format on daily, weekly, and monthly bases. These reports are used when having carrier reviews to discuss the performance and agree on corrective and/or preventive actions. KPIs give information about the current performance, but they also provide ideas how to become more effective and efficient. Choose the right KPIs, as there can be many PIs, which can be important but not necessarily key for the success of the business. Leadership needs to focus only on the key ones, understand them thoroughly and learn what factors are driving them. It is crucial to identify areas of improvement and set challenging targets, which can be derived from benchmark information of comparable companies. Check if the corrective actions indeed led to the right results. If not, check what did not work, find out the root causes, and plan new improvement actions. Go through the PDCA cycle multiple times if needed.

There are many performance indicators shippers use. Some of them can be PIs for one shipper, while the same PIs can be KPIs for the other shipper. This depends on the shipper's strategy focus at that moment and how crucial those (K)PIs are for being successful in the business. Commonly used KPIs for all flow types are:

- Number of shipments per employee
- Transportation costs per kg, m^3 or shipment
- Outbound costs as % of sales value
- Inbound costs as % of purchase value
- Delivery reliability (% net, % gross)
- Claims value as % of transportation costs
- Correct invoice value as % of total transportation costs
- Loading degree of a truck as % of the maximum volume a truck can load
- Confirmed PODs as % of all shipments
- Traceable shipments as % of all shipments
- On-time pick-ups as % of all pick-ups
- Loading and unloading time per truck per employee
- Damages as % of all shipments
- Correct documentation as % of all shipments
- Complaints as % of all orders

From the transportation management point of view, a perfect delivery is a shipment that is delivered on time, without errors (complete), undamaged, and with the right documentation. The perfect delivery performance (%) is calculated as: delivered on-time (%) × without errors (%) × undamaged (%) × right documentation (%). Therefore, the delivered-on-time, errors, damages, and documentation performances can be considered as the main transportation management KPIs. Each individual performance part is calculated as:

- Delivered on time (%) = total number of shipments delivered within SLA/total number of shipments
- Errors (%) = total number of shipments delivered without errors/total number of shipments
- Damages (%) = total number of shipments delivered without damage/total number of shipments
- Documentation (%) = total number of shipments delivered with the right documentation/total number of shipments

Figure 3.9 illustrates some examples of the transportation KPIs: "Delivered on time" (delivery reliability) and "%Errors & % Damages" (delivery quality).

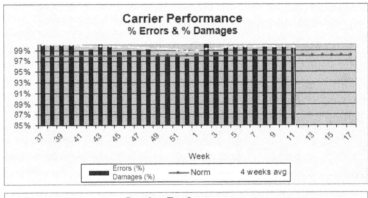

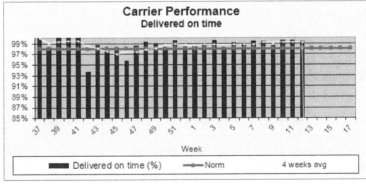

FIGURE 3.9
Example transportation KPIs.

The delivered-on-time performance, also called delivery reliability, can be expressed in a net and gross performance. Net performance is impacted by all the factors that can be controlled by a carrier such as wrongly sorted shipments, capacity issues, and planning mistakes. Gross performance includes both the carrier misses and other items that cannot be controlled by a carrier such as adverse weather conditions, late customs releases, traffic jams, and customer-related issues. This gross performance is what the receiver experiences. To find actionable improvements it is necessary to find the root causes of non-performance. Examples of typical carrier-controllable root causes, also called "delay codes," to structure transportation delays are:

• Late delivery attempt: driver showed up after the delivery address opening times.
• Connection delay: shipment missed the next truck connection at a carrier cross-dock location.
• Damaged: shipment content and/or packaging is damaged due to carrier handling.
• Driver failure: shipment is delayed because of driver mistakes such as oversleeping.
• Wrongly sorted: shipment forwarded to the wrong carrier cross-dock location.
• Lost: carrier, temporary or permanently, cannot find the shipment.
• Equipment failure: break-downs and other mechanical issues.
• Partial delivery: driver did not deliver all the shipping units.
• Split shipment: shipping units have been delivered on multiple dates and/or times.
• Customs delay: customs clearance is not completed on time by the carrier's customs department.
• No shipping label: shipping label is lost and the shipment could not be forwarded on time.
• No paperwork: paperwork is lost and the shipment could not be customs cleared on time.
• Wrong shipping label: wrong label on the packages delayed the delivery.
• No pick-up: carrier did not pick up the shipment on time.

Examples of typical carrier uncontrollable root causes to code transportation delays are:

- Customer closed: customer was closed when the driver tried to deliver.
- Holiday: the delivery could not be made on time due to local holidays.
- Customer not available to sign: customer was not in to accept the shipment.
- Customer refused the shipment: customer refused to receive the delivery.
- Delivery interception: change in address and/or service level in transit caused the delay.
- Duties and taxes: shipment is not delivered yet due to the customer not being able to pay for duties and taxes upon delivery.
- Customer's broker delay: shipment is not customs cleared on time by the customer-assigned customs broker.
- Customs delay: customs authorities did not release the shipment on time.
- Bad weather: the delivery could not be made on time due to adverse weather conditions.
- Force majeure: shipment is delayed due to unforeseen circumstances like strikes and terrorist attacks.
- Traffic jams: shipment is delayed due to too much traffic on the roads.
- Wrong address: delivery could not be made on time because the address was incorrect and/or incomplete.
- Security check: the national authorities held the shipment for an extended security scan.

Figure 3.10 shows an example Pareto diagram of root causes. Such a diagram can be created per period, carrier, lane, and more to analyze the transportation misses.

Table 3.6 shows a more structured approach of analyzing performance data on different levels such as period, carrier, country, modality, and service level.

It can be that such an analysis still does not provide enough information to take action. In that case, it is necessary to go back to the shipment data and look into the detailed issue descriptions. Figure 3.7 shows an example overview of shipment data. The same approach can be used for analyzing the delivery quality (errors and damages) and documentation (Table 3.7).

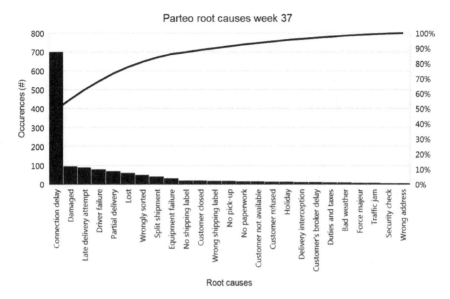

FIGURE 3.10
Example Pareto root causes.

Any carrier is expected to act proactively and continuously improve KPIs. Meeting the targets should be the minimum; the idea behind Lean is to increase the standards day by day. The improvement initiatives should not be limited to the KPIs as these represent the most important operational activities only. The scope should cover all processes, as it is impossible to capture all process performances in KPIs. This can be realized by mobilizing all the employees in the company to work on proactive daily management and kaizens. Especially in situations where the performance is below target, the carrier is expected to proactively explain the situation, provide root cause analysis, short-term mitigation plan, and resolution and target implementation date. Depending on the severity of the event, specific daily calls can be installed to discuss the progress and maintain an action list. The primary responsible and accountable carrier representative is the account manager. If the issue resolution requires a dedicated resource, the account manager can propose a different project lead but he or she remains the lead for communicating with the shipper. If the carrier is not able to improve within the agreed period, it is time to look for alternatives and prepare a phase-in/phase-out plan depending on the contract terms and conditions. Transportation KPIs should be part of the Balanced Scorecard (BSC). This is a tool for reviewing and tracking the organization's performance

TABLE 3.6

Example of a Structured Carrier Performance Analysis

	Performance by Level					Day 1			
Performance by Level	Level 1: Carrier	Level 2: Country	Level 3: Modality	Level 4: SL	Norm (%)	Shipments (#)	Late (#)	Damages and Errors (#)	Score (%)
Total performance by carrier	Carrier x								
	Carrier y								
	Carrier z								
	Total								
Performance by carrier by ship-to country	Carrier x	Country a							
		Country b							
		Country c							
Performance by carrier by ship-to country by modality	Carrier x	Country a	Air						
			Road						
			Sea						
		Country b	Air						
			Road						
			Sea						
		Country c	Air						
			Road						
			Sea						

(Continued)

TABLE 3.6 (*Continued*)

Example of a Structured Carrier Performance Analysis

	Performance by Level						Day 1		
Performance by Level	**Level 1: Carrier**	**Level 2: Country**	**Level 3: Modality**	**Level 4: SL**	**Norm (%)**	**Shipments (#)**	**Late (#)**	**Damages and Errors (#)**	**Score (%)**
Performance by carrier by ship-to country by modality by service level	Carrier x	Country a	Air	SL 1					
				SL 2					
				SL 3					
			Road	SL 4					
				SL 5					
				SL 6					
			Sea	SL 7					
				SL 8					
				SL 9					
		Country b	Air	SL 1					
				SL 2					
				SL 3					
			Road	SL 4					
				SL 5					
				SL 6					
			Sea	SL 7					

(*Continued*)

TABLE 3.6 (*Continued*)

Example of a Structured Carrier Performance Analysis

| Performance by Level | | | | | | Day 1 | | |
| | | | | | | | Damages and | |
Performance by Level	Level 1: Carrier	Level 2: Country	Level 3: Modality	Level 4: SL	Norm (%)	Shipments (#)	Late (#)	Errors (#)	Score (%)
		Country c	Air	SL 8					
				SL 9					
				SL 1					
				SL 2					
				SL 3					
			Road	SL 4					
				SL 5					
				SL 6					
			Sea	SL 7					
				SL 8					
				SL 9					

TABLE 3.7

Example Shipment Data

Shipment	Planned Pick-up Date	Actual Pick-up Date	Planned Delivery Date	Actual Delivery Date	Root Cause	Responsibility	Detailed Issue Description
4572850	23-9-17	23-9-17	25-9-17	26-9-17	Late delivery	Carrier	Customer was closed
3409576	24-9-17	24-9-17	26-9-17	26-10-17	Damaged	Carrier	Pallet collapsed in truck
3345345	25-9-17	25-9-17	27-9-17	28-10-17	Driver failure	Carrier	Driver overslept
0459123	26-9-17	26-9-17	28-9-17	29-9-17	Wrongly sorted	Carrier	Forwarded to location xyz
0998762	27-9-17	27-9-17	29-9-17	?-10-17	Lost	Carrier	Tracer pending
6234232	28-9-17	28-9-17	30-9-17	1-10-17	Equipment failure	Carrier	Truck does not start

via financial, customer, process, and people KPIs. The BSC tracks the improvement actions through monthly, quarterly, and annual reports. It consists of leading and lagging metrics, where the leading metrics indicate whether the shipper is on schedule to make the targets, while the lagging metrics show if the targets have been met. A BSC makes a company's strategy visible while communicating it across the organization. It also supports a fast decision-making process by the leadership team. Typical transportation KPIs in a BSC can be transportation costs, delivery reliability, and employee survey score.

3.4 COMPLAINT AND CLAIM HANDLING

Every business receives customer complaints in different forms. Damages and loss of freight happens with all transportation modalities. The higher the number of freight handling, the higher the risk of damage. Failing to handle complaints properly can damage the company's reputation or even create liability issues due to non-compliance. A complaint is a good source of information about process capabilities. It is a good idea to register, analyze, and report them as they can help with solution directions. There can be also a significant amount of money to recover from own and/or carrier insurance companies. Before starting complaining, claiming, and producing waste, it is necessary to know what the shipper's and carrier's responsibilities are. The first important thing to know is that the only valid transportation contract between the shipper and the carrier is the transportation document. It is possible to add additional agreements; however, the transportation document is leading. It must be clear that carriers will not pay the full cargo value. As their liability is limited, the cargo needs to be insured. The carrier will not pay the commercial damage caused by delayed shipments. The carrier will not pay if the shipper did not pack the goods properly. Carriers do not cover natural disasters, either. If, because of such a natural disaster, it is impossible for the carrier to deliver at the originally planned destination, the carrier is allowed to unload the goods at another location and request the shipper to pick-up the goods from there and take the additional costs such as the customs authorities' inspection activities. The value paid by carriers depends on what is stated on the shipping documents such as purchasing invoices. It is important to have a well-designed complaint-handling process to keep customers happy. It requires respect, timely communication, and a solution proposal to the complaining person. An unsolved complaint can lead to a claim. A claim is a letter from a customer describing the discovered loss or damage, why the carrier is held responsible, and asking the shipper to pay an amount of money as recovery. The request needs to be sent out within the time limits specified by laws and regulations for that specific modality in that country. Other words used for freight claims are shipping claims, cargo claims, transportation claims, or loss and damage claims. A loss is a situation where freight has been picked up but not delivered to its final destination. A shortage is that only part of the shipment is delivered and a damage is where the goods did not arrive in good condition. The losses or damages are a major financial loss for the shipper as it is not always possible to recover these from insurance companies and/or carriers due to their limited liabilities. Insurance companies apply own risk and pay only the lost or damaged shipment value above that own risk amount. Carriers have limited liabilities as national laws and international conventions such as CMR conditions, Warsaw Convention, Montreal Protocol, and Hague-Visby rules protect them. For example, the maximum value parcel carriers are obliged to pay for a lost or damaged package is $100. The receiver of the goods needs to declare that the goods were not in a good condition, the freight was short or damaged at delivery, and the value of loss or damage. The receiver is responsible to count and inspect the goods at the time of delivery. Some carriers require the receiver to initiate a tracer request to them, so that they can start looking and try to find the missing goods before a claim is started as it turns out that many goods are found after receiving a claim. Carriers offer standard forms for submitting a tracer or a claim. The claim value is the sales value minus any profit. A claim submission contains the following documents:

- Survey report if requested
- Police report in case of theft
- Insurance policy
- Pictures in case of a damage
- Delivery note describing the product characteristics
- Gross weight
- Packing list
- Purchase invoice with the purchase value
- Commercial invoice with the commercial value and delivery address
- At pick-up signed (full name, signature, company stamp, date, and time) freight document mentioning the missing products

- At delivery signed freight document mentioning the damaged or missing products
- Serial numbers if available
- Export documents

Any discrepancy noticed upon delivery needs to be mentioned on the transportation document and/or electronic device. In case of any irregularity, pictures need to be made and at the same time notify the carrier and the shipper within the timeframes as outlined for that specific mode of transport in that country. If the damage is discovered after signing for receipt (e.g., when opening the packages), the carrier should be requested immediately for an inspection. The receiver must keep the shipping unit and its content in the same condition as when the irregularity was found. The carrier will send an inspector to settle the claim. Transportation invoices need to be paid at any time, as it is not allowed to stop paying carriers as result of a pending claim. The portion of loss or damage needs to be included in the claim submission. It is necessary to have a solid process in place to manage freight claims from the initiation, through verification of the validity based on the provided documented evidences, submitting them to carriers and insurance companies, receiving their payments, and paying the customers. Responsibilities and accountabilities need to be clear and regularly audited. Typical KPIs are the number of open and closed claims received per value stream or carrier, the amount of money paid to customers, recovered from the insurance companies and the carriers and the amount of money, which could not be recovered, and their root causes. Laws protect the carriers from going bankrupt as result of high-value claims and prescribe limited carrier liabilities to secure their existence in the long run. Damages caused by incorrect packaging and loading are not covered by the carrier's insurance policy. A shipper can organize additional freight insurance, which covers not only the goods value but also the shipping costs.

3.5 NETWORK OPTIMIZATION

An agile transportation network is necessary to survive the severe competition, volatile sales, transportation markets, energy, and raw material cost increases. An optimized transportation network means low costs, high service, and local customization. It is necessary to review the transportation network on a daily, weekly, monthly, quarterly, and yearly basis. This function can be managed internally, but there are also consulting companies that have the IT tools to model and optimize transportation networks and calculate "what if" scenarios. The number of warehouses, their locations, and size need to be taken into account as these heavily influence transportation costs. A network study is a critical step in evaluating the overall distribution network. The intention is to define the most effective transportation infrastructure and goods flows to meet the requirements and identify cost and performance improvement opportunities. It is about conducting an objective and analytical study of alternative network configurations to support the transportation strategy. The study uses historical and forecast data to provide a cost and service performance comparison of options, which are evaluated by qualitative and quantitative tools. The study can start from an existing or a "green field" situation, which means that the study is not subject to the as-is restrictions. The study is scoped by using elements such as geography, supply and delivery points, modes of transport, key metrics, and seasonality. A study starts by creating a Statement of Work (SOW), which is a document describing the detailed requirements, activities, deliverables, timelines, prices, and other terms and conditions. The document is created and signed by the shipper and the carrier and contains elements such as:

- Purpose: description of why the study is initiated.
- Scope: explain what will be done and what will not be done.
- Timing: clarify when to start, when to end, and what activities to do when.
- Resources: note down which people will work on the study and specify the estimated hours.
- Deliverables: agree when to present what deliverables.
- Acceptance criteria: document the criteria to decide when the study is finished.
- Costs: create and agree on the budget, invoice specification, invoicing and payment terms and conditions.
- Miscellaneous: document any other relevant topic to prevent disputes between the two parties.

The first step of a study is to create a baseline model that serves as a validation process and to understand the as-is situation. After that, potential solutions can be worked out to add value to the customer and improve the key metrics such as order cut-off times, lead-times, and costs. Typical deliverables of a phased network study can be:

Phase 1: project plan
Phase 2: validated baseline model
Phase 3: long list scenarios
Phase 4: short list scenarios
Phase 5: conclusions and recommendations

In case a process redesign is recommend, it is necessary to describe the requirements, impact analyses, work out and simulate the different scenarios, and propose an implementation plan for the chosen solution. Supply chain processes are reviewed regularly as the working environment changes rapidly affecting the process performance in relation to quality, cost, and service levels.

3.6 BENCHMARKING

Shippers use benchmarking as a way to compare their performances with similar companies. This allows them to see how they are performing and find ways to become more competitive on KPIs such as sales, quality, service, and productivity. By looking at others, they can identify areas for improvement without reinventing the wheel as they have examples from other companies in their industry. Using a best practice is a way to look at a company they aspire. In peer benchmarking, companies look to businesses similar to theirs. Benchmarking is mostly used during hard times when companies have to look for every penny in the organization. It helps to figure out how the organization is performing compared to competition and best-in-class organizations. As performance targets are revised constantly, benchmarking needs to be installed as a standard tool. A potential pitfall is that the day-to-day operations distract the attention from benchmarking calling it a nice-to-know thing. Each company is not so much different from its competition and highlighting poor performance will help to improve. A point of attention when reaching out to carriers for information is to mention upfront that it is a benchmark study. It is a not a good practice to send out tenders for benchmarking purposes. Carriers receive many requests to tender, which cost significant time to process, and finding out afterwards that there was nothing to win, leads to frustration. Therefore, carriers are experienced in figuring out if it is a real tender or only an attempt to receive market information. Such a situation leads to carriers not accepting real invitations to tender, and seeing the shipper as serious partner, providing standard rates, and more of these negative effects. However, a well-communicated and organized benchmarking process is useful for both the shippers, as they can check if they are paying a good rate, and carriers, as they can get to know what rates competition is offering in the market.

3.7 OUTSOURCING

Taking a set of work, tasks, responsibilities, and functions and transferring them to an outside service provider is called outsourcing. A service provider brings a different perspective, knowledge, experience, and technology to the existing function and can work with the shipper to re-engineer processes. Shippers can realize good results by transferring part of the business to a specialized company. Organizations free up money and human resources to invest in their core business. Specialized service providers use best practices and up-to-date technology to identify issues and fix them, provide access to new markets, and scale up or down the capacity fast. They gather data and analyze these to gain insights for improvements. With outsourcing, the focus is on leveraging the relationship by exploiting the capabilities of both partners. They work together, provide visibility in their processes, and discuss improvement opportunities to complement each other's core competencies to provide more value to the customer. In transportation, most business is outsourced to a so-called 3PL or 4PL company, where "PL" stands for "Party Logistics." The commonly used PL types are:

- 1PL: First Party Logistics. The shipper has not outsourced its logistics activities, transportation, and/or warehousing to a third party and has its own logistics management department for all logistics activities. The advantages of being an asset-based shipper can be the great control and the related flexibility to change priority fast and adapt to special customer requirements easier. Being the owner of the goods can bring also a more customer-focused approach. A steady and optimized transportation network can be also cheaper than outsourcing.

- 2PL: Second Party Logistics. The shipper has outsourced the day-to-day asset-based operational logistics activities to a third party, but the management activities are still executed by its own logistics department. The shipper-service provider relationship focuses on cost control. This way of working can free up resources to focus on improving the purchasing processes, reports, performances, and other key transportation management processes.

- 3PL: Third Party Logistics. The shipper has outsourced the logistics activities, but also other activities such as inventory management and customs clearance, to a third-party service provider, which can hire other third parties for specific activities. These subcontractors are used for jobs for which the service provider does not have the capabilities. The 3PL acts as an intermediary between the shipper and these subcontractors and measures, analyses, and improves their performances. The logistics management activities are still executed by the shipper's logistics department. The shipper-service provider relationship focuses on installing a long-term cooperative partnership.

- 4PL: Fourth Party Logistics. The shipper has outsourced the supply chain activities, such as sourcing, manufacturing, and distribution of products to the market, and their management to a non-asset third party. These lead logistics providers are specialized in logistics, transportation, and supply chain management. The third party is neutral and manages logistics processes, regardless of what carriers are used, including existing 3PLs that the carrier already has. Preferred 4PL companies are non-asset-based to prevent conflicts of interest. The shipper-service provider relationship focuses on installing a long-term cooperative partnership covering all the supply chain topics and share risks and benefits.

- 5PL: Fifth Party Logistics. These are 4PL companies broadening the scope further to e-commerce. They provide innovative logistics solutions and concepts to increase sales and can do order desk-types of activities.

Another way to categorize carriers is by tiers (tier management):

- Tier 1: actual carrier is the owner of the contracts with its sub-contractors.
- Tier 2: in case tier 1 carriers cannot provide the service, tier 2 carriers are used. The tier 1 carriers manage the tier 2 carriers on behalf of the shipper. A tier 2 carrier is a carrier whose contractual ownership remains with the shipper, but who agrees to be managed by the tier 1 carrier to provide the services.
- Tier 3: carriers contracted and managed by the shipper.

In such a relationship with a logistics provider, a set of KPIs needs to be agreed upon, measured, published, reviewed, and used as a starting point for improvement actions. These activities are taken care of by the CT, which is a central department with the tools and processes to capture transportation end-to-end data and visibility enabling them to respond and act on changing environment. They manage and cooperate with the multi-tier partners to improve efficiency. Service providers are requested to share shipment information with the CT. Carrier performance management is transferred to the CT, which is also responsible for shipment delays. Common KPIs used in such a business relationship are:

- Delivery performance: a shipment is on time when the actual transportation lead-times are met. This performance (%) is defined as the number of shipments delivered on time divided by the total number of shipments. The starting position is to measure this performance on carrier level; however, it is recommended to dig a bit deeper to find issues on lane, modality, service, and pick-up level. Do not allow carriers to hide themselves behind their performance on total level, as this mostly meets the target. It is possible that a carrier is underperforming on country, state, region, city, customer, lane, or any other level, which requires improvement actions. To prevent any resistance from the carriers, it is preferred to include in the contract terms and conditions on what levels the performance will be measured, and what root cause analyses and countermeasures are expected. A customer who is experiencing delivery problems will not accept the feedback that the total carriers' performance is above target.
- Cost performance: this KPI is measured as the % of deviation from the budget. At the beginning of each financial year, a transportation

budget is created based on historical spend and planned events. A carrier is expected to operate within this budget by continuously monitoring the cost development and set out improvement actions to come back on track when the actual cost trend does not develop in the right direction. Cost trends can be measured by spend per carrier, mode, service level, volume, and destination mix.

- Quality performance: the number of shipments delivered without any damage, under- or over-delivery, correct delivery location, and documentation.

Performance targets can differ per business, country, service level, carrier, and more criteria, but these are the commonly used carrier targets:

- Green: >98%. Performance is under control, but try to reach the entitlement performance.
- Yellow: 98%–95%. Performance is below target. Immediate root cause analyses and improvement actions are needed to meet the 98% target. Actions can be a combination of temporary mitigation and structural process improvements.
- Red: <95%. Performance is out of control. Set up a dedicated kaizen event and report out on a daily basis the progress.

From the transportation management point of view, a perfect delivery is a shipment that is delivered on time, without errors (complete), undamaged, and with the right documentation. From the customer point of view, the perfect delivery definition is wider as transportation is only one part where things can go wrong. Potential customer-facing mistakes in the ordering and warehouse processing activities can be wrong number of products, non-visual inside damage, and incorrect goods invoice. The perfect delivery measurement is introduced to prevent sub-optimization and strive for end-to-end supply chain improvement. This perfect delivery KPI is defined as the number of orders that are delivered on time, in full, without damage, and with the complete and correct documentation, as percentage of the total number of orders. Striving for the perfect performance is the only way to maintain the continuous improvement culture and get as close as possible to the perfect situation. The carrier should therefore be stimulated to come up on daily basis with improvement ideas to make the next step towards this perfect situation. The number of improvement ideas can measure this activity, but as these are not implemented yet, it is better to quantify and measure only the realized savings, performance improvements, customer satisfaction increases, and lead-time reductions. Many companies hesitate to outsource, as they believe they can manage it themselves. Especially when results are needed urgently, and there is no internal expertise to make things happen, outsourcing can be a good option as it can take years of time and a significant amount of money to hire and train own people before they can add value to the company. By outsourcing the function to a partner, a company gets immediate access to sophisticated IT systems and expert knowledge enabling the shipper to move fast. An outsourced party offers a rate for its service upon successful delivery of work within the agreed time, which makes the shipper agile due to this variable cost structure. Outsourcing brings also risks with it. The shipper wants to reduce costs, while the outsourced party wants to increase sales. The outsourcing party has more business experience than the outsourced party does. Not being the owner of the goods can bring less ownership leading to less sense of urgency and delayed responsiveness. Outsourced parties stick to the agreed scope, way of working, and work instructions, which can lead to inflexibility. The outsourcing party is frequently consulted in case of non-standard situations. This can hamper the speed and productivity of helping customers. Language barriers can make communication difficult. All these elements to manage outsourced parties are hidden wastes.

3.8 SUSTAINABILITY

Although transportation is an appreciated function, traffic has negative impacts, such as air, night light, water, and noise pollution, on the environment. Carbon dioxide (CO_2) is the biggest share of all the pollution leading to the earth's temperature increase, sea level rise, and other climate effects. The amount of CO_2 emitted is calculated in ton per kilometer (ton/km) and differs per transportation modality: parcel and express and air (0.5), road (0.1), and sea (0.01). A balance needs to be found between the benefits and the negative impacts. The transportation business is working on measures to contribute to green logistics by reducing the vehicle kilometers, using environmental friendly modalities, cleaner engines, electric trucks (e.g., the Tesla truck), and less fuel consumption due to smarter driving instructions. Other solutions are solar panels on buildings and equipment, sustainable wind energy and natural gas, hydrogen, and diesel.

Sustainable transportation is necessary for maintaining livable cities and reducing the consumption of non-renewable resources and gas emissions. Especially road transportation has a negative impact on global warming, air and noise quality, and other natural lives. People working in transportation suffer from accidents and emissions, which damage their health. Congestion, a typical example of a process that is not flowing, and the loss of time are leading to higher costs. Ideas to limit this damage can be the introduction of a surcharge per driven kilometer so that the actual polluter pays, people can choose to stay out of the taxed roads to save money, invest, and promote rail freight as an alternative to road transportation. Often heard feedback is that green logistics means higher costs. In contrary, pollution reduction means less transportation and thus less cost. This helps companies to increase their competitiveness and improve their image as responsible companies. They become reliable partners for financial institutions considering new investments. The customers will benefit from fewer vehicles on highways preventing traffic jams, fewer vehicles at their docks and homes, reduced accidents, and higher quality of life. Sustainability is not only about green transportation and environment protection. It is also about committing to act fairly towards the stakeholders and respect the applicable laws and regulations. A company needs to protect the employees' health and safety by preventing personal injuries and property damages. The primary responsibility is with the employees, but it is important to set up and maintain a safe work environment by installing measures to limit hazardous processes and situations. There need to be instructions how to act in case of fire, earthquake, and injury. Sustainability is also about preventing child labor. It is not allowed to employ children, work with subcontractors employing children, or force people to work for the company. A company needs to treat its employees equally, offer them equal opportunities, and pay them equally for equal work at equal levels. Discrimination based on race, sex, religion, or political opinion is not tolerated.

3.9 QUALITY MANAGEMENT SYSTEM

The use of a quality system method needs to ensure that the quality level of a service is maintained. The first requirement is to have a clear policy manual in which is defined what is done and why to comply with the standards. Then quality procedures are created and the methods to implement and perform the policy are described. Easily understood procedures define who performs which tasks, when, and where. On a lower level, employees create work instructions how to do a task in the form of a drawing, picture, or video as employee engagement helps to suggest potential improvements. Policies, procedures, and work instructions need to be recorded by using fill-out forms, stamps, signatures, and dates to enable traceability. Quality is a key pillar for any service a shipper provides and lack of quality can hamper the image of a shipper leading to less success in the market. Only a robust process can lead to high quality. Transportation management processes can be captured in a Quality Management System (QMS), which documents the policies, processes, procedures, work instructions, records, and responsibilities needed for the planning and execution of transportation activities to meet customer requirements. Quality is a key pre-requisite to satisfy customers on daily basis and for the company's success as a whole. A clear understanding and disciplined application of QMS ensures consistency in using standard works. ISO 9001:2008 is an example of a QMS, for which a shipper can be certified and which ensures internal and external quality, legal, law, regulatory, customer, and other requirements are documented in the appropriate locations and met by the shipper. More actual requirements are the information, product and service security, and sustainability. A QMS helps to streamline the shipper's activities to become an effective and efficient organization. It specifies requirements how an organization can provide evidence of its capabilities to produce a service that meets all the requirements constantly to keep the customer happy. The transportation processes are described, measured, monitored, reported, analyzed, updated, and archived. The QMS is also used to train employees to meet the requirements and follow the procedures. The QMS content is audited on changes and performance, analyzed, and updated. The goal is to improve the quality system continuously to produce higher quality. The steps to come to a QMS are:

- Define the quality policy to meet all the requirements and realize a quality vision or mission.
- Quantify the policy into SMART objectives.
- Describe the processes, their impact on quality, potential defects, and their measurement in the quality manual.
- Document how to audit processes, communicate about and review Corrective Actions and Preventive Actions (CAPAs).
- Define the training need for a zero-defect process.

There is no standard template for a QMS, but the ISO 9001:2008 prescribes the following requirements:
Documentation of the:

- Quality policy
- Quality objectives
- Quality manual
- Other documents required for effective planning, operation, and control
- Records

Six procedures to describe the process of:

- Control of documents
- Control of records
- Internal audits
- Control of non-conforming product
- Corrective actions
- Preventive actions

Twenty-one records to share the results of:

- Management reviews
- Education and training
- Realization processes and product requirements fulfillment
- Product requirements reviews and improvement actions
- Product requirements design and development inputs
- Design and development reviews and improvement actions
- Design and development verification and improvement actions
- Design and development validation and improvement actions
- Design and development change reviews and any improvement actions
- Supplier evaluations and improvement actions
- Demonstration of validation of processes in case of no measurements
- Unique product identification and traceability
- Lost or damaged customer goods
- Process of calibration or verification process in case of measuring equipment without standards

- Validity of measurements in case of non-conforming measuring equipment
- Calibration and verification of measuring equipment
- Internal audits and improvement actions
- Product release authorization responsibilities
- Product non-conformities and improvement actions
- Corrective actions
- Preventive actions

ISO 9001:2015 requires only three documented procedures, which are "the scope of the quality system," "quality policy," and "quality objectives." However, these requirements give less guidance in how to set up a QMS.

3.10 TRANSPORTATION MANAGEMENT SYSTEM

A big challenge for shippers is to get hold of up-to-date and reliable shipment data to analyze historical flows and use this information to improve. This data is spread over various sources such as e-mails, local files, chats, and conversations in different formats. It requires quite some manual resources to gather the data in one source and format and make it useful for analyses. The improvement of such a situation needs digitalization, automation, and a central system. The transportation industry is probably the toughest place to digitalize and automate communication. This is the result of many unrelated parties, such as the shipper, warehouse provider, carrier, customs, and receiver, who need to be in the communication loop. They have their own systems and standards but need alignment on IT services like shipment data transfer, real-time tracking, and tracing, labeling, milestone, and POD exchange. This is probably also the reason why companies still use phone, fax, e-mail, and manual ordering systems. The transportation market and customer requirements are dynamic and change frequently: customers change product suppliers for better prices and/or services. Transportation systems must be flexible to respond to these changes. This can be realized by purchasing, implementing, and maintaining an in-house TMS with the analytic tools for a smarter and faster decisions making process. There is no need to build such a system internally as there are many good solutions available in this market. It is also possible to use a remote TMS and to pay the third-party service provider a rate per, for example, a transaction.

This is the System as a Service (SaaS) solution, which often already has the IT connections with carriers and allows a fast ramp up. The cloud-based solutions ensure access at anytime and anywhere allowing mobile usage. The benefits of a TMS in general are:

- Single and global data source.
- Cost reduction as result of dynamic carrier choice.
- Statistics, analytical, and scenario modelling.
- Faster and more accurate FPA.
- Transportation can be managed separately from the WHS provider preventing a lock-in.

A TMS is a data exchange platform between shippers, carriers, and customers. It simplifies the shipping process, improves supply chain visibility, and consists of three main activities: planning, execution, and post-shipment analyses. Figure 3.11 provides insight in the main and sub-processes of a transportation management cycle.

These sub-processes support the main functionalities of a TMS: automated shipment booking via an EDI or a web portal interface, FPA, paperless invoicing, self-billing, cost calculation, single source of data, and standard reports. Other functionalities are EDI and web connectivity with e-logistics portals, exchange of e-documents, and shipment status updates. The goal of a good planning process is to efficiently use the available trucks and reduce the number of driven kilometers by taking into account carrier rates, number of trucks and their sizes, loading and unloading time windows, shipment sizes, origins and destinations, driver working times, opening times of transshipment points, and traffic jams. Planning helps companies ship goods in an efficient, reliable, and cost-effective way. A TMS helps to find the best way to send each individual shipment using all

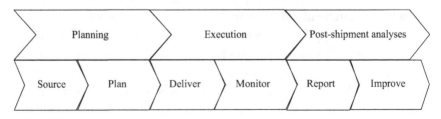

FIGURE 3.11
Main and sub-processes transportation management cycle.

available modalities, service levels, and carriers. It offers tools to tender loads, choose carriers, and create bills of lading and labels. Typical elements of planning are document creation, transit time calculation, carrier and modality selection, shipment consolidation, forward and backward scheduling, and tendering. After planning, the shipment is booked and shipped with the proposed carrier. It is then proactively monitored by using visibility and real-time shipment status tools. Typical elements of execution are shipment booking and monitoring, proactive exception management, milestone exchange, and tracking and tracing. Post-shipment analysis is executed to evaluate the decisions made and optimize the future way of working. Typical elements of post-shipment analyses are root cause analysis, KPI reporting, spend analysis, and network optimization. Cost reduction impacts on customer service and the other way around can be simulated. Many shippers manage to implement the shipment and cost visibility modules, but they struggle to proceed with probably the most important, but also the most difficult to install, added value of the tool: dynamic carrier choice. This is the process where the tool calculates and assigns the best carrier per individual shipment. The TMS processes are described in more detail in the next paragraphs.

3.10.1 Master Data Management

TMS works only if there is a proper management process to keep master data up to date. The data creation and maintenance of the shipper, receiver, carrier, and decision-making criteria is key information for a seamless process from order receipt until invoicing. In addition to financial information like rates, it is essential to maintain material master records such as hazardous material, weights, pallet sizes, and package dimensions. Examples of receiver master data are delivery addresses, slot times, phone numbers, availability of ramps, opening times, and appointment-taking process. The main purpose of transportation master data is to define the exact characteristics of a shipment in order to select the optimal way of transportation. Incorrect master data leads to operational issues like insufficient space to load, wrong equipment, longer lead-times, and deliveries to wrong addresses. Transportation master data such as the correct weights, dimensions, packing types, and number of products are used to calculate the shipment volume, weight, and size to assign the correct service level, modality, equipment type, and carrier.

3.10.2 Complete Transportation Order

For a perfect delivery, a perfect transportation order is required from the shipper. In this stage, the order is checked on the availability and quality of the order data to ensure a perfect execution. Availability elements can be the timely exchange of EDI, goods invoice, customs document, and AWB numbers. Quality elements can be the correct and complete data formats, ship-from and ship-to addresses, weights, and dimensions. Missing data is collected from the relevant stakeholders such as suppliers, customers, and warehouses. The preferred communication tool is EDI, but manual or web entries are also supported. A receiver often requires the inclusion of own references, such as handling, batch, PO, and order numbers, to follow up the shipments.

3.10.3 Document Verification

Missing and/or incorrect documents are retrieved and/or corrected and re-distributed. A TMS allows the creation, digitization, exchange, and storage of these documents online. The documents are accessible for all parties in the supply chain who have access to the system.

3.10.4 Order and Capacity Planning

The forward and backward planning criteria, such as the requested delivery date, are defined and updated in TMS. The outcomes of this process are clearly defined tasks to execute in the right order and on the right date and time. Besides the single order planning, a longer-term capacity planning needs to be prepared in case of events such as seasonality and holidays. Based on historical data, customer forecasts, market trends, and other planned events, the right transportation capacity is reserved at the carriers.

3.10.5 Order Consolidation

Consolidating orders can be cost efficient in case there are multiple orders on the same day for the same receiver. This way of working leads to less individually invoiced transportation movements, handling, and documentation. Such order combination can be done by a WMS or a TMS. Physical consolidation means that goods are physically packed together and invoiced by the carrier as one shipment. Virtual consolidation means that the goods are not packed together, but the carrier invoices them as one shipment. This allows the shipper to benefit from the lower transportation costs, but to prevent the additional work to physically consolidate the packages as one shipment.

3.10.6 Carrier Selection

There are two ways to manage the carrier selection process:

1. The carrier is allocated to a pre-defined lane (e.g., all shipments towards France are transported by carrier x).
2. Dynamic carrier choice: the carrier is chosen based on the cheapest and/or fastest option taking into account the shipment characteristics and customer requirements.

3.10.7 Non-Standard Order Management

Contracted lane agreements and master data are set up upfront in TMS to enable a perfect order processing. New lanes and exceptional heavyweight and/or oversized shipments will pop up and need to be managed properly to allow a perfect delivery. Request carriers for a quotation and select the best one. Agree on loading and unloading dates and time, enrich the revised order with the additional data, and transfer it to the carrier. Notify the receiver and monitor the shipment.

3.10.8 Supply Chain Visibility

Real-time supply chain visibility is crucial for lowering inventories, improving service levels, and managing risks. When receiving timely and accurate shipment status information it becomes possible for a shipper to orchestrate the supply chain. When, for example, a big shipment is expected to arrive earlier than planned by the supplier in the Far East, it could be a good idea to delay the next purchase order to prevent high inventory levels in the pipeline. The other way around, when a shipment is expected to arrive later than planned, it be could a good idea to temporarily source a limited quantity from a local supplier to prevent a stock-out situation. This capability requires the supply chain partners such as suppliers, carrier locations and various modalities, warehouses, and customers with their different roles and systems to be EDI-linked to each other and transfer shipment status information preferably real-time. Insight in the transportation processes helps a company to identify issues and inefficiencies allowing it to create improvement plans. Mid-term to long-term visibility provides actionable information about cost, service, and quality performances in the recent period, which can be used as input for generating logistics and/or transportation strategies and policies. Short-term visibility is required for the proactive day-to-day follow-up of individual shipments. The main reason why shippers cannot be proactive in sharing information is that they do not get this on time due to slow, complex, and error-sensitive phone-, e-mail-, or paper-based manual processes. This situation is caused by limited system integration between the supply chain partners as all of them have their own systems: people need to check several systems for updates. Other root causes, mainly at sub-contractors, are the limited real-time information exchange and digitalization, which means the move from analog to digital tools. Such situations delay the process of managing shipments by exception as it takes too much time to work through the systems and data to get to the problem shipments. It is possible to find the most recent shipment status codes in TMS, but this capability depends highly on the ability of the carrier to share shipment statuses in an electronic way. With the bigger transportation companies, this is normally not a problem as they do have EDI capabilities and do exchange milestones electronically, although the reliability of the data is still an improvement area. Smaller carriers are linked to a TMS by sending them fill-in formats by e-mail, which are uploaded automatically once received back, although up-to-date and accurate data is a bigger challenge with this way of working. Access to TMS is managed by specific user rights set-up. People can monitor shipments and take corrective and/or preventive measures. There are many and different shipment statuses, which can be captured by the carrier and communicated with the shipper and other stakeholders. Table 3.8 shows example shipment statuses as reported and shown on carrier websites.

Shipment statuses are expressed in dates and times; however, some carriers make also pictures of the goods as they come in at and leave a transshipment point. This information is also used to settle complaints and claims between the transshipment points. Once a transshipment point accepts the shipment at inbound and no remarks have been made, it is the responsibility of this location to pay for any damage or loss. The receiver is not always interested in all these status messages, as they do not always add value. The number, sort, and availability of milestones depend on the

TABLE 3.8

Shipment Status Messages

Arrived at sorting center
In customs clearance process
At destination hub
Held for collection by recipient
Shipment is cancelled
Customs authorities clearance delay
Clearance delay due to missing paperwork
Customs clearance completed
Customer refused delivery
Delivered
At customer broker for clearance
Delivered with exception
Planned for delivery
Out for delivery
Goods and documents received
In transit
Delivery is delayed
No delivery possible
Partial delivery
Picked up
Returned to shipper
EDI data received
Shipment is on hold

---

agreements between the carrier and the shipper. The milestone on time availability performance is measured through a PI as a percentage of milestones sent within the agreed time. The time windows differ from a few minutes to a few hours. Table 3.9 shows an example of milestone set-up.

A very important milestone is the POD. The perfect delivery reliability calculation is based on a high availability of this information, also called "POD coverage," which is the number of PODs received as % of the total number of PODs expected within the agreed time window in a period.

3.10.9 Proactive Shipment Monitoring

TMS gives the opportunity to identify and communicate potential shipment delays. This process is based on comparing the planned with the actual milestone date and time as reported by the carriers. When a milestone is not

TABLE 3.9

Example of a Milestone Set-Up

Milestone	Planned	Updated	Actual
Shipment booking confirmed	01-10-2017 13:00	01-10-2017 14:00	01-10-2017 14:21
Pick-up truck arrival	01-10-2017 14:00	01-10-2017 15:00	01-10-2017 15:11
Goods picked up at origin	01-10-2017 15:00	01-10-2017 16:30	01-10-2017 16:32
Pick-up truck departure	01-10-2017 16:00	01-10-2017 17:30	01-10-2017 17:39
Goods arrived at the first carrier hub	01-10-2017 17:00	01-10-2017 17:30	01-10-2017 17:31
Flight details provided	02-10-2017 13:00	02-10-2017 13:30	02-10-2017 13:32
Goods arrived at the second carrier hub	02-10-2017 13:00	02-10-2017 13:00	02-10-2017 13:03
Goods arrived at the airport	02-10-2017 13:00	02-10-2017 14:00	02-10-2017 14:04
Flight departure	03-10-2017 13:00	03-10-2017 13:00	03-10-2017 13:05
Flight arrival	03-10-2017 21:00	03-10-2017 21:00	03-10-2017 21:06
Customs in	04-10-2017 09:00	04-10-2017 08:00	04-10-2017 08:07
Customs out	05-10-2017 10:00	05-10-2017 11:00	05-10-2017 11:08
Goods arrived at the third carrier hub	05-10-2017 13:00	05-10-2017 13:00	05-10-2017 13:09
Delivery truck arrival	06-10-2017 13:00	06-10-2017 14:00	06-10-2017 14:10
Actual delivery (POD)	06-10-2017 14:00	06-10-2017 15:00	06-10-2017 15:11
Delivery truck departure	06-10-2017 15:00	06-10-2017 16:00	06-10-2017 16:12

reported on time, a potential delay notification can be sent out to the stakeholders before they find out themselves. The notification includes a shipment reference number, issue description, resolution action, and new ETA.

3.10.10 Customer Service

In this process, questions from all stakeholders are handled. There can be standard or specific questions about the status, timeliness, and quality of the shipment. Complaints and claims are monitored until their resolutions and/or settlements. Requests to implement process changes are deployed internally while keeping the customers updated. Customer service can support the decision making by systematically analyzing complaints and claims on their root causes.

3.10.11 FPA

After the shipment has been picked up and a POD is received via the TMS to confirm the delivery at the receiver, the freight payment process is initiated. Key information for a correct billing process are weights and dimensions. The shipper is often not capable to deliver the correct information as weighing and measuring goods is a labor-intensive process. Shippers accept the by carrier confirmed weights and measurements as they are equipped with automated weighing and measuring systems. Where the standard is that the carrier creates and sends invoices, a TMS offers the possibility of pre-invoicing, which is a process where the shipper notifies what the carrier can invoice. Potential disputes are captured, analyzed, and settled in the following periodic invoice to allow a fast payment process as the majority of the invoice amount is correct. The purpose of this process is to gain time and limit the administrative work such as checking invoices. A typical pre-invoicing process works as follows:

- Step 1: prepare the shipments overview. This is the process to gather all the shipment data in a week or month, which will service as input for the calculation of the pre-invoice amounts.
- Step 2: calculate the pre-invoice amounts. The amount per shipment is calculated based on the rate file. This calculation is done automatically by the TMS.
- Step 3: send the pre-invoice to the carrier. The shipper sends the pre-invoice, including a PO number if necessary, to the carrier by e-mail or any other Internet-based solution.
- Step 4: carrier receives the pre-invoice. The carrier receives the pre-invoice through its finance department. Carrier will send an invoice for exact the same amount on the pre-invoice. Potential corrections will be incorporated in the pre-invoice of the following week or month.
- Step 5: shipper receives the invoice. Shipper books the invoice and pays it within the agreed timeline.
- Step 6: process corrections. The shipper agrees with the carrier what adjustment to make in the next invoicing cycle.

Another billing process is self-billing, which allows the shipper to pay the carriers without the need to receive an invoice. The self-billing process is to calculate the transportation costs and hand them over to the finance department with the request to pay the pre-calculated amount. This process is not available in all countries due to legal restrictions such as the requirement to receive and store physical invoices for potential audits. Both the shipper and carrier are recommended to implement an auditing process to monitor the processes mentioned previously as these depend highly on correct master data management. This auditing process, which can be done internally or outsourced to a third party, is necessary to check if the agreed rates are applied correctly.

3.10.12 Tendering

Big lanes are tendered regularly and the agreed rates are imported in TMS. However, there are small and/or new lanes and/or events like a promotion action. These out of the contract scope lanes are tendered directly in the market, where carriers are requested to quote. It is possible to limit a RFQ to only the preferred carriers, specific carriers, or go-to logistics market places where any carrier can offer a rate. Rates are assessed and the shipment is allocated to the best carrier in terms of price, quality, and service. Rates and other relevant data are imported in the TMS to proceed with the shipment and/or benchmark purposes.

3.10.13 Process Standardization

Using a TMS to centralize transportation activities helps to streamline processes over multiple shipping and receiving entities. The dedicated transportation team behind the TMS will help both the shipper and the receiver to improve performance by providing better visibility and process control. TMS allows the stakeholders to have access to the system instead of calling and e-mailing. This visibility helps also improve the communication between all the supply chain partners, who can anticipate on potential issues. TMS reduces the amounts of manual communication significantly. The use of pre-billing and pre-invoicing in combination with FPA avoids billing errors.

3.10.14 Reporting

TMS can be used to create and send data and performance reports automatically on pre-defined days and/or times to predefined addresses. It is possible to create customer-specific reports. The quality of these reports depends highly on the carrier capabilities to provide the shipper milestone messages and root cause analyses electronically. There is the possibility to use a dashboard in the TMS to monitor the performance and drill down to a geographical area, period, 3PL, type of product, or transport by clicking on the specific lane item.

3.10.15 Performance Reviews

The previously mentioned reports are used as input for the periodic business reviews with the carriers, where the accomplishments, issues, and improvement actions are discussed. TMS provides the information to analyze complaints, claims, and timeliness of milestone exchanges, carrier performance, and trade compliance.

3.10.16 Sustainability

TMS allows the measurement and calculation of the carbon footprint per shipment, which can be used as input for discussions to reduce it. The carbon footprint can be used for modality selection, as, for example, the carbon footprint of air is higher than sea. By optimizing the supply chain, the number of kilometers travelled are reduced leading to a lower carbon footprint and lower costs.

3.10.17 Managed Transportation Services

Using a Managed Transportation Services (MTS) provider offers the benefits of a TMS as well as the people to manage the day-to-day operations. The implementation of a TMS can be difficult, time consuming, and requires a learning curve. This is typically true for small transportation management departments. This is probably also the reason why many shippers still do not use a TMS to manage and automate their transport operations. Aside from benefits like immediate access to a TMS and day-to-day operations relieve, a MTS provider knows how to implement and operate a TMS efficiently to meet the targets.

3.10.18 EDI and Interfacing

When considering a TMS implementation it is important to think about the new process. The data interfacing between the ERP, WMS, and TMS is considered to be the hard part. As changing these interfaces afterwards is complicated, it is crucial to define the to-be situation on time. Gather all the requirements at the beginning of the process to end up with an IT template to use as reference by all the supply chain partners. Typical questions to be answered are: does the shipper want an interface from the ERP to TMS and then to WMS to enable physical shipment consolidation? Why does the shipper want to go for a physical consolidation in the warehouse? Does this offer any additional benefits? Is virtual consolidation possible in TMS? Does the shipper want shipment status updates only in the TMS or also in the WMS and/or ERP system? Does the shipper want to print shipping labels from the TMS or the WMS? What information level does the shipper want to retrieve in the different systems: shipment, delivery note, invoice, order, order line, and/or product number? The most crucial element in interfacing is the standard EDI implementation to streamline the communication between the supply chain partners through IT. A smooth EDI set-up requires the use of a project approach and an implementation guide to agree on the exact way to set up the information exchange process. An initial meeting is planned with the project team to align on the project plan, discuss the EDI requirements by going through a questionnaire, and review the implementation guide. The outcome is an agreed and signed SOW. Generally, an International Forwarding and Transport Message Instructions (IFTMIN) message is used to communicate shipment information from the shipper to the carrier. Once the shipments have been picked up, the carrier sends back International Forwarding and Transport Status (IFTSTA) messages to the shipper to exchange shipment status information. Both messages are international EDI standards developed under UN/Electronic Data Interchange for Administration, Commerce and Transport (UN/EDIFACT). After IT has developed the transaction messages, protocols, and scripts, the EDI set-up is tested through multiple scenarios such as:

- IT testing: IT needs to check if the individual solution, as mentioned in the deliverables part of the project charter, is doing what it is supposed to do from the IT point of view.
- Functional testing: based on the elements the user wants to test, a test plan is created and executed. The results are shared with the IT team, which will check if any IT change is needed. If so, then a new functional test needs to be executed including the feedback to the IT team.

- Integration testing: when the IT and functional tests are successful, it is time to move to the integration testing, where the individual IT solution is tested if it is cooperating with other IT systems.

It is recommended to describe upfront clear and measurable acceptance criteria to decide if the test is successful or not.

As starting immediately with the hardest part of the TMS implementation, which is the EDI set-up, can be too challenging, it is possible to go for a gradual but longer implementation approach such as:

1. Manual booking
2. Track and trace and delivery status updates
3. Management reporting
4. Exchange of documents
5. EDI and web interfacing
6. E-invoicing, self-billing, and freight audit and pay

To remove the shortcomings of EDI—being complex and time consuming to implement, high maintenance costs, and inflexibility to change—a new communication technology, named Application Program Interface (API), is being implemented.

3.10.19 TMS and MTS Providers

Several service providers, such as Descartes, Transparix, Kewill, JDA, Oracle, and SAP offer TMS solutions. MTS providers who offer both the IT system and people to manage operations include DHL, Kuhne&Nagel, GEODIS, and Penske. Take into account that service providers who offer both a TMS and a MTS solution and at the same time act as a carrier can be perceived as not neutral by the other carriers. They are often not willing to share their rates with the MTS providers as they see them as a direct competitor.

3.11 TRANSPORTATION MANAGEMENT MATURITY

Process Survey Tools (PSTs) are used to assess the maturity of the transportation management processes against the world-class benchmarks. PSTs are maturity grids describing processes in, for example, 10 levels, where the presence of only basic processes scores a "1" and the presence of world-class processes scores a "10." Another way to indicate the maturity level is to use the four stages as explained by Dr. Robert Monczka and his co-authors in their book "Purchasing and Supply Chain Management" (6th edition, page 237 and further): "1. Basic beginnings," "2. Moderate development," "3. Limited integration," and "4. Fully integrated supply chains." Process experts assess processes and advise what and how to improve to achieve the next level of maturity. The advisory market offers various PSTs. The following strategic and enabling processes of Dr. Robert Monczka's are applied to transportation management:

- Category strategy development
- Supplier evaluation and selection
- Supplier quality management
- Supplier management and development
- Worldwide sourcing

To reach the world-class levels with the strategic sourcing processes it is necessary to facilitate a set of supporting processes. These enabling processes are:

- Human resources
- Organizational design
- Information technology (IT)
- Measurement

3.11.1 Category Strategy Development

Another word for "category" is "commodity." A commodity strategy is a plan how to achieve both short- and long-term goals such as the number of carriers, their characteristics, contract periods, and cost targets. The plan is based on the commodity classification as "leverage," "strategic," "routine," or "bottleneck" and includes timelines, responsibilities, accountabilities, and measurable performance targets. To reach the world-class level it is necessary to have a written action plan, which includes customer, business, process, and employee requirements, goals, and targets. This action plan contains a SWOT analysis, how the strategy will give the shipper a competitive advantage, a communication plan, intermediate reporting structures and timing, a review process, market studies with benchmark and trend information, performance targets by time, and who will do what when.

3.11.2 Supplier Evaluation and Selection

The outcome of this process, which is discussed more in detail in another section of this book, is the selection of the optimal number of carriers with the characteristics and capabilities to meet the business needs. The carriers are categorized as "commercial," "preferred," or "strategic" to define the type of supplier relationship management to deploy with them. Commercial suppliers offer a standard service, which can be purchased elsewhere. No proactive initiatives are started to improve as long as the agreed performance levels are maintained. A shipper and its preferred carriers have mutual and confirmed benefits. The focus is on meeting the price, quality, and service targets. A strategic partnership is a situation where both parties are open to share confidential information and work on mutual benefits on longer terms. A supplier rating system, which includes the what, when, and how to measure the weighted criteria such as delivery performance, costs, responsiveness, and innovation, rates all the carriers. The objective measurements are built into and downloaded from an IT system. They are regularly shared with the carriers and other stakeholders. The subjective criteria are scored in a cross-functional team. Based on the product classification ("leverage," "strategic," "routine," or "bottleneck") and how the carrier sees the shipper ("core," "development," "nuisance," or "exploitable"), the companies can define their strategies for the different services and carriers to close the gap between the as-is and to-be situation. To reach the world-class level it is necessary to have a documented process to evaluate and select carriers and to generate and maintain carrier portfolio analyses, carrier rating systems, and product portfolio analyses.

3.11.3 Supplier Quality Management

Carriers often do not have the full overview of their strong and weak points. It is useful to help them by identifying improvement opportunities on which they can work to increase their performances and capabilities. Typical tools are audits and assessments. To reach the world-class level it is required to have a documented process to measure and guide the supplier development efforts, offer resources to help, and create a continuous improvement culture including review and follow-up processes.

3.11.4 Supplier Management and Development

Based on the supplier classification, the shipper needs to work on how to cooperate with the carriers to realize a world-class supply base. The critical path is to build up a partnership with the strategic suppliers. Not all commodities require a partnership: an extensive form of cooperation between a shipper and a carrier. It is a way of working in which both parties are open to share confidential information and closely collaborate for mutual benefits by leveraging the capabilities of both companies. It is based on confidence as the shipper commits to the carrier with long-term contracts, while the carrier commits himself to improve price, service, and quality in a continuous improvement culture. To reach the world-class level it is necessary to organize the companies for long-term relationships, depend on and trust each other, have shared objectives and improvement plans, and train and educate each other. A good account management structure is needed to manage processes and projects with the objective to deliver the customer the right product on the right time within the agreed performance and cost targets. The carrier account managers should be in the driving seat to deliver the necessary service solutions and develop the business relation towards a partnership. These employees should be trusted, empowered to take decisions, and not go back to senior management for each customer request or idea. A good account manager has sufficient knowledge of the shipper's organization and processes. He or she acts as a result-driven advisor for both organizations and should not focus only on sales increase. The account manager is in the lead to drive change and improvement actions by having access to and using carrier resources. This is especially required when KPI targets are not met and action is needed to find out the exact issues, their root causes and work on countermeasures. The manager works on cost reduction and new service road maps. The status and progress reports are not shared only during the periodic business review meetings but are worked upon and shared regularly. The operational KPIs reflect in a way the account manager's performance and he or she is accountable and responsible for making the targets. The account manager has an important job regarding communication between the two parties. He or she is the first escalation point to go to, informs the stakeholders about changes in the two companies, plans business review meetings, visits the shipper, offers new services, works on new service requests, and acts as the lead in case of emergency situations. To reach the world-class level it is necessary to have a documented process to classify carriers and to allocate resources, based on how important the carrier is for the business, to work on improvement initiatives.

3.11.5 Worldwide Sourcing

If a company has multiple sites and business units over the globe, it is key to organize itself in such a way that it can benefit from the volume leverage and global sourcing opportunities. A good starting point is to standardize KPI targets, contract terms and conditions, rate comparisons, benchmark and tendering processes, and carrier implementations. To reach the world-class level it is required to have a global council, which includes key stakeholders from the various sites. This organization is needed to get the maximum out of volume leveraging, install global contracts, assign global business process owners, standardize processes, implement best practices, and develop carriers to become global players too.

3.11.6 Human Resources

To execute the transportation strategy in a proper way and meet the related targets, it is necessary to hire, educate, and train people. The starting point is to create function profiles including capability requirements such as analytic, customer-friendly, creative, innovative, flexible, efficient and effective, team-oriented, communicative, and influence skills. To reach the world-class level the shipper has to have a documented process to set up and maintain recruitment, training, education, succession planning, and assessment processes. There is the need to have job profiles and function descriptions for key positions. A review process is in place to map the current and newly required skills and have a plan to close the gap. Other elements are management development and career plans, job rotations and interpersonal, functional, integration and strategic skills, team building performance, rewarding, and appraisals.

3.11.7 Organizational Design

To make things happen it is important that transportation management is well positioned and structured in the organization. If transportation is defined as a strategic differentiator then there have to be empowered cross-functional teams in place to play this strategic role in evaluating, selecting, implementing, and developing suppliers. To reach the world-class level here it is necessary to have a documented process to assign the logistics/transportation manager as member of the leadership team to coordinate the improvement processes such as purchasing, contracting, procurement, and related processes throughout the organization. Purchasing is the process to assess and select carriers, while procurement is the daily activity to order transportation. Other processes are market research, technology roadmap, and commodity strategy development.

3.11.8 Information Technology

IT systems need to be in place to support an effective and efficient automated procurement and order realization processes such as transport ordering and invoicing. It is necessary to have EDI and other fast communication tools such as Internet and intranet solutions. It is required to set up and maintain global databases to make the data available for everyone around the globe. To reach the world-class level it is necessary to have a documented process how to link value stream, business unit, customer, and supplier enterprise systems, via IT networks.

3.11.9 Measurement

The requirement is to have a set of KPIs to measure carrier performance regarding costs, service, and quality in both the order realization and new service creation processes. To reach the world-class level it is required to have a documented process to measure, gather, aggregate, communicate, and compare KPIs with the targets. The KPIs are regularly reviewed and the PDCA cycle is applied to improve where necessary.

3.11.10 Transportation Strategy

An important goal of assessing the transportation management processes is to create a transportation strategy document, which describes the strategies, directions, resources, key initiatives, and performance targets for financial, customer satisfaction, improvement, and capability processes to realize the transportation management goals. A prerequisite to create such a living strategy document is to assess the transportation processes continuously and update it where necessary as the supply chain environment is changing rapidly. To prevent a static strategy and stay ahead of competition it necessary to regularly answer questions like:

- Is there a need to apply a specific transportation strategy based on the product life cycle phases such as high delivery speed in the introduction phase, service improvement in the growth phase, cost reduction in the maturity phase, or lower delivery speed in the decline phase?
- Does the company give customers the possibility to choose from and pay for express and/or economy service levels? If not, why not? Is there an opportunity to gain a competitive advantage by doing so?
- Is the value of the products increasing or decreasing? Does this development justify the current mode of transportation or is a change of modality required?
- Are all the products shipped by one modality? If yes, is this still a good approach or will more differentiation lead to a higher service, better quality, and/or lower costs?
- What is the current number of carriers? If the number is high, then why is this? Is it possible to reduce the number to increase the buying power and decrease carrier management efforts?
- What new technologies are there to use transportation management as a strategic differentiator? Can the company use (some of) these? If so, what is the added value for the customers?
- What transportation flows are actively managed: only outbound or also vendor inbounds and returns? If not, why not?
- How is the company performing against competition? How have they organized their transportation management? What carriers do they use? Are they customer or cost focused?
- Is the transportation function outsourced? If not, would there be any benefit by doing so? If yes, is it possible for the company to differentiate itself even more from competition if (part of) transportation is insourced?

One of the questions the strategy document needs to answer is what activities to insource or outsource. In case of insourcing, a company decides to bring back the activities that have been outsourced before. Outsourcing is to stop doing some activities within the company and let a more specialized company do this work, to focus on the core competencies. A company depends more on its partners than before. The insourcing versus outsourcing decision-making process is not the same as the make versus buy trade-off, which is used in a situation of temporary resource constraints or lack of knowledge and is a short-term solution, while the insourcing versus outsourcing process is a longer-term direction. It is crucial to define the core and non-core competencies, base the decisions on total cost of ownership, and have clear objectives and plans. These plans indicate how and when to involve carriers to optimize, simplify, and standardize processes to increase the quality and service and reduce costs. It is also important to involve carrier on the right moment in the new service creation process to benefit from their design capabilities. New services can be new transportation and/or distribution services. Do not involve the supplier too early in this process to prevent demotivation due to not being able to add value to the process. Carrier involvement is necessary as the final cost, quality, and service levels are "planned" during the design phase. It should be clear that the purchasing of transportation services should not be based on price only, but on the total cost of ownership, which is a process to include all the costs involved during the life cycle of a service.

The previously mentioned questions are only a subset of many more questions to be answered before a deployment plan can be defined in the form of commodity strategies, purchasing plans, and other improvement activities to realize the strategic goals within a period of one to three years. The Hoshin Kanri tool can be used for this process as it links strategies and objectives of value streams in one overview including the deployment approach. It is necessary to have a documented process to define business objectives in a cross-functional team, how top management will communicate, support, benchmark, monitor, and prioritize the key activities and their progress throughout the organization. Figure 3.12 illustrates an example summary of a transportation strategy.

Customer service	Trade compliance
Delivery reliability >99%	Compliance failures = 0%
Complaints <0.1%	Customs master data errors
Error rate <0.2%	<0.5%
	Hold at customs <0.3%
Costs	Processes
Increase economy service by 30%	Extend order cut-off times by 2 hours
Reduce gross volume by 50%	Simplify rate structures by 40%
Eliminate overdue invoices by 80%	Increase EDI usage to 90%
Quality	People
Incorrect paperwork <0.5%	80% Lean basics training
Damage rate <0.1%	50% Lean transportation training
Planning accuracy >99%	100% Management development plans

FIGURE 3.12
Example transportation strategy summary.

3.12 MARKET TRENDS

What was state of the art a few years ago is a basic capability now. To keep pace with changes, it is crucial for the transport management professionals to stay informed about and to adapt to market trends taking place now and in the near future. They also need to keep senior management engaged and informed about the new advanced transportation capabilities that proactively can be used as the new strategic differentiators in the market. The Political Economic Social Technological Environmental Legal (PESTEL) tool can be used to analyze the changing business environment and view these external factors, which can have an impact on the organization, from different angles. Political factors indicate to what extent governments regulate the economy. Important elements can be political stability, trade, and tax and labor policy. Economic factors can give an idea about the potential financial success a company can realize. Relevant topics can be inflation, exchange rate, and market size. Social factors provide insight into what drives customers, their behaviors and how they can be approached best. Typical attention points are the population size, growth, and age. Technological factors are new ways, tools, and methods to communicate about, source, manufacture, and distribute goods. Environmental factors are related to how sustainable a company is when it comes to taking care of the planet and people. Example subjects can be CO_2 emission, recycling, fair trade, and ethics. Legal factors are regulations and laws related to safety, working conditions and consumer rights. The output of the PESTEL analysis can be used as input for the SWOT analysis mentioned elsewhere in this book. Table 3.10 shows an overview of the main market trends and their potential impact on transportation.

3.12.1 Fewer Trade Barriers but More Regulations

Although promoted by economists, free trade is not encouraged everywhere and by everybody. Some countries protect their industries from foreign companies. They impose restrictions on services and goods flows. A well-known trade barrier is the tax on imports to make these products more expensive then the local ones. Governments give also subsidies to lower their own product prices. However, the positive impact of less trade barriers is offset by the increasing regulations such as the stricter packing, documentation, and shipping requirements for lithium batteries, screening the cargo for security reasons before flying, and the introduction of ELDs to drivers for strictly logging and adhering to the official working hours.

3.12.2 Increasing Political Instability

In situations where human rights are not respected and the wealth is not equally divided, people start actions to change. Their actions, such as strikes and roadblocks, can end up in violence leading into production and logistics disruptions. Companies will move and look for safer and more reliable locations for their businesses.

3.12.3 Increasing Supply Chain Complexity

Supply chains become more complex due to the increasing number and locations of product suppliers, customers, and service providers. A change at one partner can have an effect on all the other partners in the chain.

TABLE 3.10

Market Trends

Area	Trend	Description	Potential Impact
Political	• Fewer trade barriers but more regulations. • Increasing political instability.	• Trade barriers disappear. • Political conflicts and volatilities.	• Companies entering new markets and offer more and better services. • Cancelled services due to safety issue.
Economic	• Increasing supply chain complexity. • Global sourcing. • Omni-channel business models. • New centers of economic activity. • Segmentation. • Mergers and acquisitions.	• Connecting more global and long-distance facilities. • Sourcing and other facilities closer to customers. • Different networks for different channels. • Sourcing regions become also markets. • Product, supply requirements & regulations need dedicated solutions. • Big global logistics service providers become bigger.	• Higher need for CTs due to trade lane explosion. • More disruptions, lanes and third-party supplies require more control tools. • More dedicated transportation networks. • Unbalanced cargo flows. • Dedicated transportation designs to comply with the needs. • Negotiation power shift from buyers to sellers.
Social	• Crowd funding. • Share economy. • Mass customization. • Urbanization.	• Crowd-concepts offer new opportunities. • Sharing culture requires new logistics needs. • Complex customer demand. • Environmental and traffic control.	• Logistics providers will speed up innovation by crowd sourcing. • Infrastructure and service sharing with competitors. • Higher demand for convenience logistics. • Home and in-room deliveries require tailored urban solutions.

(Continued)

TABLE 3.10 (*Continued*)

Market Trends

Area	Trend	Description	Potential Impact
Technological	• Big data/open data. • Uberization and online logistics marketplaces. • 3D Printing. • Robotics. • Internet of Things and cloud computing. • Crypto currencies, payments, and block chain technology.	• Digitization, cloud services. • Global services. • Integrate 3D facilities in logistics flows. • Less manual work. • Use available data on Internet and cloud computing. • Alternative to banks and credit card companies (e.g., bitcoins and storage of encrypted records).	• Real-time route and capacity planning. • Less investment to enter new markets (Uber Freight, Teleroute). • Integrate 3D with the traditional parts flows. • Self-steering trucks, planes, and ships driving solely or in pelotons, drones, flying warehouses, delivery robots. • Trucks use traffic info on Internet to bypass traffic jams. • Faster payments reduce the number of outstanding invoices.
Environmental	• Circular economy. • Resource and energy limitations. • Fair trade.	• Climate change challenges. • Higher energy demands, material resource scarcity. • Fair use of the earth's resources.	• Better optimization and utilization of resources and assets. • New cooperation models will arise. • Benefits by revenue, less donations.
Legal	• Sustainability. • Safety.	• Stricter regulations. • Supply chain security enhancement.	• More trade compliance activities. • Stricter security requirements.

The higher the number of partners, the more difficult it becomes to predict the impact of a change. The resources and tools to manage these dependencies create additional costs. Even worse is the increase of lead-time variance and uncertainty, leading to a less reliable supply chain.

3.12.4 Global Sourcing

Companies source their products from their own and from other countries to maximize their competitive advantages by lower labor and raw material costs, duties, and taxes. As other companies do the same, competition is increasing in international markets. This development continues although many companies find out that global sourcing has hidden costs such as time spent to develop suppliers, learn culture, increase efficiency, decrease reaction time, and protect intellectual property.

3.12.5 Omni-Channel Business Models

The increase of e-commerce requires shippers to offer mixed services as the consumer has different views on when, how, and where to receive the purchased goods. Some want them to be delivered at home, others want to pick-them up somewhere else, and some are travelling and want to receive the goods at their hotel. However, a multichannel distribution model offers the sellers a chance to increase their sales by getting rid of the brick-and-mortar store limitation such as limited opening hours, few stock items, and fewer ways to reach new potential customers around the globe. These new concepts require dedicated logistics networks. Instead of investing in new networks, it is also possible to use the existing networks in the market. Examples of omni-channel fulfillment solutions are:

- Buy online or order at a physical shop, ship order from an outsourced DC to a customer location, which can be a home, office, or any other address.
- Buy online or order at a physical shop, ship order from an outsourced DC, ship to an owned or third-party store or locker from which the buyer picks up the shipment.
- Buy online at a seller's supplier or order at a physical seller's supplier shop, ship directly from a vendor's facility to a customer location, which can be a home, office, or any other address.

The advantage of buying online and getting it delivered from a central distribution center is that the customer has access to the full range of products. In a physical store, it is impossible to store the full product range due to the high stock-keeping costs and complex inventory management. Shops become more and more places to see and try. Once a product is purchased, it is delivered from a DC.

3.12.6 New Centers of Economic Activity

The new world's economic center shifts east due to the continuous rise of India, China, and other East Asian countries. Until recently, Europe and the U.S. were responsible for the majority of the world's production. It will continue to move as the lower production outperforms the additional logistics costs. There is trade imbalance between west and east, leading to price shifts and the increase of logistics networks in the east.

3.12.7 Segmentation

The objective of segmentation is to group potential buyers in groups and target them with specific services. It is not realistic to compete on all services in all markets. Market division enables focused marketing initiatives to satisfy customers, leading to a better service, higher sales, and the efficient and effective use of resources.

3.12.8 Mergers and Acquisitions

When two or more companies decide to become one larger company, it is called a merger. When a company buys another one, it is called an acquisition. The number and the value of mergers and acquisitions in global transportation increases year-over-year. Although the market shares of individual logistics service providers are still low compared to other industries, the negotiation power moves more and more from the buyers to the sellers. This development can lead to higher rates. Examples of recent mergers and acquisitions are the takeovers of TNT by Fedex, Norbert Dentressangle by XPO, and Coyote by UPS.

3.12.9 Crowd Funding

An innovative way to finance new initiatives is to use the financial capabilities of social networks. This development opens doors to an enormous potential capital enabling both businesses and consumers to gather the necessary resources for new business opportunities.

3.12.10 Share Economy

A new culture development is to share assets to decrease the need for investments and reduce operational costs. The creation of such new cooperation models, such as sharing trucks, cars, or houses, enables companies to offer a wider range of services around the globe. Another positive impact is the carbon footprint reduction. A good example is the Dutch company Picnic, which delivers meals to home addresses and has no return flows. To fill in this gap, they are now taking back return shipments for the online business-to-consumer retail store www.wehkamp.nl.

3.12.11 Mass Customization

Customization is about transforming individual customer requirements into a service. More and cheaper serve-to-order techniques change this approach from an exception to a standard process. There is now the opportunity to target a big number of individual customers, replacing the mass production approach. Supply chains, which are often designed around standard services, need to develop capabilities to handle the additional complexity.

3.12.12 Urbanization

The increase of e-commerce and the number of home deliveries creates traffic and environmental issues. These need to be thought through and fixed to support these developments without compromising the quality of life.

3.12.13 Big Data/Open Data

The availability of data is huge, but companies did not find a way to benefit from it yet. Several initiatives have been started to see how this data can be used to improve, for example, the capacity usage, anticipation on traffic situations, and predicting demand versus supply development.

3.12.14 Uberization and Online Logistics Marketplaces

Uberization is the move towards an economic system in which carriers exchange their underutilized capacities through online platforms. These marketplaces bring new opportunities to offer additional global services without the need to invest in assets. Companies share their networks with competition to improve their efficiency and capacity utilization. For them it is a new opportunity to sell transportation capacity online. In the 80s, a French company started for the first time the electronic freight platform Teleroute to allow road freight exchange and payment between carriers. The New York Shipping Exchange (NYSE) allows shipping lines to sell transportation capacity online. Another example is Uber Freight, which is an app for shippers and carriers to offer and accept loads, including the online and digital payment and administrative processes. There are also shipping web portals (e.g., INTTRA, GT Nexus) to find out shipping schedules, book shipments, create shipping documentation, and track and trace shipments. However, there are still many transportation companies that do not like to pick up other carriers' loads as they see it as helping competition. They quote high prices and take driving empty kilometers for granted. Another issue is the difference between the planned and actual volumes, weights, and measurements. Trucks turn out to have less space available than the planning system indicates. The consequence is that shipments are not picked up on time. Another challenge is time. Even if the truck has space to load the shipment, it cannot spend time on extra loads due to the tight planning. Carriers prefer not to take any risk, which might lead to missing deadlines and potentially losing a customer.

3.12.15 3D Printing

Potential disadvantages of outsourcing to low-cost countries can be long lead-times and high transportation costs. To get rid of these issues and manufacture products at nearby locations it is sometimes possible to use 3D printing, which is a computer-controlled process to create a three-dimensional object in layers of material. However, as these printers are costly they are concentrated in a limited number of manufacturing sites, which generates additional production locations and goods flows. More sophisticated supply chain tools are needed to manage the extra complexity. 3D printing, also referred to as additive manufacturing, allows a company to keep virtual inventories (products in the cloud) meaning that products are only made when there is a customer order to support a JIT delivery.

3.12.16 Robotics

Automation technologies enable the reduction of defects, increase of productivity, and improvement of safety. This becomes a serious alternative of the costly and error-sensitive manual work. Both the number of opportunities to use robots and their availability are increasing. Some live examples are the self-steering trucks, planes, and ships driving solely or in multi-brand pelotons (also called "platooning"), drones, flying warehouses, and delivery robots.

3.12.17 Internet of Things, Cloud Computing and Industry 4.0

The Internet of Things (IoT) is a situation where electronic and smart objects are connected and automatically send and receive data between each other via Internet to manage a process without the intervention of a human being. The availability of data and information on the Internet ("cloud") enables smart objects, such as self-steering trucks, to benefit from information about traffic jams, plan the shortest and/or fastest routes and the location of the transportation equipment. Cloud computing is the delivery and use of IT services such as software, databases, analyses, and data storage over the Internet. Storing data on the cloud is safer than using external physical hard drives as data can be retrieved from the cloud in case of loss. It is also cheaper as shippers are relieved from the investment in and the maintenance, security, and management of local hard drives, upgrades, servers, IT licenses, and personnel and other infrastructures, as the cloud computing service provider is taking care of these. The costs are stable and predictable as the shipper pays a fixed amount per month. The combination of IoT and new smart industry technologies such as sensors and artificial intelligence is expected to lead to Industry 4.0. This is the new, fourth (4.0), Industrial Revolution with self-learning machines, and predictive analyzing capabilities to realize a self-managing "smart factory." The starting position is that based on the available data and technologies the electronic objects can manage and control the production processes better than human beings can. However, some trend watchers think that Industry 4.0 will lead to Lean 4.0, where people receive better information from the smart objects to support a better decision-making process. In this scenario, it is said that the thinking capabilities of people will always be needed. An example approach is that the smart objects gather real-time data, analyze them immediately, detect the non-performing process, and alert the operators to anticipate. It is not possible to move an organization without a Lean culture immediately to a Lean 4.0 level, as the number "4.0" indicates that a company needs to mature first from levels zero, one, two, and three to four. The combination of Industry 4.0 and Lean 4.0 would then lead to the future Logistics 4.0.

3.12.18 Crypto Currencies and Payments and Block Chain Technology

This development was initially not trusted as an underground community started it. More and more transactions take place in this way as it is fast and does not require real money. It (e.g., bitcoin) forms a serious alternative to governmental and financial institutions like banks and credit card companies. Block chain technology allows a company to store records in an encrypted and timestamped way. Only the owners of these secured records have access to and the rights to edit them. Any change in a record is updated in the other related records. All changes can be track and traced. This technology is used to protect valuable digital assets such as contact information, intellectual property, passwords, and insurance documents, bank transactions, contracts, and logistics data (expiration dates, storage temperatures, handovers, locations, etc.).

3.12.19 Circular Economy

Energy and material prices are increasing, markets become volatile, and competition is severe. Companies are looking for ways to re-use and recycle material to extract value out of it. This waste reduction lowers the demand to purchase new products and has a positive impact on the environment.

3.12.20 Resource and Energy Limitations

As the world population is increasing, the demand for energy and other natural resources increases too. As these are limited and will disappear over time the price will increase too. Finding new alternatives will be crucial to maintaining the same quality of life.

3.12.21 Fair Trade

To deal with the limited earth resources, supply chain management will have to support fair trade by investing in, instead of donating to, low-cost countries and allow local people to benefit from the extra work generated by the supply chain companies. This regional empowerment shows respect to the local community and allows them to build their own local businesses preventing social unrest due to unequal division of income.

3.12.22 Sustainability

Sustainability includes business, political, economic, legislation, technological, environmental, and social aspects. It is about looking into ways to protect the environment and the planet ecosystem by reducing carbon emissions and finding renewable fuel sources. The first step is to make people aware to have a good quality of life, while protecting the earth from damage and destruction. People want to cooperate, but without compromising their quality of life.

3.12.23 Safety

Global trade security risks and regulations, such as the recent introduction of the Electronic Logging Device (ELD) for the truck drivers in the U.S. to log their working hours (and in some countries it is not allowed anymore to sleep in the truck during the weekend) are increasing. The ELD records the driving time of a trucker automatically to better control the driver's hours of service and increase the general traffic safety. Other reported advantages are a faster matching of the fuel receipts, insight into how much time was needed for a customer stop, how many stops there were, and the amount of empty driven kilometers. However, where previously time spent waiting in, for example, a traffic jam was often not registered as driving time, the ELD does. This reduces the driver's productivity. Managing risks becomes an important part of a successful supply chain management. Companies are re-designing their supply chains to adapt to the stricter global trade security challenges. Shippers map their goods flows, identify threats and vulnerabilities, and create a supply chain security plan to become compliant. Typical security measures are screening and sealing containers and trailers before shipping, locking doors, blocking access for unauthorized people to storage areas, and archiving shipment documentation.

Storage locations need to have secured gates and parks, alarms, lights, locks, and video monitoring. It is important to check the background of both the current and new employees. In some countries, it is required to handover a "certificate of good behavior." People need to receive an awareness training to detect possible risks such as terrorism and smuggling. There must be IT security policies for passwords and onboarding of new employees. Goods need to be secured in transportation, carrier hubs, and storage locations.

3.13 RISK MANAGEMENT

When moving goods around the globe, there are many potential disruptions that can have a negative impact on the supply chain reliability. Shipments can be delayed, lost, damaged, stolen, and more. Root causes are terrorist attacks, piracy, theft, social unrest, strikes, roadblocks, and adverse weather conditions. The risks can be grouped according the PESTEL structure:

- Political: regional, ethnic, and/or religion issues
- Economic: inflation and non-payment issues
- Social: bribery, corruption, and theft
- Technological: cyber-attacks, system down, and connectivity issues
- Environmental: hurricanes, tsunamis, and volcanos
- Legal: bureaucracy, need for permits, and in-transparent procedures

Although it is not easy to allocate scarce capacity to prevent and/or mitigate something that might not happen, it is crucial to reduce the threat or minimize its impact by creating a risk management plan to identify, analyze, and mitigate the transportation risks by avoiding, reducing, transferring, or accepting them. Although protection is the best approach to prevent events from taking place, a plan is required to improve the supply chain resiliency, which is the ability to recover from a disruption, to plan the mitigation of a worst-case scenario impact as response. A mitigation action can have a (temporary) negative impact on costs and lead-times. An example can be that due to civil unrest in one country, the goods are rerouted via another country, but as this means driving more kilometers the shipment will be delivered later and cost more.

However, this is still better than running the risk that goods are stuck in the country with the civil unrest. The first step is to identify the potential risks by gathering the officially reported incidents, but also by reaching out to the employees and the supply partners to ask them what they think is a risk or which issue they experienced recently. Example incidents can be cargo losses, damages, delivery delays, or safety issues caused by theft, traffic accidents, hurricanes, transportation capacity shortages, traffic jams, equipment breakdowns, poor handling, or sellers' market situation. After the potential risks have been identified, it is necessary to prioritize them to plan on which ones to work first. Such an assessment can be done by answering the questions of what is the chance that the risk will occur, how big its impact will be, and when the risk can become a real threat. The starting position is that these risks are classified in a qualitative way, meaning that people try to prioritize the risks without complex tools. However, in case of a high number of identified risks and the challenge to grid them, it can be difficult to proceed this way. In such a situation, a quantitative tool is used, where people score the probability, impact, and proximity by numbers. Table 3.11 shows a risk assessment matrix that is the result of such a process.

Based on the risk assessment matrix, a risk management plan, specifying the strategy, plans and actions, is worked out to mitigate the risks by avoiding, reducing, transferring, or accepting them. By avoiding a risk, the risky activity, such as a delivery to a warzone, is not executed or an action is taken to remove the risk such as using a hard-sided truck to prevent thieves from cutting synthetic truck curtains. To reduce the risk of, for example, a truck arriving too late, it is possible to start driving earlier than the standard planning tool prescribes, use a new truck, or two drivers.

TABLE 3.11

Risk Assessment Matrix

		Impact		
Probability		**Minor**	**Moderate**	**Major**
	Likely	Medium risk	High risk	High risk
		Sickness	Traffic jam	Bad weather
				Capacity constraints
	Unlikely	Low risk	Medium risk	High risk
		Fire	Truck accident	Theft
	Highly unlikely	Insignificant risk	Low risk	Medium risk
		Fight	Strike	Terrorism

Risks can be transferred to other parties such as insuring the goods via an insurance company, asking the buyers to pick up their purchases themselves, or requiring a bank-guaranteed letter of credit. Minor risks are accepted, as the impact and probability are low. Even if the risk results in an incident, the company can deal with the consequences. This is, for example, the reason why shippers do not insure small amounts and accept these as their own risk to keep the insurance premiums low. These analyses lead to a business continuity plan for what to do in case of disaster. As risks can change, fade away, or pop up irregularly, it is important to review the risk management plan by applying the PDCA cycle regularly, define the concerns, their root causes, and the temporary and/or permanent countermeasures. In the transportation industry, it is likely to encounter freight capacity constraints that can lead to serious business issues such as loss of deals, customer claims, and production stops. An example mitigation tool of tackling this risk and preventing that the highest bidder gets the capacity, is to work together with the carriers on a capacity management plan to safeguard the availability of transportation capacity. Such a capacity protection plan can consist of actions like:

- Establish a long-term shipper-carrier partnership in which both parties trust each other and share sensitive information such as margins (open book policy) and operational issues.
- Share and focus on the issue lanes, their root causes, and co-operate to prioritize partners above incidental customers.
- Implement a forecasting system to provide expected volume estimations on daily, weekly, monthly, quarterly, and yearly basis.
- Level out volumes to prevent peaks and prioritize shipments, which need to go first, and work on temporary solutions. This action is not limited to the shipper and the carrier, but the shipper needs to work on the same with the customers and the carrier has to align with the charters and sub-contractors.
- Install daily, weekly, monthly, quarterly, and yearly capacity management calls to detect (potential) problems on time and anticipate accordingly.

4

Lean Transportation Management

The transportation management function has to deal with many challenges such as fluctuating volumes on a daily basis, faster deliveries against lower costs, zero defects, and world-class delivery reliability targets in a rapidly changing market where customers have individual and diverse requirements, countries implement stricter compliance regulations and complex customs processes. On the other side, there are many opportunities where the function can make a difference as good transportation management has the potential power to improve the customer experience leading to higher sales due to retaining customers for a longer period and winning new ones in the market. The delivery performance is just as important as, and in some industries it is even more important than, the product quality for winning deals in the market. Therefore, transportation should not be seen as a special capability of the logistics department, which decides how to use it for moving goods from one location to another. Instead, it is a business enabler representing the company when meeting the customer upon delivery, available for the company's leadership team to use it as a strategic differentiator in the market. This approach does not mean that cost control is not relevant. Fast growing, innovative and high-margin industries can absorb higher than average costs, but stable, mature, and low-margin markets cannot. Fortunately, there are enough new technologies in the market to better control costs and improve service and quality levels. It is possible to increase supply chain visibility by using IT systems (e.g., TMS) to lower inventory levels, reduce manual work through automation and digitalization (e.g., e-CMR), improve sustainability with electric equipment (e-bike), and reduce costs by smarter repacking (pack assist software) and more. Proven management concepts help to improve the span of control (control tower) to continuously reduce waste (Lean methodology), limit the number of suppliers (global carriers), standardize processes (global process owners), compare performance with competitors or world-class companies (benchmarking), and use IT tools for sourcing processes (e-tender). There are many best practices to enable at least basic capabilities such as flexibility, agility, and responsiveness. To mitigate the risks and at the same time seize the opportunities in the market, it requires the leadership team to create a vision and a mission to guide the employees towards the common goals the company wants to reach and share with them what needs to be done to realize those. The next step is to translate the vision and the mission into a story that is recognized by the employees, who must feel energized to do something with them. Then the people can think about what it means for their own functions such as production, marketing, and logistics. They use this input in their strategic, tactical, and operational plans. Keep on doing what previously has been done, but in a slightly faster and better way is not sufficient to survive over the long run. There is pressure to reduce costs and lead-times and increase quality and service in challenging market conditions. The business is more customer centric, high-quality products are necessary, supply chains change rapidly by innovations and customized solutions become the new Unique Selling Point (USP). The shipper needs to transform its operations into a world-class company by deploying the Lean philosophy and tools. There is waste within any shipper's organization: inefficient truck space utilization, volume increase due to inappropriate packing, waiting for loading and unloading, several handovers of copied paper sets, and many check processes. Other examples are wrong deliveries, damaged goods, vehicle breakdowns, non-availability of loading or unloading equipment, and incorrect routings. Asking a transportation manager to ship smaller quantities more frequently might feel counter intuitive. It contradicts the traditional large lot sizes and "cost efficient" approaches as managers are rewarded when meeting the cost reduction targets. To prevent such sub-optimizations, it is necessary to reward managers on the overall value steam results. It is also not a sustainable strategy to squeeze partnered carriers by lowering their rates as this means a direct decrease of their already low single-digit margins. Instead, shippers need to cooperate with their carriers to reduce waste in the whole supply chain and share the benefits. This leads to lower rates for the shipper and higher margins for the carriers due to lower supply chain costs. The most important wastes in transportation processes are:

- Waiting times: mainly at loading and unloading locations.
- Manual work: both shippers and carriers are still calling, faxing, printing, copying, e-mailing, and posting hardcopy paperwork

and retyping multiple forms with the same data. A related waste is delayed and/or unclear communication.

- Limited visibility: not knowing the most recent shipment statuses, loading degrees, truck location, etc. complicates an optimal planning of resources.
- Half-empty trucks: due to sub-optimization by shippers and carriers, multiple trucks, heading in the same direction or coming from the same origin, are often not fully loaded. Another example is driving an empty truck from the unloading address to the next loading address, which can be far away, as there is no closer loading address at that moment. The truck can even drive home empty, as there is no loading option at all.

While there is already the need to work on the previously mentioned improvement areas, the fast-changing e-commerce trends are making this job even more difficult. The Business-to-Business (B-t-B) volumes remain a significant part of the global transportation networks, but the Business-to-Consumer (B-t-C) shipments are increasing rapidly. More and more people buy their products via Internet, instead of at a physical store, and they want to have it fast, cheap, and delivered at any possible location. These are highly customized flows with many delivery points making the transportation networks more complicated. The delivery points can vary from a home or work address, restaurant, sports club, and hold for pickup location. It is now possible to receive the purchased goods on the day ordered, next-hour after, on Saturday or Sunday. Customers can change the delivery time and location online on the very last moment just before the actual delivery would take place. E-commerce companies offer their consumers the option to choose between different modes of transport, lead-times, and rates and use transportation as a service differentiator to increase sales. Originally, transportation networks have been set up to deliver relatively big shipments from factories to storage locations. The average shipment size has decreased, but also shops and other businesses are holding less inventory as carriers can deliver fast. This trend forces carriers to think about how to adapt existing and set up new networks to support customer requirements. E-commerce companies find the traditional carriers not innovative enough and tend to set up their own transportation networks. The biggest challenge for carriers is how to control the transportation costs on a day-by-day basis. The number of small shipments to any possible destination varies daily and the shipment information is known only a few hours before pick-up. The delivery points are often not dense enough to justify a fixed network, which creates pressure on planning the right transportation resources, routings and on time deliveries. To make the network a bit denser, carriers offer consumers the possibility to pick up their goods from a hold-for-pickup point. This allows the carriers to ship big volumes to those concentrated points and prevent home deliveries. Carriers use more and more the existing public networks.

4.1 PREPARE FOR THE CHANGE

It is clear that there is waste in transportation networks. Supply chain partners can benefit from this opportunity to reduce waste when they cooperate. To have an idea how much there is to win by implementing Lean, it is possible to score a Lean opportunity assessment as shared in Table 1.4. The transportation management processes are scored on the 14 Toyota principles. A low score of "1" means that there is a traditional way of working with many potential improvements. A high score of "10" means that the company is using the Lean best practices and that there are limited potential improvements. Once the organization is convinced that there is something to win, it can start preparing the Lean journey. Firstly, introduce Lean to top management, which informs the leadership team about the burning platform, upcoming change, Lean philosophy, and the stretched targets and that they are expected to take part in kaizens. Then inform the rest of the employees about Lean, what is expected from them and the approach to follow. All functions, including management, need to follow a Lean basics training. People have to understand that removing waste will deliver more value to customers and secure their jobs on the long run. Guarantee that making the processes more efficient will not lead to job cutting and that people will get new work where the focus is on improving processes. Another way is to grow business and absorb the additional work without hiring new employees. The strategy is to implement Lean, meet the stretched targets and work on breakthrough improvements by mobilizing all the people in the organization. The shipper starts with creating value streams based on a logic approach such as service types, product families, businesses, and markets. Change the company

from a functional into a value stream organization to support ownership and prevent finger pointing in case of issues. Focus on an end-to-
end approach to maximize the span of control. Each value stream has
a manager, who is responsible for making the targets and results. This
organizational change sends a strong message to the people: we are serious about this change. Now that the organization is ready to work on
kaizens and reduce waste, it is important to think about what to tackle
first. There are many proven concepts, best practices, and ways of working to reduce waste. For supporting the policy deployment, these basic
Lean tools can be used: values stream mapping, 5S, daily management,
problem solving, standard work, and kaizens. The complete set of strategies, tactics, operations, and tools will have to result into better quality,
higher service, and lower costs. Managers do see the benefits of Lean,
but they often do not know how to get there as they continue doing what
they have always been doing in a slightly better way. Implementing Lean
requires a radical change of thinking and doing. The shipper needs to
create a learning organization where people become independent problem solvers, although preventing problems instead is still better than
solving them. Choose the right timing for starting a Lean change as all
supply chain partners, such as unions, need to be involved to prevent
roadblocks. Managing a Lean journey is not a part-time job. It needs
focus and daily management to make it a success. If there is no Lean
knowledge within the organization, hire an external Lean consultant,
who will help to get things started and select external candidates to
bring in more Lean resources to lead the upcoming kaizen events. It is
important to find a senior Lean transformation manager, a Lean master,
outside the organization, who has implemented and sustained Lean for
a long time. As this change agent is not able to change the organization
culture solely, he or she needs resources to help the organization with
the first steps on a project-by-project basis. The organization can get
Lean knowledge in the form of consultants and experienced Lean practitioners. As in any change process, it is key to have or create a burning
platform, which means that there must be a good reason why people
need to change, as they will ask what is in it for them. A potential starting point can be a benchmark, which shows that the company is behind
competition, less profitable, and has higher costs and/or lower revenue.
When the transformation manager has the authority and responsibility
to start the Lean journey, he or she received the necessary resources,
and people understand the reason of change, the shipper can install

kaizen event teams. Experienced Lean practitioners lead the kaizens, map the value streams, work on improving them, and show results fast. Share the benefits of reduced waste with the employees. To change "them" (management) vs "us" (employees) into "we" culture, it is crucial to get the employees on board as fast as possible and start working on kaizens, releasing the company's power to work with each other in the same direction. Everyone, including senior management, participates in kaizen events every day. Increase targets once met, as finalizing a kaizen for a process is not the end station. Start new kaizen events for the same process and strive for perfection. Use daily management and visual control tools and gemba walks to follow up on results and agreed actions. Do not blame people and allow them to make mistakes. To realize the maximum impact of this big potential improvement power, the company needs to install a solid Lean learning curriculum starting from the starter level, via a generalist, advanced user and finally the specialist level. Each level indicates the ability to market the Lean philosophy and use Lean tools, the capacity to lead kaizen events and teach others and act as a coach. Use the "train the trainer" approach to speed up the Lean culture implementation. When a company reaches a good Lean maturity level, it can include suppliers and customers in the Lean enterprise as the more partners involved in the supply chain, the bigger the benefits of Lean deployment become.

The summarized Lean implementation action plan can look like:

1. Introduce Lean to top management.
2. Top management informs the leadership team about the upcoming change.
3. Leadership team informs the employees.
4. Appoint a Lean master as change manager, source more Lean knowledge, and organize for the change.
5. Provide Lean basics training to leadership team and employees.
6. Change the organization in value streams such as inbound, outbound, returns, and repair.
7. Assign value stream managers.
8. Train kaizen event leaders and teams.
9. Select kaizen events with stretched targets.
10. Assign kaizen events to kaizen leaders and teams.

11. Kick-off kaizen events, start working on them, and learn by doing.
12. Install daily management boards and gemba walks.
13. Kaizen leaders to present progress in daily calls.
14. Review processes and results with shop floor.
15. Share success and inspire the rest of the organization.
16. Use "train the trainer" approach and increase the number of kaizen events.
17. Implement a recognition and reward model.
18. Increase the targets.
19. Train people on advanced Lean tools.
20. Work on kaizen events that are more complicated.
21. Increase the Lean maturity level of the organization.
22. Work on kaizen events with partners outside the organization.

This Lean implementation specific action plan needs to be synchronized with the development plan for the transportation management function:

1. Know the business strategy.
2. Review the logistics strategy.
3. Deeper understand the customer, employee, process, and business requirements.
4. Define the customer value from the customer's perspective and express that in terms of quality, service, and costs.
5. Learn about the key processes, markets, technologies, and trends.
6. Define the potential use of transportation as a strategic differentiator in the market.
7. Rethink, document, communicate, and implement a transportation strategy.
8. Set up KPIs to measure, monitor, and improve performances to meet the customer requirements.
9. Map the value stream loops: visualize the value-added and non-value-added activities to deliver a service to the customer.
10. Eliminate non-value-added activities and add value to the customer through kaizens.
11. Daily management and problem solving.
12. Strive for perfection: try to eliminate waste completely so that only the value-adding activities remain.

4.2 SUCCESS FACTORS

4.2.1 Lean Leadership

A successful Lean deployment process is only possible if the Lean leaders successfully practice the following habits:

- Share the vision and inspire all the employees to actively contribute as one team.
- Focus on the required culture change, not the implementation of the Lean tools.
- Visible management commitment by actively and physically driving the change on the shop floor.
- Clear communication, measurement, and review of stretched team targets to encourage teamwork.
- Celebration of Lean wins by recognizing and rewarding people in a town hall type of setting.
- Continuously review the progress made, provide help where needed, and share lessons learnt.
- Engage everybody in the organization, but respect resistant and incapable people. Allow them to share their problems and try to solve them. Allow people to try out things, make mistakes, and learn. Do not punish them.
- Lead by example: go to the gemba, see for yourself, and learn how processes work to teach others and challenge employees with detailed questions.

The most important tool is probably the daily gemba visit as it allows the leadership team members to see things for themselves and do a reality check to verify if what their people tell them is in line with their understanding. Such visits allow them to talk with people who do the real work and come up with their own improvement ideas. However, a gemba visit should not be used as an exercise to stretch legs and requires a good preparation. It is important to define upfront what exact part of a process is going to be observed. This choice can be based on, for example, customer feedback, both positive and negative, processes with long lead-times, capacity problems, high illness rates and safety issues. Create a relation with the workers, introduce yourself, explain what you are trying to do and why, ask them what they see as a problem and what their improvement suggestions are; however, take sufficient time to just stand still and observe what is happening on the shop floor and try to understand what and why each process step is executed. These extensive observations allow the observer to come up with innovative out-of-the-box improvement ideas. It is required to write down the observations, concerns, causes, improvement ideas, and follow-up actions, but above all, it is crucial for the leadership team to block time in the agenda for these daily visits.

4.2.2 Lean Value Stream Manager Transportation

A key change agent in the Lean journey to make transportation management a strategic differentiator is the value stream manager of the transportation function, previously called transportation manager. In the past, this function was often filled in with a functionally trained employee with a background in finance, engineering, or production. Nowadays it is a requirement to hire people with a supply chain management background as the industry became complex and requires specific knowledge and skills, more than only cost control and managing the day-to-day operations, to use transportation more as a strategic differentiator in the market. Where transportation management was considered a back-office activity in the past, it is now a front-office priority where the function talks directly with customers about how to serve them best. This new transportation manager is responsible for creating, implementing, in cooperation with the supply chain partners and in line with the logistics strategy, and adhering to a transportation strategy and policy. This includes the global solutions design, implementation, standardization, maintenance, improvement, optimization, measurement, and monitoring of sustainable networks, process, and performance management. The transportation manager knows the processes and proactively asks for, and listens to, the customer, process, and employee and business requirements and uses the Lean methodology to meet these by reducing costs, improving service, and increasing delivery quality. Other key areas of responsibilities are trade compliance, export control, master data, auditing, freight audit and payment, complaint and claim handling, supply chain security, outsourcing, analyzing and optimizing networks, capacity planning, benchmarking, selecting and reviewing carriers, negotiating contracts, sustainability, market studies, developing transportation and commodity strategies, teambuilding, managing supplier relationships, managing quality systems, teaching, standardizing processes, reporting, and innovating. He or she is a customer-focused team player who makes problems visible, benchmarks performances with the best-in-class companies, defines problem statements, looks for root causes, tries out and implements countermeasures, reports out KPIs, standardizes and sustains processes, and monitors the performance on a daily basis. He or she is a reliable partner and has strong communication skills and masters English, verbally and in writing, to build up relationships and align with multi-cultural and multi-national partners such as customers, customer demand managers, warehouse managers, carriers, TMS/MTS providers, trade compliance departments, quality and regulation functions and customs authorities in the global supply chain. The transportation manager holds these partners responsible and accountable for the performance of their contribution to the end-to-end processes, participates in daily transportation operations calls to help fixing daily issues, manages supplier sourcing, contracting and review processes, leads periodic business review with suppliers to develop them, initiates, prioritizes, and coaches projects to realize the Hoshin Kanri goals. He or she manages outsourced parties through good supplier relationship management and is capable of using multiple data-driven analyses, can think in concepts and strategies, and is flexible to re-prioritize his or her activities to work on customer escalations. The focus can move on a daily basis from operational and tactical to strategic topics. Only an experienced and successful transportation manager with demonstrated Lean leadership skills, a proven record of accomplishment with measurable and confirmed results in transportation management, and knowledge of the transportation industry and the company's processes, is able to build, lead, coach, and teach his or her team of seasoned and young professionals and global process owners. He or she is a university or bachelor supply chain management educated and skilled people manager with analytical, project, change, process, and performance management capabilities to optimize transportation management towards perfection.

4.2.3 Lean Value Stream Organization Chart Transportation

Probably the best way forward is to change the physical distribution organization into end-to-end value streams such as inbound, outbound, returns, and repair where the process starts at order drop and ends upon POD receipt. However, if this is a bridge too far for some shippers, it is possible to see transportation management as one value stream and approach this function as a single end-to-end flow preventing sub-optimization of individual processes. The value stream manager reports to the supply chain director, a member of the company's leadership team representing the transportation. The manager leads this value stream, which is split in manageable value stream loops, which are based on the transportation modalities: air, parcel & express, road, sea, train, and intermodal, as they are seen as one complete service ("product family") and managed end-to-end by one leader on all performance aspects: service, quality, and costs. To show one face to the customer it is recommended to also define customer service and handle complaints and claims end-to-end, as a separate value stream loop. The other functions reporting to the value stream manager are part of enabling processes to support the value stream loops and realize the performance targets. Figure 4.1 shows an example of a Lean organization chart for the transportation value stream.

4.2.4 Lean Metrics

Companies deploying Lean philosophy believe that good processes lead to good results. Applying only results management to make the short-term targets and calling for actions to make the periodic numbers is not enough to survive in the long run. Managers are then tempted to take decision, such as delaying investments, using improvement capacity for additional production capacity and hold more inventories, which are not good for the company's future. The processes, which led to the results, are not touched meaning that the root causes of their low performances are not analyzed and the problems are not solved leading to the same outcomes as before. Therefore, it important to spend sufficient time on both the results and the process led to these. A Lean implementation is not supposed to deliver other results than the current business needs. The successful adoption of Lean will have to lead to improved standard business KPIs such as:

1. Delivery: picked up and delivered on time (%)
2. Customer: satisfied customers (%)
3. Financial: transportation costs per kg ($/kg)
4. Quality: damaged and incomplete shipments (%)
5. Compliance: negative audit results (%)
6. People: happy employees (%)

Although preferred in many companies, it is not helpful to show all KPIs in green. Such a situation will not trigger the organization to look for better ways to organize a process. It should not be a problem to show KPIs

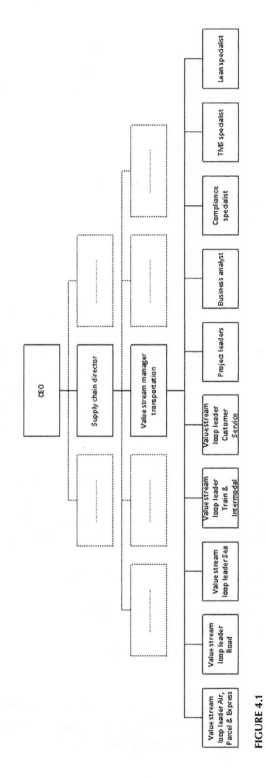

FIGURE 4.1

Lean value stream organization chart transportation.

in red, and do not blame any person but blame the relevant process, to challenge the organization to make the next step as according to the Lean philosophy there is always a better way.

4.3 TRANSPORTATION HOUSE OF LEAN

The pillars of the transportation house of Lean are JIT and Jidoka, requiring the delivery of goods in the right quantity, quality, time, and place. In other words: use high quality carriers to transport only what is needed, when it is needed and in the amount it is needed. In the Lean concept, goods arrive in smaller quantities on a more frequent and predictable schedule. Lean carriers need to support this philosophy by being a flexible, reliable, capable, and stable partner, who is fixing problems quickly and without disruptions. Lean transportation is possible by moving away from the push to the pull strategy and support the business by providing reliable, fast, frequent, and small quantities only when needed to prevent high inventory investments and inventory holding costs. Increasing supply flexibility towards demand fluctuations will reduce also the need for warehouses. Table 4.1 shows how traditional and Lean shippers use the

TABLE 4.1

Transportation Management Key Drivers

Key Drivers	Traditional Transportation	Lean Transportation
Transit-times	Long	Short
Modality	Predefined	Flexible
Scheduling	Long term	Short term
Volume leveling	Big shipment size	Small shipment size
Frequency	Weekly	Daily
Visibility	Limited	Full transparency
Responsiveness	Re-active	Proactive
Packing	Ex-factory packing	Dedicated packing
Stacking	Random	Stacking plan
Documentation	Manual	Automated
Loading	Random	Loading plan
Shipping	Many carriers	A few carriers
Unloading	Random	Unloading plan
Complaints and claims	Headache	Good information to improve

transportation management key drivers. Improving these drivers will lead to higher quality, better service, and lower costs.

Transportation strategy needs to support the logistics strategy by implementing the pull system as that provides the best value over the whole supply chain. The starting point is to derive this strategy from the company's logistics strategy giving a direction for the key transportation driver. Example questions, which need to be answered by the strategy document, are:

- Transit-times: is transportation going to deliver fast or slow? Will the shipper allow the customer to choose the service level and pay for it? What is competition doing?
- Modality: will the shipper use road, air, parcel & express, train, intermodal, or sea freight or does this depend on product values?
- Scheduling: will the shipper use forward or backwards scheduling? Will this be manual or automated? What IT systems to use?
- Volume leveling: will the shipper allow customers to order small shipments on a daily basis? How is the customer demand shared with the suppliers?
- Frequency: does the customer ask for daily, weekly, or monthly shipments? Will the shipments be consolidated?
- Visibility: which track and trace tools will the shipper use to increase the visibility of goods in the pipeline? Does the shipper consider using a TMS? How to give customers more visibility in their shipment statuses?
- Responsiveness: what approach and/or tools to use to be flexible and anticipate proactively on issues?
- Packing: will the shipper deliver full pallets or also smaller quantities? What does this mean for transportation costs and product prices?
- Stacking: do the products and their packaging allow the shipper to stack pallets on each other? What impact does this have on the transportation equipment to use and potential damages?
- Documentation: what documents does the company need to create to be compliant with the regulations? Does the shipper have the IT systems to manage this?
- Loading: will the shipper use load plans? How to measure loading degrees?
- Shipping: what kind of carriers will be used: asset based or non-asset based? Is there a tender roadmap?

- Unloading: do customer ask for making slot times? Do receivers allow the exchange of pallets?
- Complaint and claim handling: will the shipper use an IT tool? Is this a centralized department or will each value stream loop handle its own complaints and claims?

In Lean, it is common to use a house and its pillars to visualize the building blocks of a management system. Figure 4.2 shares the transportation management house of Lean.

The fastest way to reduce transportation costs is by negotiating better rates and selecting the right carrier, modality, and service level for each individual shipment. Also, better carrier performance management and automated transactional activities deliver considerable improvements. However, the exact improvement potential depends on the maturity level of an organization. In the coming paragraphs, many improvement ideas to reduce waste are shared and explained. The phrase "to reduce waste" can be replaced by "to eliminate waste," but be aware that the perfect situation will probably never be reached due to changing business environments. However, only this strive for perfection will allow a company to reach excellence. Keep in mind that all these elements are relevant for all maturity levels, only the focus can be different. In Lean, it is more about creating and sustaining the right culture than the use of tools: the following improvement ideas are not standalone and need to be seen as part of

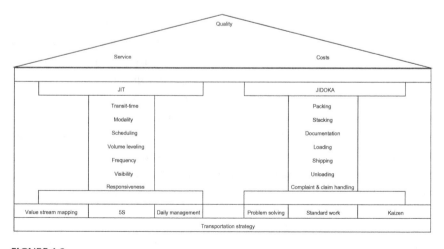

FIGURE 4.2
Transportation management house of Lean.

an integrated Lean transportation strategy. After selecting kaizens, assigning them to kaizen leaders and their teams, senior management needs to kick-off the first kaizen week and join the teams as members only. During the kick-off meeting, the team leaders present their kaizens and the team members. A daily call or meeting in the late afternoon is installed to discuss the progress and the plans for the day after. It is good to understand that it is more difficult to observe the work in logistics, compared to production processes, as activities are executed behind a desk and a computer, in people's minds, and on the phone. It requires asking more open questions and the use of the "5 times why" tool more often. Office employees turn out to be more difficult to change than people in a shop floor area are. In an office, there is often no standard work and people realize the same results in different ways.

4.4 REDUCE WASTE: LEAN CUSTOMER

The only reason why a company exists is that there are customers who are willing to pay for its high-quality products and/or services, which deliver at the first time right what they have been purchased for. These are demanding customers, who want to receive value for their money, while relying on their suppliers to hold themselves to the high and ethical standards. This does not mean that the seller needs to have the lowest prices in the market, but it does mean that the supplier must have the best cost, quality, and service combination. As the business environment is constantly changing, it requires a continuous improvement culture to maintain the best offer. This is the basic reason why Lean exists and why it is adopted by an increasing number of companies. Especially when a customer is an experienced Lean practitioner, the requirements are even higher as the customer is able to assess the potential improvements in the supply chain. Mature Lean companies try to extend the improvement focus from their internal organization to the enterprise level from the suppliers' suppliers to the customers' customers and reach out to their partners to collaborate and reduce waste for mutual benefits. They often ask for yearly cost, quality, and service improvement targets and offer their help to work together on kaizens and realize the goals. The help can exist of providing Lean knowledge, trainings and/or kaizen leaders and more. If a partner is not cooperating or not developing fast enough, there is a risk that the customer moves to another provider. To prevent that and enhance the customer-supplier relationship, it is crucial to adopt the Lean philosophy, proactively reach out to the customers, and develop a joint continuous improvement plan. In the following paragraphs, a few Lean customer-related improvement ideas are shared. The amount of added value can differ per company and its maturity level.

4.4.1 Develop and Deploy a Transportation Strategy and Policy

The starting point of any good process design is to know upfront what the deliverables need to be and how these fit in the bigger company's picture. The same is valid for the transportation management function, which needs to have a clear answer on questions like: what is the added value the customers are expecting from the company and how can transportation be a strategic differentiator in this journey? What systems and tools are needed to enable what capabilities when? Once the questions have been answered, images, graphs, and charts are used to capture these in a living and interesting to read transportation strategy document. Then it becomes time to work out a roadmap with the tactical and operational details in a transportation plan with goals and timelines to fully seize the strengths and opportunities and mitigate the risks and weaknesses. The transportation strategy serves as input for the transportation policy document, which provides guidelines to all employees about Incoterms® to use, modalities to implement, service levels to choose, shipping frequency to maintain, and more.

4.4.2 Collaborate with the Customer

Supply chain collaboration offers the opportunity to benefit from synergies between two or more partners by working on shared objectives and sharing the savings. It is possible that a change means a bit higher costs for one party, while the costs for the other party are reduced significantly leading to overall lower supply chain costs. An example is a customer who orders ten products and wants them repacked in individual solid boxes to receive them undamaged and have them sent as separate parcel shipments, because it is easier to identify them at inbound and speed up the receiving process. This leads to high repacking and transportation costs for the shipper, who proposes to put all the boxes on a pallet and send it as a LTL shipment. The shipper saves money on less time for repacking, less repacking material, and lower transportation rates as the boxes do not need repacking once put on a pallet and the LTL costs for one pallet are lower than the total parcel costs for the individual shipments. However, the new way of working requires a bit more sorting time at the customer's inbound department. To realize a win-win situation, the shipper offers the customer lower product prices and the customer accepts the proposal. The more parties cooperate in a network, the higher the potential savings. One important and often overlooked partner is the customer. It is therefore important to proactively reach out to the customer and better understand its requirements to deliver to its expectations. This contact gives also the opportunity to collaborate on reducing transportation costs by analyzing its order and delivery behavior and come up and/or ask for improvement ideas. Try to understand the key drivers of the transportation costs and how customer order behavior impacts these. High transportation costs per m^3 can indicate that the average shipment volume is low and/or the more expensive modality is used. Transportation costs as % of sales is not always a good indicator as in case the product value is high as this percentage can be low, while the transportation costs per m^3 can be high. Key drivers affecting the transportation costs are:

- Order quantities: the smaller the order quantities, the more repacking activities and expensive mode of transportation is needed.
- Modality: parcel and air transportation are expensive (350 $/$m^3$); sea and road are cheaper (100 $/$m^3$).
- Delivery frequency: the higher the delivery frequency, the smaller the order quantity per delivery, the more expensive mode of transportation needed.
- Customer requirements: special services such as labeling, re-palletizing, article clean pallets (only the same products on a pallet), and rush deliveries generate extra costs.

Transportation costs can vary per business unit, business line, distribution channel, customer category, and mode of transport. A business line can have the lowest transportation costs as % of sales but can generate the most transportation costs and at the same time the lowest transportation costs per m^3. The same is valid for distribution channels like consumer, prof, and oem. Customer categories are based on sales value, where category A includes the customers with the highest sales, followed by category B with less sales, then categories C and D. Having the transportation costs per customer enables the shipper to calculate the customer profitability to prioritize the list of customers to approach for improvements. Potential improvement areas to tackle these situations can be:

- Delivery frequency reduction: investigate the possibilities per customer to deliver less frequently while preventing higher inventory levels.
- The introduction of surcharges for small orders, third-party deliveries, rush orders, and special services.
- Consider the special services when sending quotes to customers.

4.4.3 Pack Properly and Prevent Damages and Losses

Waiting for a delivery and then finding out that the packages are cosmetically damaged and/or the products arrived as defects leads to frustration and a less positive brand image. Customers want to be taken seriously and expect their purchased products to be sent out in solid packages to survive the travel. Prevent damages by using proper packing, stacking, and handling and transportation solutions. Do not ship out damaged goods or packaging, as the customer will reject them. Use the customer feedback, also in the form of complaint and/or claim, to improve the packing designs. Make use of recyclable material, design re-usable packing, and adhere to market standards to keep the purchasing price low. Drop test the packing before going live. Use standard handling equipment and instruct the workforce how to handle the freight and where to load it in the truck. Apply standard procedures and work instructions making this activity clear and predictable. Instruct the driver to reduce shifting during transportation preventing goods from collapsing upon each other leading to damages. Prevent cargo damages and claims as it can have a significant negative impact on the profitability and customer satisfaction. Involve the transportation function early in the process design phase to bring in the requirements and agree on the optimal packaging, stacking, loading, space utilization, and shipping solutions. All outgoing shipments should be checked for damages as it still happens that the damage did not occur in the transportation network as it was already damaged when handed over to the driver. Every package should be packed in such a way that in case of, for example, accidents, turbulence, bad roads, and immediate braking, the content is protected against damages or the impact is reduced. Typical internal packaging materials used for cushioning are plastic bubble wraps or paper foils. Besides cushioning, it is important to fix the internal product in such a way that it cannot move when the package shakes. And it will. It is possible to use drop tests to check if the package is good enough. A more sophisticated approach is to hire a packaging company to do the complete design and testing of packaging material. It may seem sustainable and cost-effective to reuse packages, but this is not recommended as they already lost their cushioning, fixing, and positioning strengths. Optimal packaging helps to protect goods on the same pallet or truck from getting damaged as heavy weights and oversized shipments can fall on each other. Other issues can be spilling of liquid goods and dangerous goods. The outside package needs to be hard enough to survive the impacts of goods falling on each other, loading and unloading drops, and other movements. The combination of a hard-outer box, positioning, and cushioning should help to prevent damages. Adding a label containing a text such as "do not stack other goods on this package" will not help much. The number of labels on packages has increased dramatically due to requests, which cannot be managed system wise. The impact of adding another label is limited as drivers and other logistics workers do not have time to read all of them. The package can be also too small to cover all the labels in a readable way. When designing packages, it is necessary to know if the packages will travel as single units in parcel transportation networks or on full pallets. If packages will travel as single shipping units, they require a more robust and expensive packaging. Moving goods on pallets requires less robust packaging. If the package is moved on a mixed pallet with multiple sort of products and packaging, it will still require a proper packaging and stacking plan. Some guidelines are: put the heavy parts first on the pallet, distribute them equally over the pallet, and use cardboards between layers as they help to distribute weight, position packages against each other and avoid holes as result of different shapes, keep all products within the pallet boundaries, and use shrink wraps or plastic for sealing. Position the pallet in the truck in such a way that it cannot move by using hard-sided trucks, airbags, double-floor trucks, and other stacking material.

4.4.4 Improve Visibility

Download shipment status reports from carrier websites to speed up the availability of information and share this with the supply chain partners in the early morning, before the actual delivery should take place. Provide customers, suppliers, and employees access to visibility systems to get information they need preventing e-mailing and calling. Investigate the possibility to exchange information in a 24/7 environment as both customers and carriers are extending their working times. In addition to visibility, transport operations require the systems to provide easy-to-use workflows enabling them to execute customer service activities, such as informing customers and making new slot times, in an efficient way. The transportation industry has a long way to go here, as more than half of the trucks of mainly small sub-contractors still do not have automated onboard telematics to communicate their positions and movements allowing the planner to see, on a geographical chart, shipment statuses such as green (on schedule), red (late), and yellow (at risk). There are a significant number of manual activities, as some drivers use mobile devices to communicate by sending SMS codes, while others use smartphones or web-interfaces. The other challenge is that there are many telematics, TMS, WMS, and planning system providers requiring their own ways of integration with other systems and devices. So far, the track devices register the locations and movements of trucks, trailers, or mobile devices, but not at the shipment, pallet, or package level. This functionality seems to be more interesting for the carrier, assuming that all the planned deliveries are actually in that equipment, than for the shipper who is interested only in a specific shipment.

4.4.5 Extend Order Cut-Off Times and Customer Service Availability

Extend the order cut-off times until late in the evening (e.g., 22:00) with the carriers, who can afford this so that the customer can keep on initiating new orders as needed enabling same-day processing. Try to work only during daytime to prevent labor cost surcharges but set up a process for urgent orders dropping in the warehouse after the regular opening times or in the weekend. It is possible to process orders dropped after Friday evening until Sunday afternoon/evening, on Sunday to be delivered on Monday as some carriers are capable to pick up goods on Sunday afternoon/evening and process them on the same day. Offer as much as possible a 24/7 customer service availability to support customers with urgent orders, shipment follow-ups, and first-line help.

4.4.6 Reduce Transit Times and Their Variances

Eliminating variability frees up resources. Reduce transit times and their variances to improve the on-time delivery performance, as about one-third of the abandoned e-commerce shopping carts are caused by insufficient delivery options. Use carriers with the shortest possible transportation times and the highest delivery reliability performance, while meeting the cost targets. Reducing variances increases supply reliability and reduces safety stock leading to less inventory in the total supply chain. Allow customers to order same-day deliveries, or even deliveries within a few hours, if they are willing to pay for the additional costs.

4.4.7 Plan for Adverse Weather Conditions, Peak Seasons, and Holidays

Get proactive insight in and plan for adverse weather conditions (in the winter), peak seasons and national and local holiday schedules, and related disruptions in intercontinental airfreight flows, by temporarily increasing or building local stock and re-planning around holidays to prevent delivery delays. Although increasing inventories is not Lean, it is still better than not being able to deliver to customers. Holiday information is retrieved in a regular cadence and standard format from the carriers. It is then shared with the Sales and Operations Planning (S&OP) team members for internal alignment. National holidays of both the shipping and receiving countries can be managed in their separate ERP systems such as SAP; however, they need to align between each other to make sure that the warehouse and transportation planning allows an on-time delivery, which often means an earlier manual release of orders. Managing local holidays in only part of a country requires a bit more manual intervention as in most systems it is only possible to manage holidays on the national level, not on the local (zip code) level. An effective holiday management approach around, for example, the Chinese New Year is required as the demand for airfreight capacity just after these holidays is high leading to longer transit times. A shipper can prevent such a situation by building or increasing local inventories in China a bit more just before the holidays. What also helps to reduce a few days lead-time is to prepare the customs clearance documentation during the holiday period so that the clearance process can start immediately on the first working day.

4.4.8 Other

- Go back to the basics of transportation management: deliver on time, complete, undamaged, at the right location, and respect the other customer requirements. Track and trace shipments, proactively inform customers about their shipment statuses to prevent unpleasant surprises, measure the delivery performance on a daily basis, find root causes of issues, and take countermeasures to improve. There is not much added value to be occupied with actions to increase sales, market share and profit, implement a TMS, pilot drones or 3D printing, when the basics are not in place. The perfect delivery remains the key driver for a customer to select a supplier. It should be also the first block for a shipper to build on a world-class supply chain.

- Ask the customer how he or she wants to be served. Use the outside-in customer-centric approach and apply a customer survey for each shipment or period.
- Implement forward-looking, leading, and customer-centric KPIs (e.g., "if we continue like this, will we be able to deliver all the shipments on time?") in addition to measuring the lagging performance afterwards (e.g., "did we deliver all the shipments on time last week?"). Make sure that KPI reports are well explained to and understood by all the stakeholders, automatically generated, and communicated in accordance with a pre-agreed rhythm.
- Channel customer feedback and contacts via a single point of contact and allow them to talk with customer service employees. Use standard and automatically generated customer feedback reports and review these in the daily calls with the customers. Do not use functional e-mail addresses with the "Do not reply" e-mail receipt confirmation. Use personal e-mail addresses to increase the sense of urgency and ownership. Use social media tools to communicate with the customers.
- Use only sealed hard-sided, no curtain, trailers, and rest only at predefined secured truck stops to prevent theft. The trucks and trailers are preferably equipped with GPS tracking to locate them, by the shipper as well as the police, in case of unplanned movements. Provide the driver, or two drivers in case of high value shipments, the person whose identity has been confirmed upon pick-up, the route to take, and instructions how to act when driving. If theft occurs, investigate where (e.g., during loading or unloading) and when (e.g., while sleeping or fueling) it took place and take countermeasures to prevent re-occurrence.
- Offer the option to deliver in-room, (or in-house in case of B-t-C), to lockers and other (pick-up) locations, in the evening, on Saturday and Sunday and holidays where possible. Standard parcel and express weekend delivery options, where available, are cheaper than taxis and courier drives and can cover longer distances.

- Instruct drivers to check the quantity and quality of the goods picked up and the robustness of the loading before leaving. Train the drivers to act as the shipper's "salesman" in the contacts with the customer and treat each delivery as a chance for marketing.
- Visit the customers regularly to know more about their organization, processes, and requirements. Do not leave this task only with the sales people or account management.
- Protect the goods by using airbags, strapping, blocking, and bracing, but limit the use to prevent inefficient truck space utilization.
- Use backward scheduling to maximize the economy service planning for orders with a delivery date in the future. Do not wait with releasing these orders to prevent the use of express services. Use the economy service for timely planned preventive maintenance, customer deliveries to a stock location, shipments from vendors, and returns. Allow the express service only for system down, back-order, and out-of-stock situations.
- Babysit critical shipments from pick-up until delivery and allow carriers to inform customers directly, and cc the shipper, to speed up the information exchange. Use mobile track and trace and scan apps on the widely available smartphones to speed up and digitalize the communication of real-time shipment status information with the supply chain partners. It is now already possible to replace the Cash on Delivery (COD) service by allowing the consumer to scan the package label and pay by using its mobile device. This way of working is faster, more efficient, and safer compared to the traditional e-mailing and paperwork.
- Do not judge carriers on their total performance for all services to all destinations, as this aggregated figure mostly looks good, but can hide performance issues on lower granular levels such as lanes, countries, customers, service levels, imports, exports, or combinations between these.

4.5 REDUCE WASTE: LEAN FINANCE

The objectives of traditional finance teams are budgeting, controlling, and preparing periodic reports in line with the internal standards and external regulations and providing data to support managerial decisions on company level. Lean finance sees these basic activities as only the starting point for the main goals: continuous cost reductions and cash-flow improvements. The Lean approach requires the financial teams to move away from the departmental accounting structure to allocate revenues, inventories, and other costs to end-to-end value streams instead of departments. They need to organize themselves in an effective and efficient way around these value streams and use the Lean tools to eliminate waste from their administrative processes by simplifying, standardizing, accelerating, automating, and potentially outsourcing these activities to spend more time on supporting Lean transformations. In addition, they can lead cost reduction programs and projects or participate in teams to help calculating the end-to-end long-term financial impacts of by kaizen teams proposed changes. The financial teams should not focus too much on the short-term Return on Investment (ROI) metrics. They need to support the development of a long-term continuous improvement culture by allowing the company to hire Lean transformation leaders, bring in Lean experts with the knowledge to facilitate kaizens, develop new kaizen leaders, and invest in the train-the-trainer approach to accelerate teaching the employees the Lean philosophy and methodology. In the following paragraphs, a few Lean customer-related improvement ideas are shared. The amount of added value can differ per company and its maturity level.

4.5.1 Consider Modal Shifts

Try to use the right mode of transportation. Take the delivery requirements, such as lead-time, to select the cheapest modality. Consider the move from the expensive air, parcel, and express to the cheaper road, sea, train, and intermodal. Transportation alternatives for air are:

- FCL: longer transit time, lower reliability, suitable for replenishment flows and big volumes.
- LCL: longer transit time and lower reliability compared to FCL. Suitable for smaller volumes.
- Parcel: potential substitute of small airfreight shipments. Breakeven points, the weight at which it becomes cheaper to use air instead of parcel, differs per trade lane and carrier combination.
- Sea-Air: one shipment and two commodities: ocean and air. Cheaper than airfreight. Faster than sea freight. Not suitable for urgent shipments. Not available on many trade lanes. Good alternative for poor airfreight availability, capacity constraints, and congested ports.

- Rail-Air: one shipment and two commodities: rail and air. Cheaper than airfreight. Faster than sea freight. Not suitable for urgent shipments. Not available on many trade lanes. Good alternative for poor airfreight availability, capacity constraints, and congested ports. Shippers using rail-air are the European clothing retailer H & M, supplier of cellular phones and network systems Ericsson Mobile Systems, and the multinational technological manufacturer Flextronics, which have a supplier base in China.

4.5.2 Consolidate Shipments

Maintain a healthy partnership with the warehouse. Agree with them the optimal and flexible pick-up times. The activity of consolidating shipments in the warehouse might take longer and require more resources but can lead to lower transportation costs. Create together a business case and decide on the best way of shipping. Consolidate and increase shipment sizes from parcels to pallets, from pallets to LTL or LCL, and from LTL or LCL to FTL or FCL without increasing inventory levels. The bigger the average shipment size, the lower the freight costs per product. Be aware that there is a break-even point between these modalities when it becomes cheaper to move, for example, from LTL to FTL or from a 20' to a 40' container. It can be that there is more than 6 m³ to ship and that it is potentially cheaper to purchase a FTL instead of shipping it as LTL instead of receiving every day several LTL shipments with different carriers combine these in a milk run FTL for inbound and outbound. A milk run is a roundtrip that facilitates the distribution of goods from one location to several customers and/or collection of goods from several suppliers to one location. Such a set-up works only in a high-density area, where the distances between the addresses are short and the carrier can plan the optimal route to minimize loading and unloading activities, trips, trucks at the docks, and lead-times.

4.5.3 Set Up Tender Roadmaps

Set up and prepare tender roadmaps to tender lanes regularly. The more precise the shipment data and forecasts shared with the carriers are, the more interesting the quotations will be as with this data the providers can calculate the costs more accurately. If the data is just an estimation, or the carriers know from history that the shipper provides incorrect and/or incomplete data, service providers build safety in their cost calculations leading to higher rates for the shipper. However, do not select carriers only on rate basis. Take the total cost of ownership into account. Go for the dual-sourcing approach, a leading and a back-up structure, to encourage competition but be aware that they do not use the same sub-contractors to prevent issues with both carriers at the same time in case of disaster. Consider regional and local carriers as they often have lower rates as result of lower overhead, better utilization of owned equipment, and more knowledge of the local market and requirements. Go directly to carriers who are actually executing the transportation, instead of forwarders, for lower rates, but watch out for the extra overhead as more contacts with more carriers means more people to manage. Agree on simple rate structures and all-in prices preventing hidden costs and surcharges, which can be a significant part of the shipment cost. Surcharges can be applied for fuel, extended areas, residential addresses, non-conveyable goods, and hazardous material. Consider joint procurement within or outside the organization to reduce rates as result of leveraged volumes. Contract steady lane volume and do not ask a quotation for every shipment. Spot quote big shipments but watch out for creating additional overhead. Tender warehouses in combination with transportation as a warehouse location has a big impact on transportation costs.

4.5.4 Negotiate Fuel Surcharge Costs

Fuel costs as part of the total truck operating costs variate from around one tenth for courier vans to one third for big trucks. Since the rising of fuel prices, transportation companies started charging customers a fuel surcharge as compensation for the increasing diesel costs. Today it is an industry-accepted practice, but this should not recover more than the additional fuel costs for the carrier. A FSC should give money back to the shipper in case of a diesel price lower than the baseline. Allow the carrier to propose a mechanism and benchmark its competitiveness. Companies who are best able to manage fuel costs have a competitive advantage.

4.5.5 Leverage Purchasing Volumes

Centralize sourcing, source globally, and manage contracts centrally. Leverage purchasing volumes, as higher volumes lead to lower rates, but also to more attention and customer service from the carrier. This is especially advantageous for enterprises with multiple business units and sites, but small companies can also increase their buying power by forming and sourcing as a group of small businesses. Remember that carriers are willing to offer lower rates for big and steady volumes to create a guaranteed flow for maintaining their basic network. Shop for the best rate-service level combination in case of big volumes and projects. Use the spot quote process: buyers send out a request for quotation to several carriers, who will provide their best possible rates. Carriers are willing to accept lower rates in case of challenging market circumstances and over-capacity. Spot rates change frequently and significantly. Install a globally accessible online tool (e.g., a simple Sharepoint location or a more sophisticated TMS) to communicate with approved carriers, their rates, volume and lane allocations, contract terms and conditions, performance reports, and contract compliance metrics.

4.5.6 Improve Loading Degrees

Make sure that the maximum available truck space is used by introducing a stacking plan and prevent sending out half-empty trucks due to an inefficient loading process. Stack the goods as high as allowed by the carrier to benefit from lower transportation costs, but also to prevent other customers' goods from being stacked on these and potentially leading to damages. There are IT-based stack assist tools in the market to support this process. Define how many pallets fit in a truck and how many products fit on a pallet. Consider double-floor trucks for non-stackable pallets to prevent damages. Make sure that the pallet space is fully utilized. Think about using a Long Heavy Vehicle (LHV) for big volume flows such as line haul equipment between big sorting centers or cross-dock locations. A LHV is a truck of up to 25.25 m in length, which can handle a maximum weight of 60 tons, although these metrics vary per country. There are also long road trains, 20'/40' container combinations and other big equipment, which is even longer, wider, and higher.

4.5.7 Apply a TCO Tool

Implement a tool to calculate the TCO of a service, carrier, and process combination. Prevent one part of the supply chain from benefitting at the expense of others. Shift from looking only at the purchase price to the total costs of a service in operation. Get rid of the practice of selecting carriers on price only. Remember that purchasing prices account for only part of the total costs. Look at the entire process of procuring and consuming the service with costs occurring in the operations such as set-ups, trainings, and maintenance.

4.5.8 Do Not Accept General Rate Increases and Price Indexations

Do not automatically accept General Rate Increases (GRIs) or price indexations. Asking for a rate increase means either the carrier did not manage to implement productivity improvements or the carrier did manage this but uses these generally accepted increases to generate higher margins. Both scenarios are not acceptable. Instead, work together with the carriers to reduce costs for both companies by sharing the benefits. Some shippers request their carriers to reduce costs every year by applying cost reduction targets.

4.5.9 Introduce Direct Deliveries

Deliver orders from factories directly to customers and bypass warehouses. Consider triangular shipments, which are deliveries from product suppliers directly to customers. The orders can be big, but also small orders can be shipped directly. This concept is possible for B-t-B and B-t-C flows. The Belgian hardware store-chain Hubo delivers goods from its suppliers directly to its consumers. This way, it is possible to deliver faster and avoid transfer and handling costs. This leads also to lower inventory levels and fewer warehouses. Another potential concept is the drop shipment option, where a backorder is delivered to customers from another continent than where normally the goods come from (e.g., deliver from a DC in AMEC to a customer in APAC).

4.5.10 Check the New Silk Route

This is a railway connection between China and Europe. It offers opportunities for the east-to-west transportation flows as the lead-time is 14 days, which is just between those of the faster but more expensive airfreight and the significantly cheaper but slower sea freight. The train stops at the main European seaports of Warsaw (PL), Hamburg (DE), Rotterdam (NL), Antwerp (BE), Calais (FR), and London (UK).

4.5.11 Other

- Negotiate acceptable payment terms (e.g., 30 days end of month) to allow both the shipper and the carrier a proper cash flow and working capital management.
- Prevent that purchasing teams solely negotiate with carriers, as big potential savings detected during the sourcing process are often not realized due to inappropriate process knowledge, the requirements, and unfavorable terms and conditions.
- Reducing costs is in a way also a wasteful activity, which can be compared with quality inspection. Finding out at the end of a process that there is a defect, read higher costs, it too late. It is better to prevent cost increases, which need to be corrected afterwards. Re-assess and validate too optimistic business cases before implementation, value-track cost impacts of projects to verify if these materialize as planned and potentially reverse the change if not, measure adherence to the agreed shipping policy and contracts, and, only in the very worst-case scenario, install an approval process to assess any spend.
- Know the customer, employee, process, and business requirements and processes to be able to identify cost-saving opportunities: what and how much is shipped from where to where against what costs and so on.
- Assign a dedicated business analyst to the transportation value stream to help prepare AOPs, periodic financial reports, analyze the spend and actuals, value track events, bridge the actuals with AOPs, detect problems or opportunities and co-operate with colleagues to initiate improvement actions.
- Implement forward-looking, leading, cost KPIs (e.g., "if we continue like this, will we meet the target of logistics costs as % of sales at the end of the year?") in addition to measuring the lagging KPIs (e.g., "did we met the target of logistics costs as % of sales in the last year?"). Make sure that KPI reports are well explained to and understood by the stakeholders, automatically generated, and communicated in accordance with a pre-agreed rhythm.
- Ship prepaid for lower rates as carriers are willing to offer these, as there is a higher chance that they are paid for the service.
- For air and sea freight, it is not necessary to source transportation on a door-to-door basis by default, as it can be cheaper to do this per leg:

door-to-port, port-to-port, and port-to-door. There is a limited of number of big carriers that dominate the port-to-port market, while there are many players in the market for the door-to-port and port-to-door transportation. This results in more competition and lower rates. It is also possible to use cheaper modes of transportation for the last-mentioned legs (e.g., use the train instead of road freight to move freight to and from ports).

- Minimize the number of internal intercompany replenishments: maintain stock levels by shipping directly from the product suppliers to the final stock locations. Ship repairable and/or scrap products directly from the market to repair and/or scrap vendors.
- Use the outbound taxis and courier trips to pick up returns and/or vendor inbounds on their way back against no or limited additional stop costs as the taxi rates are based on the total number of kilometers driven back and forth.
- Do not buy insurance from carriers; buy it from a third-party insurance company, as the rates are significantly lower.
- Try to tender outside the peak seasons, as carriers tend to offer higher rates when demand is higher than supply. Agree on a long-term contract period if the expectation is that the market rates will increase and agree on a short-term contract period if the rates are expected to decrease.
- Discuss with the carriers the possibility of implementing virtual consolidation, which means that goods going on one day to one address are not packed together and leave the warehouse as multiple shipments, but the carrier invoices them as one shipment. This allows the shipper to benefit from the lower transportation costs but prevent the additional work to physically consolidate the packages as one shipment.
- Make sure that only one carrier is organizing backhauls as this is cheaper, also for the carriers, than two one-way trips organized by two different carriers. Look for opportunities to combine outbound with inbound shipments.
- Watch out of the minimum charges for small shipments. Some airfreight carriers charge, for example, a minimum of 30 kg, even if the shipment is only 5 kg.
- Include structural Value-Added Services (VAS) costs, such as accessorials for deliveries to extended areas and Saturday and in-room deliveries, in the bill towards customers.

- Enable shipping systems to show the transportation costs of a shipment to employees, when selecting a service, to increase their cost awareness.
- Do not physically ship software, manuals, and documents. Allow the receivers to download these from and sign documents via online platforms.
- Validate cost reduction business cases and value track them for a minimum of one year as many cost saving projects do not materialize for different reasons. Value tracking enables the organization to learn and timely anticipate and safeguard the planned savings. Not all benefits can be expressed in financial figures. Actions to improve, for example, the customer service and delivery performance are vital for the company's future existence; however, it is not easy to translate these into financial gains.
- Do not replenish stock locations by the parcel or airfreight modalities unless the goods values justify this. Use sea freight and/or road transportation to ship goods with low values.
- Use postal services for small packages as they generally have lower rates compared to parcel and express carriers due to their wide reach and extensive transportation network.
- Use light packing material and prevent sending "air." Big and/or heavy packing material results in higher payable (volumetric) weight. There are IT-based pack assist tools in the market to support this process.
- Load and unload quickly and get rid of the standard two-hour window in carrier quotations to lower the rates as faster loading and unloading means lower waiting cost.
- Know the Incoterm® of a shipment upfront to define to whom the carrier should send its invoice, the shipper or the receiver, and include this check in the invoice verification process to detect potential errors and act accordingly.
- Look for nearby located carriers as this reduces the empty driving kilometers from the carriers' to the shippers' locations leading to lower costs and rates.
- Not all shipments need to be delivered urgently and as soon as possible. Use economy service levels as default and express service levels for urgent deliveries only.
- Regularly model and simulate distribution networks. Use software to optimize delivery and transportation routes.

- Investigate the possibility to cross-dock shipments instead of putting them on stock to prevent inbound, stock, and outbound handling.
- Check the potential use of a merge-in-transit center, which receives the goods from different origins, groups and forwards them to customers as one shipment against lower transportation costs per unit.
- Agree premium pricing with the carriers and customers for urgent shipments but minimize its usage. Limit the number of taxis and courier shipments.
- Get refunds from carriers for not meeting service levels with money-back guarantees, damages, and lost goods.
- Do not let the shipper suffer from increased surcharges and handling fees in the peak season. Get guarantees from the carriers during the contracting phase that they will offer sufficient transportation capacity at pre-agreed rates.
- Leverage supplies, such as packing material, to decrease purchasing prices.
- Do not ship "air": minimize the package sizes by optimizing the portfolio of the packages in house. It is possible to use a packing machine, which measures the loose boxes to repack, cuts the right-sized package from a roll of carton, repacks the goods, and prints and pastes the shipping label on the final package. In addition to transportation cost reduction due to lower chargeable volumes, this way of working lowers the total amount of carton needed. The cut and unused carton pieces are recycled. Also, the environmental conscious customers do not like to receive too much repack and fill material.
- Reduce or eliminate the filling of empty parts in the package with sealed air, paper, or any other material. In addition to extra transportation costs due to shipping "air," the more fill material the higher the material purchasing costs.
- Use lighter packaging material: move, for example, from heavy wooden to light synthetic crates as parcel and airfreight rates are per kg.
- Agree with nearby shippers with the same customer base to consolidate and co-load shipments.
- Get rid of fixed costs. Accept only transactional rates. Minimize or even better eliminate accessorials and surcharges.
- Structurally check carrier invoices against rates and quotations. Set up cost calculation tools to forecast shipment costs and compare these with actual invoices.

- Consider a robotic loader and unloader. This is a sensor-based lifting platform at the dock on which mostly uniform pallets are put manually by using a lift truck, an automatic belt, or an Automated Guided Vehicle (AGV). The platform has the same maximum length, width, and height as the trailer. When the platform is full, it lifts up automatically, rolls into the truck, drops the pallets, and rolls back to the dock. The reverse process can be used for unloading trucks.
- Do not combine standard goods with hazardous and/or heavy and/or oversized goods in one shipment as the (airfreight) carriers can invoice the whole shipment against the higher dangerous goods and/or upper deck rates. Instead, send the three types of goods flows as separate shipments to realize lower costs as this way the standard goods will be charged against standard rates and only the (limited) hazardous and/or heavy and/or oversized goods will be charged against higher rates.
- Know the carriers and shippers in the market for benchmarking rates against world-class levels. Know also the exact definition of the various rates to compare "apples with apples." When a rate seems to be too low to believe, then there is a big chance that the rate is indeed incorrect or it is used to win the customer against any cost and will not hold for a long period.
- Re-assess if the products have been classified by the right HS code to prevent paying unnecessary high duty rates.
- Allow carriers to do customs clearance for shipments with them for a fast throughput time, but benchmark if they have competitive customs clearance fees.

4.6 REDUCE WASTE: LEAN PROCESSES

Lean processes need to be capable, stable, and reliable to satisfy customers by adding value through the production of affordable, innovative, and high-quality products and/or services in line with their requirements. There is no room for high inventory levels of raw material, overproduction of (semi-) finished products, defects and reworks, unsafe workplaces and accidents, access of transportation, waiting on each other and over processing such as approval cycles. Processes need to be waste-free, starting from the design phase. Any prevented waste does not need to be corrected later on. The same is valid for project implementations: do not allow projects to go live and leave the "last bits and pieces to be fixed by the operations" as this is also a form of "built-in waste." In the following paragraphs, a few Lean customer-related improvement ideas are shared. The amount of added value can differ per company and its maturity level.

4.6.1 Consider in- and Outsourcing

Consider outsourcing of owned vehicles and its management as maintaining the equipment, staff, and state-of-the-art IT systems is difficult, costly, and requires up-to-date knowledge. For most companies, transportation management is not their core business. Outsourcing does not mean that the shipper is relieved from being responsible for the transportation performance as it is a critical function, which can be used as a service differentiator. Uncontrolled processes should be controlled before outsourcing them as the outsourced party could be blamed for non-performance, which was already an issue before the transfer of activities. These become clearly visible in an outsourced situation. Transportation can be quite complex as it involves several supply chain partners, networks, systems, and processes. If not handled in the right way it can lead to significant inefficiency and ineffectiveness. It is good to know that there are companies for which transportation is their core business and who have the organization, knowledge, IT systems, and technology to play a leading role in this market. It can be a good idea to outsource transport management to these specialists. Outsourcing to a knowledgeable partner allows the shipper to prioritize and allocate the limited resources of its best people to the core business activities. The partner is able to advise on the most cost-effective planning and efficient solutions. Besides micromanaging shipment by shipment, partners relieve the shipper from investing in equipment and infrastructure allowing the shipper to allocate this money to its core business initiatives. Outsourcing makes transportation flexible as partners have the global network to allow the shipper to grow and downsize operations fast. The shipper can also benefit from lower rates due to the partners' buying power as they work for many other shippers. Consider also the outsourcing of FPA to a specialized company. Bear in mind that American companies can only process invoices, which can be paid by the shipper (also called "prepaid") or the consignee (also called "collect") of shipments towards embargoed or sanctioned countries only if the export license number is mentioned on the invoices. American companies are not allowed to ship goods to these countries themselves, but with a license, they are allowed to pick and pack these. Watch the freight bills as some of them are incorrect. Check also the possibility of insourcing part of transportation and/or its management, which require limited management effort and/or can be a strategic differentiator in the market. The Dutch company Coolblue recently decided to insource part of the distribution of its domestic appliances. It uses now its own transportation equipment, depots, and people to improve the customer delivery experience by offering a free of charge next business day in-house delivery to get more control on the last mile, which is probably the most important part of the transportation chain as it has a direct impact on the customer in case of non-performance. Coolblue sends the customer a delivery pre-notification by SMS to confirm the delivery within 60 minutes meaning that the recipient needs to wait maximum one hour. The two delivery persons call 30 minutes before arrival, bring the shipment in house, test, install the machine, and take the old one with them.

4.6.2 Implement Daily Performance Reporting and Proactive Exceptions Monitoring

Install a daily proactive shipment status reporting and monitoring process to save shipments from delays and/or inform the customers timely and efficiently by using the mail merge option. Mail merge is a process to personalize and send pre-addressed mass e-mails on multiple times in a day to many customers from one template with fixed and variable text parts. The variable part comes from different databases and includes customer-specific information such as order references, AWBs or Pos, and their shipment status. Have an eye for waste and problems and eliminate them immediately. Maximize the use of carriers with track and trace systems to improve visibility and order desk responsiveness towards customers. The word "track" refers to "which route did my shipment take?" and the word "trace" is about "where is my shipment now?" An example proactive monitoring process is the automated delay notification, which can be communicated in different ways to customers:

- For every shipment that received an exception in the carriers' network is potentially at risk and an automatic delay notification is sent out to the receiver of the goods. This is a system set up on the carriers' side and includes tracking and customer reference numbers, exception description and resolution. The advantage is that all delays in the network are captured and communicated. The disadvantage can be the high number of delay notifications. Most of them will not lead to an actual delayed delivery as they are recovered further in the supply chain.

- Receive the automatic delay notification only for shipments with a confirmed delayed and revised delivery date. The advantage is the limited number of notifications. The disadvantage can be a late notification due to the reactive modus.
- Proactively search for potential delays in the network at preset times and milestones. Based on the most recent milestone scans the shipment received in the network, the shipper can estimate if a shipment will be a late delivery and if communication towards the customer is necessary. It is possible to babysit critical shipments until final delivery. The advantage is a limited and accurate number of notifications. The disadvantage is that it is a labor-intensive process.

4.6.3 Level Out Demand

Level out demand by planning for one-time events and promotions. Receive downstream forecasts, real-time demand is even better, on time and send them upstream to reduce ups and downs in the supply chain preventing the bullwhip effect. This impact describes the effect on inventory levels and costs when orders move from customers, via manufacturers, to product suppliers. The further back in the supply chain, the higher the demand variance is due to forecasting errors, working with batch sizes and long lead-times. A customer order of, for example, 10 pieces can lead this way to the product suppliers' sub-contractors producing 120 pieces. Prevent the traditional peaks in the morning for unloading and in the afternoon for loading as this generates waiting time for the driver at the pick-up and drop off locations and/or in traffic jams. Ship on off-peak days (e.g., Monday) to prevent higher rates due to limited transportation capacity in the market on the other days. Traditionally, people make the highest number of purchases in the weekend. To have then sufficient stock, and not too much in the rest of the week, dealers require transportation on mostly Thursday and Friday leading to higher rates on those days. Offer, for example, night, using electric trucks to prevent noise and carbon emissions, or mid-day pick-ups. Agree with customers beneficial loading and unloading days and times. Request product suppliers to send an ASN for each shipment latest the day before delivery. An ASN includes information like the number of pallets, loose boxes, POs, and PO lines to enable the inbound process to plan resources equally over the day. Train people to be multi-skilled giving the company the flexibility to plan more people in the morning at inbound and in the afternoon at outbound. Install fixed loading and unloading day and time agreements with carriers. Reduce the number of carriers to focus the improvement efforts to eliminate waste in the supply chain.

4.6.4 Limit and Manage Returns

A return is often the result of a delayed shipment and/or a defect on arrival, which can generate huge wastes such as lost revenue, re-shipment of the correct products and time spent handling the complaint. Unmanaged returns lead to inefficient warehouse and inventory control processes. Not knowing what products will come back when and what to do with these leads to resource planning issues, space problems, delayed information exchange flows, and slow customer complaint settlements in the form of a new shipment or money-back process. In the meantime, there are high inventory levels as many products are in the pipeline but cannot be used yet as they are waiting to be processed. In the worst case there are backorders waiting for the products, which cannot be used, although they are in the company's position. Such a situation leads also to incorrect overview of inventory levels, production plans, and financial reporting. Limiting returns starts with a perfect outbound delivery performance. However, in case of returns a process is needed to support the reuse, resale, or repair of returned products. Return flows can be up to 40% of the outbound volume. Although reverse logistics gained more attention recently, there are companies that perceive this process as headache. They do not have the right systems in place, overlook the added value, and manage it as a cost center with low visibility. Proper returns management results in improved customer satisfaction due to higher availability of goods on stock as result of faster returns. The company needs less working capital by reusing products instead of buying new ones, lower inventory levels and less scrap. It is recommended to route the Return to Sender (RTS) goods through the returns warehouse to be checked, resent, and/or stored at good stock. This inspection process is necessary to check the numbers, packaging quality and as the goods have been outside an unsecured area, they have to be made secure again. Expected returns, the shipper is notified that the goods will be returned, can be managed by using return reference numbers, return labels, and inbound processing instructions. Unexpected returns are more difficult to process as they are not planned and it is unclear what to do with them. Consider installing national consolidation centers for returns instead of shipping them one-by-one trans-border, as this is more expensive.

4.6.5 Optimize Vendor Inbounds

Inbound transportation is one of the most overlooked aspects of logistics. Shippers can gain more control by agreeing to use the Incoterms® rule FCA, meaning that the consignee pays the inbound transportation costs, to identify inefficient processes and potential improvements such as reducing lead-times, more efficient dock scheduling, and shipment consolidation. If the vendors are responsible for shipping, provide them a preferably web- or TMS-based routing guide specifying the approved carriers and shipping process. Regularly update the guide and audit the vendors on their adherence to the guidelines. The inbound transportation costs are normally hidden in the product price, but by paying them separately, they become transparent making it easier to work on cost reduction programs. Other reported benefits are lower inventory levels due to shorter lead-times, reduced transportation costs by using own contracted carriers with better-negotiated terms and conditions, maximized usage of economy service levels, and improved supply chain visibility. Insight in the shipment statuses of POs and supplier delivery performances allows the company to manage inventory levels more accurately and reduce them. Do not stock damaged packaging, as the customer will reject them. The product supplier should use proper packaging material and not send out goods in damaged packaging, but if the damage occurred during transportation do not send them back to the supplier. Instead, build up the required skills internally to fix the issue at the inbound process and agree with the product suppliers on settlement rules. Prevent 100% inbound inspection and target for the first-time-right approach: challenge the product suppliers for a perfect delivery with zero defects and agree on a settlement process in case of errors and/or damages. Check the feasibility of pick-up logistics, where the receiver manages goods from product suppliers to its own locations. The goods are picked up and exchanged between the trucks in a cross-dock facility so that each truck going to a store has products from all suppliers. Receivers use their own carriers in order to reduce costs and optimize service by integrating outbound with inbound deliveries in a backhaul, which is any return load taken after the delivery has been made. It is a change from a supplier to a customer driven logistics. Picked up shipments synchronize inbound space optimization, better staff planning, reduction of dock contacts, elimination of waiting hours, improved delivery reliability, reduction of lead-times and less damages, higher goods availability, and less inventories. Companies using this concept are, for example, Metro, Baumax, and Albert Heijn. Service providers supporting this way of working are, for example, Masped Group, Logmaster, DHL, and Dachser. Typical concepts are:

- Carrier management: the customer, supplier or 4PL manages the carriers.
- Warehouse management: one logistics company for transport and warehousing or a carrier for transportation and a logistics company for warehousing.
- Supply chain management: a product supplier delivers at a central cross-dock platform of a carrier/4PL or the goods are picked-up from the product supplier site and then delivered to a customer outlet.

Pick-up logistics can be used in combination with the Vendor Managed Inventory (VMI), Supplier Managed Inventory (SMI), Supplier Managed and Owned Inventory (SMOI) and direct delivery concepts, the product suppliers own, and stock inventories at their warehouses. When there is a market order, it is forwarded to the supplier, who at that moment sells the product to the purchasing organization, which picks up the product to deliver it directly to the end customer. A step further is to ask the supplier to organize also the transportation to the end customer.

4.6.6 Implement Smart and Re-Useable Packing Material

Rethink if the currently used pallets are still the best ones for your business as the standard wooden pallets can be contaminated with bacteria or cracked, leading to damaged goods or fire. Consider the usage of smart light, strong, and easy-to-clean pallets with a wooden content, but a fire-resistant synthetic surface equipped with a tracking device to monitor their locations, temperatures, and humidity enabling the shipper to anticipate, for example, rerouting a truck to bypass vibrate roads and helping the identification of potentially recalled pallets. Implement re-useable and returnable containers or other packing material, to and from repetitive delivery locations, to limit the investments. For domestic flows, it is possible to set up pallet exchange agreements with the carriers, as the shipper remains the owner of the pallets. Carriers have the option to physically return the pallets to the shipper or buy them for a pre-agreed rate. To eliminate or reduce the amount of "lost" pallets, it is also possible to join pool systems, where logistics providers, against a transactional fee, offer shippers the possibility to administratively exchange pallets without moving them physically around. Make sure that there is a well-managed pallet administration preventing disputes with carriers. This is also valid for agreements with rental companies. The best way of working for international shipments is to use TAPs, as bringing them physically back is costly. There are also no or limited parties who are willing to install an international pallet exchange procedure.

4.6.7 Plan Docks

Preliminarily assign docks to arriving trucks enabling the workforce to load and unload trucks in the right order. Use flexible docks for any kind of transportation equipment such as vans, side loaders, and standard trailers. Make sure that there is a sufficient number of docks to prevent waiting times. When the pallet is picked up from the truck, drive directly to the storage or staging areas and prevent the several put-away and pick-up handovers in-between. Install and measure the dock-to-stock lead-time. Create a process to book goods in an urgent way in case of stock-outs or backorders. Implement express desks for loading and unloading small and/or urgent shipments to prevent driver-waiting time and speed up the inbound handling process.

4.6.8 Other

- Take full control of the outbound flows by using the CIP incoterm to benefit from using a limited number of preferred carriers and better-negotiated rates due to leveraged volume. Reduce the number of carriers to consolidate planning, invoicing, shipment consolidation, loading, unloading, complaint, and claim handling activities. The additional visibility enables the shipper to plan, execute and create service, quality, and cost reports more efficiently.
- Assign global process owners. Global processes can be created for network design, FPA, complaint & claim handling, trade compliance,

master data, carrier performance management, and sourcing. Use standard work templates to standardize, document, and audit processes.

- Require the part suppliers to use economy service as default. Express service can only be used after approval. Part suppliers need to consolidate shipments towards the receiver and not send them out as individual parcel or pallet deliveries.
- Investigate the option to build ULDs at the shipping location and transport them directly to the airport. This reduces handling activities such as unloading the incoming truck and loading the outgoing ULDs at the airfreight carrier and allows the shipper a later truck departure time, which gives the customer more time to order products to be shipped out on the dame day.
- Use Internet-based carrier-shipping tools to digitalize the supply chain and increase the shipments' visibility, reporting capabilities, and EDI connectivity.
- Implement a shipping policy such as "deliver expensive products by air," "ship replenishment flows by sea," "use economy service for preventive maintenance," "implement express service for corrective maintenance," "send returns by road," "justify deviation from the policy by filling in the 'approval tool' for monitoring," and so forth. This process requires the organization to set up and implement the policy, but also to manage its adherence by creating and maintaining a compliance report with countermeasures in case of non-compliance.
- Ask the carriers to provide a Disaster Recovery Plan (DRP).
- Containers from Asia to Europe and the U.S. are often loose loaded as the transportation cost savings due to higher loading degrees outweigh the additional handling costs of loading and unloading these manually. A potential solution to speed up the unloading process is to instruct the shipper to use cardboard slip-sheets on the container floor and stack the loose boxes on them. The recipient can then manually drag these out of the container and use a clamp truck to grab the boxes on the slip-sheets and stack these on pallets. A more sophisticated way is to use a stacking robot.
- Use the availability of early orders to plan for shipping by economy services. Do not allow orders to be picked, packed, and shipped by an express service on the very last moment before the requested delivery date and time.

- Use SOPs and SLAs with carriers to document and standardize processes. Agree on an updating process.
- Use forklift trucks with lithium batteries, as these charge faster and require less frequent charging events compared to the traditional ones. This means more availability time and higher labor productivity. These batteries use also less energy.
- Innovate and try out new solutions in the logistics market. Look at onboard cranes, belts, automatic loaders and unloaders, and other tools to speed up the loading and unloading processes. Consider Radio Frequency Identification (RFID) and GPS tracking for high value products to retrieve them in case of missing, but also to include these inventories in the pipeline for end-to-end inventory management process. If the RFID tags are expensive, attach them to the packaging material (e.g., a pallet or a crate), return, and reuse them.
- Consider road trains for bulky lanes.
- Agree on a checklist for the handover of new processes from the project status to operations. This should prevent that projects with "loose ends" are transferred to operations and create confusion, gray areas, and process gaps.
- Investigate the possibility to use pack, stack, and load-supporting software.
- Get rid of manual weighing and measuring. Start using automated industrial systems.
- Reduce the number of carrier account numbers to prevent complexity and do not provide these to the goods suppliers or other parties to prevent inappropriate usage.
- Measure and review carrier performance. Implement daily management, MBRs, QBRs, and ABRs with the carriers. An example agenda content list can look like as (1) Recognitions, staff, and organizational updates, (2) Customer feedback, (3) Performance review and concerns, (4) Root cause analyses, (5) Countermeasures, (6) Improvement initiatives, (7) Innovation projects, and (8) Risks and DRP.
- Consider local scrapping of returns when the goods value is lower than the transportation costs.
- Use drop trailers and other equipment to prevent waiting times for the drivers and warehouse personnel. Drivers dropping off and picking up trailers from the shipper premises means a short turnaround time.
- Organize a single point of contact at the carriers and the shipper. Show one face to the customer.

- In case of own drivers, allow them to go to professional driver trainings to reduce fuel consumption and damages.
- When shipping, remove old labels used by, for example, the vendor to ship goods from its location to the receiver, on the packages and pallets as this confuses the carrier's operations and leads to the shipment delivered to a wrong address due to scanning the old label.
- Share the forecasted volumes with the carriers to allocate capacity on time at lower rates.
- Map the transportation flows, challenge the points where the goods are delayed, and decrease the number of delays in transit.
- Ask carriers to move two 20′ containers in one pick-up. A carrier can also pick up a combination of a 20′ and a 40′ container by one truck as a road train.
- Make network studies part of daily management. Install post-analysis processes to review and improve the transportation networks.
- Minimize firefighting and "temporary" solutions and workarounds. Maximize process standardization by using standard work and implementing structural process designs.
- Eliminate gray areas between end-to-end value streams and process owners. Agree on clear Responsibilities and Accountabilities and who needs to be Consulted or Informed (use the RACI matrix). Share this with the stakeholders.
- Find a balance between the "easy" to manage, but more expensive, one-stop-shop and the "complicated," but cheaper, cherry-pick (use the cheapest carrier per shipment) concept.
- Implement control towers to manage flows end-to-end. Separate the control function clearly from the operations, as this prevents the tower from working on forward-looking and structural improvements. Control towers are not supposed to babysit shipments and handle urgent delivery escalations.

4.7 REDUCE WASTE: LEAN IT

Although logistics is one of the most dynamic industries, it is still lagging behind on the implementation of digital- and data-based technologies. One of the main reasons for implementing IT solutions in the past was to make processes more efficient to reduce headcounts. Shippers increasingly gathered and described process requirements, built business cases, initiated IT change requests, waited for prioritization, waited for budgets to become available, waited for approval, waited for project leads, and waited for many more actions. IT did their best to satisfy everybody, but they were not able to process the backlog of requested changes on time and with the right quality levels. Instead of helping the organization, IT itself became a bottleneck for implementing process improvements driven by fast-changing business needs. To reverse the trend, it is important that also IT becomes Lean, reorganizes itself, and moves quickly to contribute to the daily continuous improvement culture. IT needs to focus on adding value to the customer by being flexible and fast to support value streams with the tools and processes to adapt quickly to changing customer requirements and eliminate waste. Shippers who have outsourced this key enabling IT function might need to rethink part of this strategy and question themselves if this set-up can effectively support the continuous improvement philosophy. In the following paragraphs, a few Lean IT-related improvement ideas are shared to be checked for feasibility in each individual shipper's situation as the amount of added value can differ per company. Remember that process improvement comes first and that IT comes second meaning that technology needs to support the most optimal process design and not the other way around. Many companies had to change their processes into a less efficient design to support the implementation of an IT system. In the following paragraphs, a few Lean customer-related improvement ideas are shared. The amount of added value can differ per company and its maturity level.

4.7.1 Consider a TMS

TMS is the new basis, first building block for almost any innovation-related new opportunities such as IOT, Artificial Intelligence (AI) where a customer can negotiate with a computer about a new delivery date and time or address, machine learning, predictive analytics, telematics by using GPS and onboard diagnostics to register and monitor truck movements, and tracking devices. An example tracking technology is geo fencing where a real-time alert is triggered to a shipper's or carrier's TMS via a mobile device or onboard telematics once entering or exiting by GPS- or RFID-identified geographical boundaries. By offering supply chain partners access to TMS, it enables all parties to have the same and most recent whereabouts preventing confusion due to information gaps.

Consider optimizing transportation management by using a TMS, which calculates the best cost, transit-time, carrier, and modality combination automatically. Making these comparisons manually is labor intensive and can be difficult due to complex rate structures and shipment characteristics. Many shippers use weight as the only selection criteria and ship parcels up to 70 kg with a parcel; shipments up to, for example, 7,000 kg with a LTL; and everything above that with a FTL carrier. However, for specific shipment and lane combinations it might be cheaper to ship everything above 4,000 kg by a FTL instead of a LTL carrier. Review the processes and select the technology that meets the needs to manage transportation in a better way and without workarounds. A TMS should give the shipper valuable information for a good decision-making process in a workflow set-up. Other benefits can be the reduction of manual work, faster document creation, and communication by default e-document set-ups. The financial accrual process is more reliable as result of the real-time information availability and there will be fewer customers requesting a shipment status update due to their direct access to TMS. The system supports also the elimination of human errors, real-time pipeline visibility, and prevention of data retyping and faster generation of standard performance reports.

4.7.2 Use a Dynamic Carrier Choice System

A dynamic carrier choice system is a cost-efficient transport-planning tool to determine which shipment will be shipped with which modality, service level, and carrier to what destination. Normally this is a standard TMS functionality, but if this is not available, a shipper can use simpler off-the-shelf multi-carrier selection tools such as ShipItSmarter and ConnectShip, manual instructions such as the use of carrier x for deliveries up to 30 kg to a certain country can work too, but this process is less accurate and inefficient. A more sophisticated tool can make this decision for each individual shipment automatically. The calculation rules and criteria, such as chargeable volume and weight, the number of shipping units, rates on the zip code level, modality, and carrier, can be programmed in the tool. The decision-making process can be based on only the transportation costs, but it is preferred to add also the warehouse costs as preparing a parcel shipment involves different warehouse activities compared to preparing a LTL shipment. Consolidate shipments on the same day to the same customer. Take into account the customer requirements such as delivery frequency, time windows, and preferred modalities and carriers. Make the decision-making process globally applicable and automated as much as possible. Carrier allocation needs to take place before picking, packing, and shipping. Estimate the gross volumes, weights, and measurements if not known upfront.

4.7.3 Automate and Digitalize More

Communicate online with carriers, use EDI, automate, and digitalize more to free up capacity for other value-added services, but also to become more agile. The success for a company depends more and more on how well it can adopt new technologies as it enables, besides real-time information and visibility to anticipate events, new business models to differentiate from the competition. Get rid of manual work. Stop faxing, phoning, paper orders, and retyping data. In some countries is it already possible to use digital transportation documents (e.g., the Dutch e-CMR TransFollow). Exchange delivery note information between product suppliers and customers by DESADV messaging. It is faster, easier, and cheaper to create, sort, and archive these. It leads also to fewer typing errors, paper damages, and loss. Automate ASNs and the exchange of invoices. Agree on paperless transaction-based invoicing by EDI to reduce the non-added value work of creating invoices, printing them, sending them out, receiving them, scanning them, processing them, and so on. Additional benefits are reporting and managing cost developments on a daily basis and taking immediate corrective and preventive actions where needed. This technology can also be used to create paperless communication, shipping and receiving processes by exchanging invoices, packing lists, and other documents by EDI instead of printing and attaching them to the goods. Use existing carrier web tools such as the claims registration systems. Integrate mobile image-capture apps in the IT systems to increase visibility and reduce manual handling costs by photo-documenting shipments including labels, pallet conditions, and product and trailer conditions. Warehouse personnel and truck drivers can photograph shipments and upload photos with information about the date, time, and load details. The images are shared with the supply chain partners to improve the visibility of goods conditions and determine the responsible parties in case of irregularities. Many shippers do not receive chargebacks because they have no way to prove compliance at shipping. Use digital tools to increase the efficiency of the procurement process, become agile to repeat this cycle more often to improve the sourcing results. A digital procurement process allows a better understanding of the shipment data; helps to handle complexity in case of many lanes, sites, products, and so forth; supports a faster and clearer communication; makes it easier to analyze and compare bids; enables fast calculation of what-if scenarios; and executes e-auctions.

4.7.4 Consider a Yard Management System

A Yard Management System (YMS) enables the shipper to efficiently plan, execute, and track loads based on shipment type, dock, and warehouse capacity. For small shippers this process can be executed manually, but for large yards, an YMS is required as the process becomes complicated and labor intensive. An YMS can be used in combination with a WMS or TMS. It helps to efficiently manage truck movements when entering and leaving the facility, finding the closest empty trailer, free docks and digitally instruct shuttle drivers what equipment to move from where to where. The planning process starts before the truck and the driver arrive at the gate as they have been pre-announced, by using an app or manually, so that the truck can enter the premises immediately and without long-lasting entrance formalities. The system provides information on the vehicle and employee location and their movements by using RFID or other tracking means. A YMS provides fast and real-time visibility in continuously moving trucks, trailers, and employees to plan for a fast throughput, preventing waiting times for the drivers and warehouse personnel. There are also cost savings involved such as better asset utilization, shorter communication and planning time, less drivers' waiting times, demurrage, and detention costs. Transportation equipment makes money only when it is moving. Carriers invoice demurrage costs to the receivers or shippers, depending on the agreed Incoterms® rules, when they have not taken the fully loaded containers from a seaport or container terminal within the allowed, in general five, free days. The costs per container per day vary per location and carrier. These costs are the results of process wastes such as missing or incorrect documents, delayed customs clearance process by the local customs offices, extended security scans by authorities, and disputes between the seller and the buyer. Prevent such costs by preparing the customs clearance process for the incoming goods on time and thoroughly. Start by requesting the seller to send the shipment documents and shipment delivery details by e-mail. If it is necessary to exchange original documents, use an express carrier. Check the import requirements and permissions for the specific products in the specific country and agree with carriers more free days in case more time is needed. Potential disputes between the seller and the buyer can be prevented by hiring a special company like SGS to inspect the cargo at the seller before shipping. The carrier invoices detention costs to the receivers or shippers when they have taken the containers from a seaport or container terminal to their locations for unloading and they did not return the empty container back to the carrier location within the allowed free days.

4.7.5 Use Online Transportation Market Places

Use Internet-based transportation market places to tender shipments, although there are more and more platforms offering also the planning, execution, and post-shipment analyses. Look out for the extra overhead as more contacts with more carriers means more people to manage this. There are so many lanes, carriers, and trucks that it is key for carriers to optimize their planning, not only within their company and fleet, but also with other carriers to match demand and supply on a daily basis. This will reduce the number of empty kilometers, lower rates for the shipper, and generate higher margins for the carrier. A shipper offers a shipment on the website, potential carriers place a quotation, and the shipper accepts one and allocates the shipment to the winning carrier. The advantages are a faster dispatching process and a more efficient use of the dispatcher at the shipper and carrier. It is replacing calling multiple carriers and comparing their quotations manually. Especially small shippers, who have a limited number of deliveries to ship, can significantly benefit from lower rates due to the uberization of the transportation market, where imbalanced demand versus supply situations are made visible offering the incidental shipper the opportunity to shop around for the best deal.

4.7.6 Other

- Keep master data, such as HS codes, product weight and dimensions, carrier communication matrices, customer contacts, delivery addresses and prices, and Incoterms® up to date and share these with the stakeholders.
- Upload carrier restrictions, such as maximum weights and dimensions, non-serviced destinations, and DG classes, in the TMS to prevent shipment rejections by carriers and delays but watch out for overcomplicating the system.

- Enable the use of social media-type tools such as Facebook and WhatsApp to communicate with customers.
- Do not try to copy the current way for working into a TMS. Be practical to enable a fast implementation. It is possible to try building complex rate structures in this system, but this requires quite some IT resources and development time. It might be faster to agree new simple rate structures with carriers. It also happens that shippers start measuring shipments' weights and dimensions costing them quite some additional resources, as the new system requires this. However, it is also possible to rely on the carriers' automated weighing and measuring systems and use that information preventing additional work.

4.8 REDUCE WASTE: LEAN ORGANIZATION

The mindset of a Lean organization is to be customer focused, strive for perfection, and employ leaders and employees who are aligned on goals and strongly believe that there is always a way to improve processes and eliminate waste to add more value to the customer. In Lean organizations, there is no room for silos, egoism, management by objectives, and heroism. Instead, empowered and engaged leaders and employees work together in cross-functional teams and communicate vertically and horizontally to align on goals, collaborate to reach these, teach people the Lean philosophy and methods and allow them to become responsive problem solvers, prevent layoffs in bad times, and proactively look for better ways in good times. A Lean organization is not necessarily a flat organigram with a minimum number of employees and management layers. A Lean company needs Lean masters to guide the Lean initiatives, Lean experts to coach kaizen leaders, team leads to lead, and employees to work on kaizens. In the following paragraphs, a few Lean customer-related improvement ideas are shared. The amount of added value can differ per company and its maturity level.

4.8.1 Hire Qualified Employees

Hire only multi-skilled people with capabilities to communicate, design and implement solutions to increase the chance of success. This approach increases the first time right percentage by preventing personal mistakes. The person needs to have sufficient knowledge of and experience with the Lean philosophy, complex transportation networks, regulations, and other requirements, which can vary over the globe. He or she needs to be an effective communicator between the many supply chain partners and a networker to build long-term relationships with its partners by being reliable, flexible, and dependable. The employee takes care and confirms on time what has been promised and gives the partners the trust and confidence that he or she will do everything to find a solution for their problem, request or need, as he or she has developed his or her problem-solving skills. Install a learning curriculum supported by training on the job, class trainings, and workshops. Allow people to go to these trainings and work on their personal development. The limited extra costs will bring significant savings. Pay the people well as good people ask for good rewards and excellent people ask for excellent rewards. Transportation needs to attract and retain smart people to bring the industry to the next level. Compared to other industries, transportation is lagging behind on digitalization, big data usage, and IT. The low driver and warehouse personnel wages, hard lifestyle, and increasing number of regulations and related audits do not make the industry interesting to work in. This is probably also the reason of the limited number of women in logistics. Such a situation leads to driver shortages and other human resource issues, limiting industry growth. In addition to paying people higher salaries, it is possible to make the work more attractive by building a network of driver hotels where the people can take a shower, sleep in a bed, and eat healthy food and sport. Another way is to shorten the time a driver is away from the family at home by allowing them to exchange trailers halfway to their destinations with their colleagues driving in the opposite direction enabling them both to return back home. Reduce the working hours, time pressure, and stress by creating a realistic pick-up and delivery planning allowing the driver to do the work in normal tempo. It also helps to create and maintain safe parking places, free of thieves and criminal activities. The first impression could be that these actions lead to higher costs, but the rates in a market where the demand for transportation is structurally higher than the supply of drivers will go up faster. Not being able to deliver costs even more. The expectation is that the upcoming autonomous trucks will not replace the drivers, but only change the content of their work as driving from one location to another is not the only part of a trucker's job. New technologies will help the driver to get rid of, for example, the current driving time limitations, anticipate the traffic situations, prevent accidents, or bypass traffic jams giving him or her more time for customer service activities such as calling the consignee in case of delay and doing temperature and humidity checks. A driver acts also as a sales representative and logistician who has direct contact with the customer and receives valuable feedback about the shipper's products and services that can be used to improve the supply chain performance.

4.8.2 Develop and Co-Operate with Carriers

Shippers are typically looking for a good rate, while carriers are trying to make a good margin meaning that high rates are not necessarily their primary objective. To work towards a win-win situation, both parties should focus on reducing costs in the total supply chain. Lower costs mean lower rates, while maintaining the carrier's margin, which is necessary to invest in the carrier's infrastructure to safeguard continuous and sufficient transportation capacities. If carriers are not able to generate a proper margin, they go bankrupt leading to higher rates due to demand becoming higher than supply, lower market shares due to higher product prices and less competitiveness, and longer delivery lead-times due to insufficient transportation equipment and lower quality levels due to carrier's cost reduction measures to survive. Treating carriers fairly, and not using the power play model, is a pre-requisite for a good relationship, which is necessary for a steady rate development in all freight market situations. In return, a healthy relationship delivers significant, not easy to quantify, benefits in the long run, as carriers are more willing to support beyond the standard contract terms and conditions, invest in tools and processes, and be more open about cheaper ways to handle the business. It is no longer sufficient to adapt to changes as they come. Shippers need to be flexible to anticipate changes before these are forced upon them. The transportation branch is changing and evolving every day and will continue doing so. The proactive shippers anticipate what is coming and collaborate with their partners to develop new and optimized processes to remove waste and add more value to the customer. This is only possible with strong partners with clear missions, visions, goals, plans, and organizations. Companies with strong and flexible partners benefit from the competitive advantages of the partners' service innovations as they act fast on changing customer requirements and business environments. Start kaizens to develop carriers to continuously improve their processes; ask them to commit to the zero-defect philosophy; cooperate to eliminate waste in their processes; collaborate more by exchanging short-, mid- and long-term demand and supply forecasts; and enable and use more EDI communication. Best-in-class companies work with a limited number of carriers who have adopted the Lean philosophy, in a long-term cooperative relationship. Such an effective relationship requires a two-way communication where both parties work together to maintain a healthy relationship. The partners are preferably located near to each other, create a platform for problem solving, co-operate to achieve the KPI targets and benefit both from the realized efficiencies. Install challenging supplier cost-reduction targets and help the carrier to make it happen. Share one third of the benefits with the carriers. It makes no sense if the shipper is looking for cost reduction opportunities with the carrier while the carrier is looking for increasing sales. The shipper will try to speed up the improvement process, while the carrier will try to slow this down to minimize negative Profit & Loss (P&L) impacts. A partnership requires a different behavior from the shipper, who needs to be open, trust its carriers, and move from a transaction-based relationship to a strategic partner as carriers are only committed to invest in a long-term relation. A typical transaction-based shipper, for which the costs are more important than service and quality, continuously looks for the lowest rate offered by any carrier in the market. However, for the strategic partner, who is using transportation management as a strategic differentiator, the service and quality are more important than costs. A partner does not look only into rates, but analyzes the total cost of ownership, which is explained previously in this book. A partnership requires more carrier resources, such as account managers, process performance measurement and improvement engineers, IT and technology integration designers, and project managers, to take more time to meet, improve communication, and receive trainings to better understand and anticipate the more extended and complex customer requirements.

4.8.3 Standardize Processes

Reduce complexity and standardize processes over the globe. Minimize the number of exception processes, which are error sensitive and hide waste. Reduce transactional labor costs, manual errors, and retyping of data and speed up the communication and data interpretation by considering advancement in technology such as the automated generation of POs and EDI usage for transportation order exchange between the shipper and the carrier. Using EDI for milestone, POD and ASN exchanges shortens processing times and order-to-cash cycles.

4.8.4 Install a Key Transportation Leadership Position

Represent the transportation management function by a highly positioned supply chain director in the leadership team to bring in the transportation aspects when making decisions. The existence of the position indicates that transportation management has the leadership commitment. The director gives direction, aligns transportation with the logistics and company's strategy, and helps remove barriers to success. The key stakeholders will be more willing to support transportation management initiatives.

4.8.5 Plan to Map all the Value Streams and Value Stream Loops

The fundament of improving any activity is to understand how a process works. The same is valid for transportation management: map the value streams and value stream loops to understand the key drivers of the processes before making any change. Use the VSM tool to execute this action.

4.8.6 Other

- It is possible to organize the transportation management function into value streams such as "Inbound," "Outbound," and "Returns," but appoint a single point of contact for carriers to prevent conflicting requirements from the value streams and value stream loops towards the carriers. For the same reason, a single point of contact is also needed at the carriers' side.
- Meeting face-to-face is the best way to communicate. However, as traveling around the globe costs a lot of time it is recommended to work on virtual teambuilding activities.
- Embed problem solving in the company's culture: train people the philosophy and tools, create an overview of open and prioritized real live problems, assign these to teams, link them to an experienced Lean coach, and ask employees to volunteer as team leader or team member and/or assign people to teams. Organize a biweekly

or monthly call for the teams to share their progress, challenges, need for help, and lessons learnt for cross learning and program improvement.

- Great ideas do not come on command; they come at any moment and place. Organizing a workshop at the beginning of the year to come up with ideas to lower costs and inventories and increase the service is not sufficient. Increase the frequency and/or set up a process to come up, update, change, replace, add, and share improvement ideas on a daily basis.
- Plan to look actively for logistics market knowledge by buying market study reports, visiting seminars, exhibitions, workshops, master classes, and peer companies. This helps to develop the shipper and carriers to benefit from best practices and innovations.
- Regularly report out to all the stakeholders the transportation accomplishments to market the function.
- Get rid of approval and escalation processes by empowering people to act fast and prevent waiting for approvals and management instructions.
- Benchmark processes against the best Lean companies like Toyota, Danaher, Honeywell, and Walmart. Encourage and visit ("kaikaku" in Japanese) them to learn.
- Install an S&OP call or meeting to bring all the supply chain partners, such as planners, carriers, and customers, together to discuss operational performance, agree and take decisions on an aligned business plan in which the planning activities of all the functions are synchronized to prevent sub-optimization. Define the higher shared company's goals, such as lowering inventory levels in the whole supply chain and reducing end-to-end delivery lead-times, translate these into forward-looking actions, and provide help where needed. Typical agenda items are capacity, timing, and issues between demand and supply. Example topics to discuss can be carrier delivery issues, stock-out and backorder situations, introduction of new customers, and organization of return calls, delivering on new sales projects, new product introductions, market constraints, new regulations, production issues, and other unexpected disruptions.
- Consider the in-car delivery option: prevent engineers from driving to a location, picking up spare parts, and driving to the customer's location to fix machines and drive back to drop off repairable returns. Engineers can use their cars as mobile addresses, park them in an

accessible place and specify a delivery time window. They can leave returns in the car for collection by the carrier. The driver receives the delivery location information, the exact car's position, and a single-use access code.

4.9 REDUCE WASTE: LEAN COMPLIANCE

Being compliant has often been seen as a burden on an organization as "it did not add value" to the customer and as "something we had to do to prevent penalties and/or keep a quality certificate." Compliance has not been seen as a way to create capable, stable, and reliable processes to build high quality and safe products, prevent dual-use products falling in the wrong hands and being used for terrorist attacks, benefit from free trade agreements to prevent duty payments, and classify the products by the correct HS code to pay lower duty rates. It has also not been seen as a way to draw back the paid duties and taxes for re-exported shipments, speed up deliveries through customs processes, work only with companies that respect human rights, act with integrity, support fair trade, and take care of the environment. It becomes time that shippers start to see these benefits and actively manage these processes towards a higher performance level. In the following paragraphs, a few Lean customer-related improvement ideas are shared. The amount of added value can differ per company and its maturity level.

4.9.1 Sign a Carrier Quality Agreement

Request carriers to sign a quality agreement. The intention of such an agreement is to write down what the shipper expects from the carriers to realize the mutually agreed safety, service, and behavior goals. Make sure that the carrier is compliant with national and international regulations and laws. Request carriers to show ISO certification as evidence. The carriers can use the same approach towards their own subcontractors. Although the carriers are primarily responsible for their performance levels, it is up to the transportation managers to make sure that these are reached. By signing the quality agreement, the carrier agrees to have a certified quality management system. Such a certification is necessary to make sure that the company is compliant with the requirements and standards predefined by the certification institutes. Such a certification process requires the carrier to analyze and improve its processes. The certification is valid for only a certain period, after which the company will be audited again. This will maintain the carriers analyzing and improving activities. This maintenance process is often in the hands of a member of the leadership team who has the authority and responsibility to implement and maintain the quality system. Besides the audits by the certifying institutes, it is recommended that the carriers execute and archive internal audits to monitor the progress. A shipper can ask the carriers to visit them to audit their processes and agree on improvement actions.

4.9.2 Expedite Customs Clearance Processes

Consider the use of a global trade software system to standardize, visualize, and accelerate the import and export processes. The IT systems will help to be compliant with the applicable regulations of the destination countries and manage declarations in an automated way with the customs authorities. It gives the opportunity to get rid of manual work, calculate the expected duties and taxes, benefit from the preferential agreements, check the restricted and denied parties, and use it as a single source for reporting. Provide carriers the power of attorney to do customs clearance of behalf of the shipper and/or receiver to speed up these processes. Do not use a third-party broker as handing over documentation back and forth between the carrier and the broker is delaying the clearance process and adding costs. Implement a consolidated clearance process: all shipments towards one country with one carrier using the same modality on one day can be cleared as one shipment. Not having to pay for clearing each individual shipment results in significant savings. Incorrect product descriptions, wrong prices, incomplete addresses, or proofs of origin are pitfalls that can lead to high costs and loss of time. Make sure that the information towards customs authorities on the paperwork and physical goods are correct and in line with each other. Prevent carriers asking the receiver to pay duties and taxes upon delivery, as this cash is not available leading to the driver bringing back the goods to the carrier location. Instead, agree with the carrier to allow the receiver a credit and send invoices for taxes and duties after the delivery.

4.9.3 Manage Transportation Risks

Work on a risk management plan to identify, analyze, and mitigate the transportation risks by avoiding, reducing, transferring, or accepting them.

Create a business continuity plan for what to do in case of disaster. Assess carriers on their financial stability and assign potential back-ups. Think of alternative ports, carriers, and routings in case of congestion, terrorist attacks, strikes, or roadblocks. Plan for adverse weather conditions. Define alternative modes of transportation when capacity issues arise. Consider cargo-tracking devices and hard-sided trailers for valuable products. Get C-TPAT certified and cooperate only with certified carriers. Train employees to screen people, cargo and locations, and restrict accesses. Guarantee safe workplaces and tools. Use solid packing and describe the content in generic terms.

4.9.4 Implement the Neutral Delivery Service

Many international shippers do not want their consignees to know the seller's purchasing prices. As result, the shipment is sent to a local organization, which removes the confidential documents and forwards the shipment towards the end customer. This is leading to longer lead-times and non-added-value activities. A Neutral Delivery Service (NDS) allows the shipper to send a shipment directly to a consignee while keeping the purchasing prices on the invoice from the shipper's goods supplier confidential. Duties and taxes are billed to a third-party IOR, which can be a local organization. All documents go to the IOR and the consignee receives only a copy of the waybill, with no indication of the value.

4.9.5 Reduce the Carbon Footprint

The first step to make a change here is to measure the carbon emission to create people's awareness. It is not necessary to build a new tool. Use Internet-based supply chain carbon emission calculators, such as https://dhl-carboncalculator.com and http://www.freightemissionscalculator.com, but make sure that all the variables (e.g., mode of transportation, fuel consumption, routing, equipment utilization, service levels, weights, and dimensions) are taken into account by the tool. Example projects to reduce the negative impacts are to decrease the number of shipments and volumes; improve loading degrees; increase the average shipment volume; use more economy services; move from air to ocean, train, and/or road transportation; and hand over re-usable packing material to the driver upon delivery or at the pick-up location. Other ideas are to use delivery time windows, electrical cargo bikes and vans, share assets with competition, consolidate the final mile deliveries of multiple carriers, share loading and unloading locations, install hold-for-pickup and drop off locations, create postal offices at the ground floors of large buildings and use bicycles as a transportation modality. A good example of the e-cargo bike usage is the DHL's Cubicycle. Packages are loaded in small (80 cm × 120 cm × 100 cm) GPS- and solar panel-equipped containers in a DHL sorting location and moved to the city center hub where they are attached to e-bikes for further distribution. The GPS system provides the biker with the optimal route and allows the carrier to locate the containers and track and trace the packages real-time. The reverse process is used to handle returns. The company Dachser has implemented a comparable solution for the city distribution of pallets.

4.9.6 Reduce Duties and Prevent Delays and Penalties

Purchase products domestically or locally to prevent paying duties when importing. Ensure that shipments meet compliance laws and regulations to prevent delays and penalties. Know the potential inappropriate dual-use of a product, screen customers and other persons and partners, make sure that the relevant licenses are in place, and watch out for suspicious financial flows and parties before any negotiation, commitment, or deal. Simplify policies and procedures without sacrificing the ability to detect, for example, theft and fraud. Install and assess anti-corruption and anti-bribery guidelines and review them constantly and bring them up to date. Keep them realistic and easy to understand to ensure compliance.

4.9.7 Take Advantage of Preferential Trade Agreements

There are trade agreements between countries or regions leading to lower import duties and taxes. To benefit from these, it requires the creation and handover of proper documentation. If a product is exported to a country for rework, and it is re-exported within a certain period, the paid import duties can often be reclaimed.

4.9.8 Act with Integrity, Honestly, Ethically, and Support Fair Trade

Buyers and consumers are taking social responsibility impacts into their decisions. More and more RFQs ask suppliers to provide information about their social initiatives, paying a fair salary, and not employing children. Request carriers to sign a security agreement and act accordingly. Appoint compliance officers to create, train, assess anti-corruption and anti-bribery guidelines, and install an ethics line to report suspicious situations and guidance.

Abbreviations

ABR	annual business review
ADA	actual date of arrival
ADD	actual date of departure
ADR	accord dangereux routier
AED	automated external defibrillator
AEO	authorized economic operator
AGV	automated guided vehicle
AI	artificial intelligence
AOP	annual operating plan
APAC	Asia Pacific
API	application program interface
ASN	advanced shipping notification
ATA	actual time of arrival
ATD	actual time of departure
ATR	association Turkey
AWB	air way bill
BAF	bunker adjustment factor
BL	bill of lading
BOL	bill of lading
BSC	balanced scorecard
B-t-B	business-to-business
B-t-C	business-to-consumer
CAF	currency adjustment factor
CAPA	corrective action and preventive action
CDC	central distribution centre
CFR	cost and freight
CFS	container freight station
CIF	cost insurance and freight
CIP	carriage and insurance paid to
COC	certificate of conformity
COD	confirmation of delivery
COD	cash on delivery
COO	certificate of origin

CPI	cost price indicator
CPT	carriage paid to
CT	control tower
C-TPAT	customs and trade partnership against terrorism
CTRN	customs trade reference number
DAP	delivered at place
DAT	delivered at terminal
DD	door-to-door
DDP	delivered duty paid
DG	dangerous goods
DGD	dangerous goods declaration
DIAD	delivery information acquisition device
DM	daily management
DN	delivery note
DP	door-to-port
DRP	disaster recovery plan
EAD	export accompanying document
ECCN	export control classification number
ECO	export control officer
EDA	expected date of arrival
EDD	expected date of departure
EDI	electronic data interchange
EDIFACT	electronic data interchange for administration, commerce and transport
ELD	electronic logging device
EOD	end of day
EOR	exporter of record
EPAL	European pallet association
EPT	electric pallet truck
ERP	enterprise resource planning
ETA	estimated time of arrival
ETD	expected time of departure
EU	European Union
EXW	ex works
FAS	free alongside ship
FBA	fulfillment by Amazon
FCA	free carrier
FCL	full container load
FDA	food and drug administration

FEU	forty-foot equivalent unit
FOB	free on board
FPA	freight payment and auditing
FSC	fuel surcharge costs
FSL	field stocking location
FTL	full truck load
GDP	good distribution practice
GPS	global positioning system
GRI	general rate increase
HAWB	house air way bill
HFPU	hold for pick-up
HS	harmonized commodity description and coding system
ICC	international chamber of commerce
IFTMIN	international forwarding and transport message instructions
IFTSTA	international forwarding and transport status
IMO	international maritime organization
IoT	internet of things
IOR	importer of record
IPP	international pallet pool
IPPC	international plant protection convention
IPSM 15	international standards for phytosanitary measures 15
ISPS	international security port surcharge
ISO	international organization for standardization
IT	information technology
JIT	just in time
KPI	key performance indicator
LC	letter of credit
LCL	less than container load
LDC	local distribution centre
LSP	logistics service provider
LLP	lead logistics provider
LOI	letter of intention
LPR	la palette rouge
LTL	less than truck load
MAWB	master air way bill
MBR	monthly business review
MPF	merchandise processing fee
MSDS	material safety data sheet
MTS	managed transportation services

NBD	next business day
NDA	non-disclosure agreement
NFO	next flight out
NVOCC	non-vessel operating common carrier
NYSE	New York Shipping Exchange
PD	port-to-door
PDCA	plan do check act
PESTEL	political economic social technological environmental legal
PI	packing instruction
PI	performance indicator
P&L	profit and loss
PO	purchase order
POA	proof of attorney
POD	proof of delivery
POU	point of use
PP	port-to-port
PSS	peak season surcharge
PUDO	pick-up and drop-off
QBR	quarterly business review
QMS	quality management system
RACI	responsible accountable consulted informed
RC	repair centre
RDC	regional distribution centre
RFI	request for information
RFP	request for proposal
RFQ	request for quotation
ROI	return on investment
RTS	return to sender
SaaS	system as a service
SGI	strategic goods indicator
SLA	service level agreement
SMART	specific measurable achievable realistic time bound
SMI	supplier managed inventory
SMOI	supplier managed and owned inventory
SO	sales order
SOI	supplier owned inventory
SOP	standard operating procedure
S&OP	sales and operations planning
SOW	statement of work

SSC	security surcharge costs
SSCC	serial shipping container code
SWA	shipping with Amazon
TAP	ThrowAway pallet
TAT	turn around time
TCO	total cost of ownership
TEU	twenty-foot equivalent unit
TMS	transport management system
TPM	total process management
TPS	Toyota production system
TT	transit time
TTI	target to improve
ULD	unit load device
UN	United Nations
USP	unique selling point
VAS	value added services
VOCC	vessel operating common carrier
VMI	vendor managed inventory
VSM	value stream map
WACC	weighted average cost of capital
WMS	warehouse management system
YMS	yard management system

Further Reading

Byrne A. 2017. *The Lean Turnaround: How to Implement Lean, Create Value, and Grow Your People*. New York: McGraw-Hill.

Coyle J., Novack R., Gibson B. et al. 2015. *Transportation: A Global Supply Chain Perspective*. Boston, MA: Cengage Learning.

Cudney E. 2009. *Using Hoshin Kanri to Improve the Value Stream*. New York: CRC Press.

Ford H. 2003. *Today and Tomorrow*. New York: CRC Press.

George M., Rowlands D., Kastle B. 2004. *What is Lean Six Sigma*. New York: McGraw-Hill.

Goldsby T., Iyengar D., Rao R. 2014. *The Definitive Guide to Transportation: Principles, Strategies, and Decisions for the Effective Flow of Goods and Services*. Upper Saddle River, NJ: Pearson Education.

Liker J. 2004. *The Toyota Way: 14 Management Principles from the World's Greatest Manufacturer*. New York: McGraw-Hill.

Liker J., Convis G. 2012. *The Toyota Way to Lean Leadership*. New York: McGraw-Hill.

Monczka R., Handfield R., Giunipero L. et al. 2014. *Purchasing and Supply Chain Management*. Boston, MA: Cengage Learning.

Myerson P. 2012. *Lean Supply Chain and Logistics Management*. New York: McGraw-Hill.

Niederstadt J. 2015. *The Lean Expert: Educating and Elevating Lean Practitioners Throughout Your Organization*. New York: CRC Press.

Ohno T. 1988. *Toyota Production System – Beyond Large-Scale Production*. Boca Raton, FL: Productivity Press.

Rother M., Aulinger G. 2017. *Toyota Kata Culture: Building Organizational Capability and Mindset Through Kata Coaching*. Chennai, India: McGraw-Hill.

Rother M., Shook J. 2003. *Learning to See: Value-Stream Mapping to Create Value and Eliminate Muda*. Cambridge, MA: Lean Enterprise Institute.

Shook J. 2010. *Managing to Learn: Using the A3 Management Processes to Solve Problems, Gain Agreement, Mentor, and Lead*. Cambridge, MA: Lean Enterprise Institute.

Womack J.P., Jones D.T. 2003. *Lean Thinking: Banish Waste and Create Wealth in Your Corporation*. New York: Simon & Schuster.

Womack J.P., Jones D.T., Roos D. 1990. *The Machine That Changed the World*. New York: Rawson Associates.

Index